Dynamism and the Ageing of a Japanese 'New' Religion

Also available from Bloomsbury

Mountain Mandalas, Allan G. Grapard
The Origin of Modern Shinto in Japan, Yijiang Zhong
Shinto, Nature and Ideology in Contemporary Japan, Aike P. Rots

Dynamism and the Ageing of a Japanese 'New' Religion

Transformations and the Founder

Erica Baffelli and Ian Reader

BLOOMSBURY ACADEMIC
LONDON • NEW YORK • OXFORD • NEW DELHI • SYDNEY

BLOOMSBURY ACADEMIC
Bloomsbury Publishing Plc
50 Bedford Square, London, WC1B 3DP, UK
1385 Broadway, New York, NY 10018, USA

BLOOMSBURY, BLOOMSBURY ACADEMIC and the Diana logo are trademarks of
Bloomsbury Publishing Plc

First published in Great Britain 2019
Paperback edition published 2020

Cover design: Terry Woodley
Cover image © Ian Reader

A catalogue record for this book is available from the British Library.

A catalog record for this book is available from the Library of Congress.

ISBN: HB: 978-1-3500-8651-7
PB: 978-1-3501-7014-8
ePDF: 978-1-3500-8652-4
eBook: 978-1-3500-8653-1

Typeset by Newgen KnowledgeWorks Pvt. Ltd., Chennai, India

To find out more about our authors and books visit www.bloomsbury.com
and sign up for our newsletters.

To Toki and Anna

Contents

Figures

Acknowledgements

This project could not have been completed without the encouragement and support of many colleagues, friends and family.

The idea of this book was initially discussed during the annual joint workshop on 'Religion in Contemporary Japan' organized between the University of Manchester and Tübingen University, Germany. We would like to thank our colleagues Klaus Antoni, Monika Schrimpf, Birgit Staemmler and David Weiss for their feedback and for inviting us to share our preliminary thoughts with their students at Tübingen. We would also like to express our gratitude to colleagues who helped us complete this work by sharing research materials and publications, replying to our questions, joining us during fieldwork visits and inviting us to present our project at their institutions: Ian Astley, Alexandre Benod, John Breen, Andrea Castiglioni, Lucia Dolce, Benjamin Dorman, Chiara Ghidini, Horie Norichika, Paulina Kolata, Benedetta Lomi, Nishimura Akira and Tatsuma Padoan. Thanks are also due to various officials and members in Agonshū for patiently answering our questions during fieldwork and via email.

Our most recent fieldwork in Japan in 2017–18 was supported by a grant from the Great Britain Sasakawa Foundation, while previous visits where supported by grants from Japan Foundation, Japan Foundation Endowment Committee and the Japan Society for the Promotion of Science.

Many thanks also to Lalle Pursglove and Lucy Carroll at Bloomsbury for their help and support in producing this volume, and to the four anonymous reviewers who enthusiastically supported our book proposal and provided insightful comments on it.

We are also grateful to John Shultz and Ritsuko Tatsumi for their hospitality in Japan, to Jonathan Bunt for spiritual assistance in helping us unwind after work sessions and to Toki's Kitchen for feeding us delicious sushi.

Finally, we would like to thank our family members, Dorothy, Rosie, Phil, Toki and Anna, for their support and for diplomatically appearing to listen to our discussions.

Note on Japanese Names, Terms and Transliteration

All Japanese names are in standard Japanese order of family name first, followed by given name.

Long vowels are indicated by macrons (ō, ū) except for words and names commonly used in English (e.g. Kyoto, Tokyo, Shinto).

When talking about religious institutions in Japan associated with its two main religious traditions, Shinto and Buddhism, we follow standard conventions and refer to Shinto institutions as 'shrines' and Buddhist ones as 'temples'.

Introduction

Death of a founder and themes of this book

On 29 August 2016, Kiriyama Seiyū, the founder of the Japanese religious movement Agonshū, died. Although Kiriyama's movement originated in 1954, it became widely known in Japan in the 1980s because of its use of media technologies and its dramatic public rituals that attracted huge crowds. These, along with Kiriyama's easily accessible sermons that offered hope of dealing with misfortunes and of confronting the world's problems, his charismatic personality and his seeming ability to tap into the popular mood of the times, gave Agonshū an aura of dynamism and excitement that attracted new followers. It created a sense of optimism about the mission of world salvation that Kiriyama proclaimed – a mission of spreading a revitalized Buddhism from Japan to the world at large.

Three decades later things seemed rather different. In the years before his death Kiriyama appeared to be frail when he performed Agonshū rituals, and had to be helped to participate in them. The movement appeared to be ageing along with its founder, with a membership that looked older and seemed to have lost the momentum of earlier years.[1] Kiriyama's death, at the age of 95, presented the movement he founded and was so central to with a significant challenge. It also marked a major rite of passage for Agonshū – one that is commonly faced by religious movements after the demise of inspirational founders and as they struggle to face the future without the living presence of the person whose charismatic leadership has been such a factor in recruiting followers. As will be seen later, how Agonshū dealt with this immediate challenge, by memorializing his spirit and enshrining him alongside the historical Buddha as its main object of worship, followed a pattern of founder veneration found in many Japanese religious movements.

This book is not, however, specifically an examination of Agonshū and of Kiriyama Seiyū, so much as it is one that uses Agonshū as a case study to discuss a number of issues pertinent to movements in their early stages of development. In particular it focuses on the construction and trajectories of religious movements and their founders in the period from their founding and the dynamism and excitement that can accompany such early phases, to the ways in which they handle the ageing and loss of their founders. In such contexts, too, it looks at the role and nature of charisma as a driving force in the construction of new movements, at how movements deal with the physical loss of charismatic founders and at how a deceased founder is used in the continuing development of a movement. We use Agonshū and Kiriyama as the main focus around which to discuss these issues, but we also draw on other examples from the Japanese religious world, in particular viewing them as examples of common patterns manifested not just by the broader phenomenon of Japanese 'new religions' (a term and concept we discuss in great detail in the next chapter), but of Japanese religious movements and of the trajectories of new movements more generally.

By tracing the development of a new movement in the context of how changes in the status of its leader affect the ways in which the movement operates and positions itself, we identify and examine a number of themes. These include the roles and nature of religious founders, and the ways in which they are viewed and portrayed in the movements they establish and lead, the ways in which the ageing process – even within the first generation of leadership and membership – may be reflected in changes in orientation in terms of teaching and practice, and how charismatic leadership may be modified and recalibrated to adjust to the loss of a founder. As we examine these themes we will note, for example, how a founder may initially be portrayed in his or her movement as a teacher with new spiritual insights who points to inalienable and ancient truths and offers a new way, with new modes of presentation, teachings, rituals and practices, of dealing with problems and issues in the modern world. Yet as the movement s/he founds develops and grows, the teacher who is initially seen as a role model for followers may be increasingly elevated to higher spiritual levels and acclaimed as a deity or a Buddha and an object of reverence. In this process, the founder/leader becomes elevated beyond the realms of ordinary people and followers, while the movement s/he founded becomes centred increasingly on founder veneration. Agonshū's treatment of Kiriyama, especially in the immediate period after his death, provides a good example of this process in action and is one that has resonances across the religious spectrum.

Charismatic leadership alone is not a guarantor of success, of course. While a leader's charisma and personality play significant roles in drawing people to a movement, these are not enough for the success or even survival of religious groups. As one of us has discussed elsewhere (Baffelli 2016), Agonshū and others (e.g. Kōfuku no Kagaku, another Japanese movement that emerged in the 1980s and that will also be mentioned in this book) became popular not just because of their leader, but also because of a combination of the leader's image, the ways that they packaged their messages, their uses of media and the ways in which they managed to incorporate and manifest issues that were prevalent in the era in which they developed. How religious movements are constructed, in other words, and how they are presented to followers (existing and potential) are crucial to how they manage to attain and retain support.

As such, we pay attention to the ways in which movements mature and develop, the ways in which they adapt to new circumstances and amend and reshape their teachings and practices as a result. For instance, in this context, we indicate how Agonshū, as it increased its popularity and audience in the 1980s, amended its focus in terms of practice and developed new images of worship, which later came also to incorporate the spirit of their deceased founder. As it and its leader aged, and as it developed more of an infrastructure, it became more focused on fixed teachings and practices, such as the annual cycle of rituals, and, crucially important in Agonshū, notions of karma and the role of ancestors, both of which are themes that resonate with the patterns of established Buddhism in Japan. It also became focused on rituals related to Japanese spirits in ways that asserted an increasingly overt nationalism that appeared designed to appeal to older audiences.

We show, too, how significant themes of a movement's initial message may be displaced, amended or even dropped as the circumstances in which a movement operates change. Thus we discuss how Agonshū appeared very much in tune with many of the religious themes prevalent in the 1980s, when it experienced rapid growth and attracted widespread attention, and how, as the sociocultural context in which it operated changed from the 1990s onwards, it faced problems, started to look less in touch and lost momentum. For example, the millennialism that was evident in Agonshū's teaching in the 1980s (and that was a central theme in the messages of other new movements that captured attention in 1980s and early 1990s Japan) receded from the latter 1990s onwards. Agonshū in its earlier days emphasized a millennialism in which Kiriyama was a prophetic figure and a dynamic world saviour. As the allure of millennialism weakened in 1990s Japan (for reasons we discuss in Chapter 4) and as the movement and its leader became older, the image of dynamism and the sense of urgency that characterized its earlier millennialism became less viable to maintain. As this happened, too, Agonshū's messages about world renewal and salvation became less prevalent compared to an increasing turn to nationalism in which issues of Japanese identity and concerns about Japanese spirits of the dead became preeminent.

We thus ask whether the very fact of ageing and losing a physical power and presence may weaken the message of millennial transformation and spur a turn to a more conservative nationalism and reinforcement of the status quo. We discuss how Agonshū has moved away from a seemingly revolutionary or world transformative stance preaching universalism towards a more conservative one that not only reaffirms more traditional Japanese religious concepts but also expresses increasingly nationalistic attitudes. This is not just something specific to Agonshū but has occurred elsewhere in Japan, where there are plentiful examples of new movements that have moved away from radical millennial stances as they enter later stages of their development. All of this suggests that the ageing process of new religious leaders and their movements – and the death of such founders – tends to lead them towards an inward-looking conservatism, with the result that what begins as posing a challenge to the existing state of things and to more traditional religions frequently appears to reaffirm the patterns and nature of the established religious world.

We also pay attention to the wider religious context and market within which Agonshū operated. In an earlier article we discussed how new movements do not exist in a vacuum but operate within a wider context in which the actions and examples of other, often rival, groups can influence the directions they take. In that article, we examined the competing attitudes of Aum Shinrikyō and Kōfuku no Kagaku, in which they developed a rivalry during the 1980s and amended their millennial messages and portrayals of their leaders accordingly (Baffelli and Reader 2011). While this current study does not pay similar attention to rivalries, it recognizes that Agonshū developed and sought to express its teachings and attract followers in a context in which it was one of a number of movements competing for custom. That in turn was a factor behind the emphasis Agonshū placed, especially in its earlier years, on being an innovator that was (it claimed) ahead of the field and in the ways in which it sought to project itself and its leader through dramatic spectacular ritual events. Later, too, its transformation of the deceased founder into a powerful spiritual entity and focus of worship also showed how the movement imbibed patterns from elsewhere in the Japanese religious milieu.

The trajectory of our research

To explore these themes we draw on an extended period of observation and study of Japanese new religious movements in general, and of Agonshū in particular, that we have carried out between us over three decades. Our observations began when one of us (Reader) first became aware of Agonshū while living in Japan in the mid-1980s. After finding, in his mailbox, a leaflet from Agonshū advertising its annual Hoshi Matsuri (Star Festival)[2] he became interested in the images it appeared to be conveying and the potential spectacle promised. As such he attended the Hoshi Matsuri in 1987 and 1988 at Yamashina, just outside Kyoto, where Agonshū had acquired an extensive tract of land and where it subsequently built a large temple. He also visited Agonshū centres elsewhere in Japan, notably Tokyo, Kyoto and Osaka, attended sermons and ritual performances by Kiriyama, interviewed Agonshū members and officials and wrote a number of articles and book chapters about Agonshū, generally portraying it as representative of a particular dynamic infusing the 1980s Japanese religious world (Reader 1988; 1991: 194–233; 1994). While his observations of Agonshū ceased soon after, they resurfaced in 1995 when Aum Shinrikyō, a movement often identified alongside Agonshū as one of the new wave of religions causing a stir in the Japanese religious world of the 1980s and early 1990s, carried out a series of atrocities, including its infamous attack on the Tokyo subway in March 1995. Because Aum's founder and leader Asahara Shōkō had briefly been a member of Agonshū before quitting and forming his own movement, Agonshū became caught up in the subsequent media spotlight and maelstrom of hostility that affected religious groups in the wake of Aum's murderous activities, and as such it became a minor part of the Aum Affair as well (Reader 2000a: 13).

The other author of this book (Baffelli) began observations of Agonshū in the period after the Aum attack. This was as part of a broader study she was conducting on the ways in which modern Japanese religious movements used media forms to project themselves. From the early 2000s she regularly attended monthly events at Agonshū's main centre in Tokyo, including the First of the Month Fire rite (*tsuitachi engi hōshō goma*), the Ritual for the Liberation of the Spirit of Ancestors (*meitokusai*, held on the 16th of each month), occasional events such as *goma* (fire) rituals performed overseas and broadcast via live transmissions to Agonshū centres in Japan, the New Years' Sacred Fire Ceremony (*Hatsugoma*, in January 2009, January 2014, January 2018) and the *Mandō senzo kuyō*, the annual lantern memorial ceremony for the ancestors in July 2014. These visits, together with attendance to the Hoshi Matsuri and visits to the Tokyo centre at other times, were combined with informal conversations and interviews with members in Tokyo and Miyazaki and with former and current representatives of the movement. Her observations over the period from the early 2000s until 2014 indicated that Kiriyama was ageing and that his health was gradually deteriorating, and it led to a shift in the way he appeared at Agonshū rituals. At the same time, she started observing an increasing focus on rituals devoted to the souls of Japanese soldiers who died during the Second World War, something that indicated how the theme of nationalism was becoming more central to Agonshū. These issues are significant elements in Agonshū's recent development and will be discussed later in this book.

As we began working together, we became interested in interactions between religious movements – and more specifically on how different movements within the same milieu appeared to take note of and reshaped their views in response to what their rivals were doing and saying (Baffelli and Reader 2011). At the same time we, along with a colleague, carried out a study of the influences of the internet and online modes of communication, which were being used by religious movements in Japan and also influencing the ways in which the movements operated (Baffelli, Reader and Staemmler 2011). We began working on an informational website about Japanese new religious movements that provides extensive case studies of individual Japanese movements,[3] while giving joint talks about our mutual research on interactions between new religions, their competitive dimensions and their uses of media. As well as examining issues of competition between religious movements in Japan and the ways they projected themselves in media contexts, we also examined how Aum's activities impacted on the wider religious sphere in Japan (Baffelli and Reader 2012; Baffelli 2012). In all of these contexts, Agonshū featured prominently, and the idea of using it as a means to explore some of the above themes and to bring together various strands of our research developed.

Kiriyama's death proved the final catalyst in this process. Although he died on 29 August 2016 the news did not emerge in public until mid-September – a delay that caused us to wonder whether the movement's senior officials were unsure how to announce this event or handle the transition. The funeral was held in Yamashina on 16 October, forty-nine days after his death – a period significant in Buddhist contexts and indicative of Agonshū's assertions (see later chapters) that it represented a true and authentic form of Buddhism. Baffelli was back in Japan for a period of research at this time and was able to attend the funeral and speak to Agonshū officials and members, who queued for hours after the ceremony in order to pay their last respects to their leader. Later the body was cremated as is standard in Japan and (as is also standard in Japanese Buddhist funerals) some ashes and bone relics were preserved afterwards. These were placed in a silver casket similar to the casket in which Agonshū preserves what it claims to be the relics of the historical Buddha and which thus far had served as the movement's main image of worship.

In February 2017 Reader was able to visit Japan to follow up on the aftermath of Kiriyama's death, speak to Agonshū officials, collect materials such as Agonshū pamphlets, flyers and magazines produced by the movement after his death and attend the movement's annual all-day fire ritual the Hoshi Matsuri. Held every year on 11 February, this is the largest event in the Agonshū calendar and in 2017 Kiriyama's demise made it particularly significant. The 2017 festival incorporated a ritual service in which Kiriyama's relics were enshrined on the altar and he was declared to be the 'second Buddha' (*dai ni no budda*). This ritual enshrinement of Kiriyama's spirit and relics not only reiterated Agonshū's view that he was the spiritual leader of Buddhism in the modern day, one who had, according to the movement, received a direct transmission from the Buddha, but that he remained spiritually present in and for the movement. Indeed, as we discuss in Chapter 5, it signified how in death Kiriyama appeared to surpass the Buddha in the eyes of the movement, both physically and spiritually. His relics were placed in front of the casket said by the movement to contain those of the historical Buddha, while Agonshū teachers talked of him being more powerful spiritually than the Buddha. His continuing presence in the movement was affirmed in a series of spiritual messages known in Agonshū as *kaiso reiyu* (a term that translates as 'the founder's spiritual admonitions' or 'the founder's spiritual instructions'), which are said to be delivered by his spirit via the people who have taken over the day-to-day running of Agonshū. These spiritual messages or admonitions have been published in Agonshū's membership magazine and in flyers and pamphlets, and the messages they impart tell followers that Kiriyama's spirit continues to direct the movement. He may have died physically but spiritually he continues to guard over and guide the movement, and to exhort followers to follow the path he set out. In January 2018 Baffelli was able, during a subsequent visit to Japan, to attend Agonshū's first New Years' Sacred Fire Ceremony (*Hatsugoma*), where she talked to members, observed that Kiriyama's relics were placed in front of the Buddha's relics and noted further indications of how Agonshū continued to incorporate and emphasize their deceased founder as a continuing living presence in the movement.

Attending these events after Kiriyama's death, talking to officials and members and collecting materials Agonshū has produced in its aftermath thus enabled us to complete a cycle of observation of the movement over a period of more than three decades from its foundation to the death, enshrinement and apotheosis of its leader. This, we contend, represents an important way of examining movements; rather than being focused on a period of fieldwork during which we examine the dynamics and meanings of a movement at a particular point in time (and especially in terms of how devotees might engage with and draw from the movement), it seeks to take a longer historical perspective and to consider the trajectories of development within a movement over an extended period of time. Our focus is not to any great extent on the attitudes of members or their experiences in the movement so much as on the patterns of the construction and development of the movement as a whole and the projections of leadership and practices that have emerged in it in the context of changing circumstances over the past three or so decades. As such it provides a longitudinal study of one movement that serves as a case study through which to examine the processes whereby new movements emerge through the actions of a charismatic founder figure, build a framework of teachings, rituals and other means aimed at attracting a following, deal with various vicissitudes in their earlier periods of formation and handle the transition to a new leadership alongside dealing with the death of a founder. This has enabled us to make some suggestions about the nature of new movements, notably in Japan, but also potentially relevant for understanding religious movements elsewhere in their formative phases. We also look critically at the use of the term 'new religion', a term that has become normative in Japanese contexts to discuss movements such as Agonshū that have emerged in the modern era, but that contains numerous problems, not least when the founders of such movements person age and die, and as movements themselves grow older, enter a second generation of leadership and – as we indicate in later chapters – appear to reflect many of the normative themes associated with the Japanese religious environment rather than anything particularly new.

Chapters and themes

In Chapter 1 we contextualize Agonshū in Japan by looking more broadly at the notion of 'new religions' (*shinshūkyō*) as it has been generally used in Japan, along with the characteristics commonly associated with such movements. Agonshū has generally been viewed, in academic studies, in more popular accounts and in the mass media, as a 'new religion' in Japan – and the term itself has become one of the most common and normative ones used in the study of religion in that country.[4] We outline what is commonly meant by the term, including the historical context in which it and the movements associated with it have arisen. We also summarize some characteristic traits generally associated with the idea of the 'new religions'. Moreover, the reasons why some movements during the late 1970s and 1980s were briefly labelled as 'new' new religions (*shin shinshūkyō*), a term that suggested these movements, of which Agonshū was seen as a prime example, somehow represented a new wave in the context of Japanese religious movements, are also outlined. At the same time, we indicate that the terminology of the 'new' contains problems within it, not least because some of the movements labelled in this way are now quite old, but also because it can lead to generalizations that artificially categorize movements that have rather different orientations together under one banner. We return to the problems related with the idea of 'new religions' in our final chapter.

In Chapter 2 we provide an account of Agonshū's development, focusing on Kiriyama Seiyū's life, experiences and character. As Chapter 1 indicates, and as various studies of religious movements have argued, the role of charismatic founder-figures tends to be crucial in the formation and development of new religious movements. Founders have commonly been seen as central to this process in Japanese new religions,[5] which, especially in their early days, can come across predominantly as projections and reflections of their founders. The death of such figures in turn can serve as a critical point in the life cycles of their movements, an important rite of passage that presents new challenges. While we draw attention to several indicative examples of such founders, we focus particularly on Kiriyama who, we argue, can be regarded as an especially significant figure not simply in the context of Agonshū but more widely. Kiriyama is important not just because he established his own movement but also because he played a major role in shaping and articulating the religious agendas of the 1980s, when Agonshū first really attracted public notice, and as such he had an effect on other emergent movements of the time. In such terms we consider that he was one of the most seminal religious figures and foremost examples of charismatic religious leadership in modern Japan. In this chapter we draw attention to the example of Deguchi Ōnisaburō, the second founder/leader of Oomoto in Japan in the early twentieth century, who was an adept and innovative user of media as a way of spreading his messages, and who tapped into and shaped the prevailing ethos of his era. Deguchi has been described as a 'charismatic entrepreneur' (Stalker 2008) who expanded his movement dramatically and influenced other religious leaders – several of whom began as disciples in Oomoto before breaking away to form their own movements. If Deguchi was perhaps the most striking charismatic figure of the earlier twentieth century, we suggest that Kiriyama was a similar example from the 1980s, a founder who articulated ideas and practices that resonated with the spirit of the age, who used new technologies along with striking public ritual displays to draw attention to and expand his movement and who helped shape the context in which other new movements of the era grew. We look at various elements in Agonshū's make-up, from its millennialism and messages of world salvation, to its use of spectacular fire rituals and media technologies, and its opening up of roles to women that had been restricted in older traditions, in the context of Kiriyama's own life experiences.

In Chapter 3 we provide a general account of Agonshū's teachings and practices. We emphasize that the two operate in tandem; teachings and doctrines cannot be separated from practices and rituals. The latter are activities that articulate in overt forms the meanings of the movement's teachings. Practices serve as a mechanism through which followers can express the movement's teachings and (in their view) realize them. The centrality of beliefs about the ancestors and spirits of the dead (Prohl 1995; 2004), and of concepts such as karma and the ways in which individual lives may be influenced by such things, are crucial to Agonshū and they play a significant role not just in providing meaning for followers but in offering them a way through which such meaning can be enacted. Agonshū's messages of world salvation and its claims to be building a new centre to spread Buddhism to the world at large have been complemented by rituals that symbolically express images of world salvation and renewal alongside practices aimed at soothing the spirits of the dead. In this chapter we outline some of the ways Agonshū has set out these messages. We discuss some of the movement's core ritual practices along with its main festival, the Hoshi Matsuri, through which the movement's messages have been articulated in practical forms. In conjunction with this we also examine aspects of its membership structure and the ways in which devotees can engage in practices. In particular we pay attention to its claims of having opened up areas of practice to ordinary people that once were the monopoly of religious elites, while also noting that whereas this appears to be a form of democratization, it also makes significant demands – not least financial – on members.

Agonshū developed rapidly in the 1980s but during the 1990s this growth slowed – in part because the mood changed in Japan, especially after the 1995 subway attack by Aum Shinrikyō that created a hostile reaction to religion. Japan's problems due to economic stagnation also altered the mood of optimism that had fuelled Agonshū's earlier millennial messages of world salvation. While such messages have not been made redundant by changing circumstances, we show, in Chapter 4, that they have become somewhat less prominent while others that relate more directly to Japanese concerns and to Agonshū's orientation as a Japanese movement have become more prominent. In particular we note how themes of Japanese identity suffused with revisionist nationalism have become more central as Kiriyama (and the membership that formed the core around which the movement coalesced) aged. As Agonshū, after the early flushes of enthusiasm and dynamism related to its initial rapid growth, began to struggle to attract new followers, its orientations have become more inwardly directed towards Japanese concerns. Rituals once primarily emphasized as Buddhist and focused on world salvation have incorporated Shinto elements and centred on repatriating the spirits of the Japanese war dead, while the movement began visiting controversial Shinto shrines associated with prewar nationalism and militarism. Alongside these changes were publicly expressed regrets from Kiriyama about his own lack of participation in the Second World War and a rhetoric that lauded the sacrifices of Japan's war dead and portrayed them as integral to the well-being of the contemporary nation.

While Chapter 4 thus charts the changes in Agonshū's direction as Kiriyama aged and as the movement lost its initial impetus – something that is experienced in many new movements – Chapter 5 turns to the latest stages in Agonshū's trajectory. In 2016, as we noted earlier, Kiriyama died. In the years beforehand he appeared to be infirm and unable to carry out many of the rituals he used to perform. How Agonshū handled this initial period of infirmity and then death provides an example of the ways in which movements deal with the figure of a powerful charismatic founder, how they handle the problematic issue of the transition to a new leadership and how they seek to reconstruct themselves in the wake of a departed founder. Such periods can be highly fraught, and we cite examples of movements in Japan that have faced secessions and conflicts about who will succeed a charismatic founder. At the same time, movements face the problem of how they will henceforth regard their powerful founder figure. In the case of Agonshū we describe the response thus far from the movement, examining how a new leadership has sought to handle the transition by using Kiriyama's spirit to underpin its own legitimacy. Kiriyama, we show, has not just become elevated to a higher spiritual plain at death but remains present both physically and spiritually. His relics are now venerated as a key focus of worship in Agonshū while his continuing spiritual leadership is affirmed via the messages he is said to transmit to members via Agonshū's new leaders. We describe this process in Chapter 5 as 'losing the leader, and preserving, elevating and sanctifying the founder'. This, we argue, reflects a common pattern in charismatic movements, of elevating the leader to a status beyond that of a teacher or prophet and retaining him/her as a continuing spiritual presence, source of authority and means of legitimating and upholding the temporal leadership of his/her successors.

In our concluding chapter, Chapter 6, we discuss some of the implications of our study of Agonshū. It indicates the importance of examining movements over a period of their development, for example, by looking at them from their formation to the demise of their first generation of leaders. By examining how Agonshū has dealt with Kiriyama – by making him into a primary focus of worship – we discuss the extent to which it can be viewed as a founder veneration movement. In so doing we draw attention to founder veneration as a recurrent and significant dynamic in the structure not simply of new charismatic movements but also of Japanese religious contexts in general. Showing how similar themes pertain, for example, in traditional Japanese Buddhism as well as in new movements in and beyond Japan, we emphasize the theme of founder veneration as a recurrent pattern in the construction of religious structures. As such, Agonshū is not a unique or special case but an exemplar of a recurrent pattern.

Its articulation of themes found repeatedly across the religious spectrum in Japan – from its focus on the spirits of the dead to its use of ritual forms found in Buddhism and mountain religion, to its articulation of nationalist themes of identity and belonging – also serve to show that, despite the epithet of the 'new', Agonshū expresses normative rather than revolutionary religious themes in Japan. This, along with the evident fact that it is no longer really 'new' after having lost its founder and turned him into a figure of worship in ways that appear to memorialize the past more than they reflect visions of the future, raises questions about the concept of the 'new' in religious terms. In Chapter 6 we outline some of the arguments relating to the terminology of the new and suggest that although the term 'new religion' has become normative in Japan (and to a degree elsewhere), it is also a highly problematic concept, especially when, as with Agonshū, a movement ages and loses its founder, and when we need to distinguish so-called new religions from those that are older and more established.

1

Situating Agonshū: The Concept of 'New Religions' in Modern Japan

Introduction: the 'new' and the 'new new' in Japanese contexts

In this chapter we situate Agonshū within the broader Japanese religious context in which it is commonly portrayed, as one of that country's many 'new religions' (*shinshūkyō*). In so doing we clarify what is meant by the term 'new religion' in contemporary Japanese contexts.[1] By using this term we are following a conventional pattern in the field and are doing so for the sake of convenience, but, as this book indicates, we also feel that such blanket usage may be increasingly inappropriate, especially when movements age, founders die and they no longer appear to be at the forefront of the field in terms of dynamism. By drawing attention to such issues we establish the grounds for a more detailed examination of Agonshū and its leader in subsequent chapters, through which we can address the ageing process and development trajectories of newly formed religious movements, an area that we consider has thus far been understudied in the field.

Agonshū is a legally registered religious organization in Japan. It is commonly referred to in media and academic reports as a 'new religion', although this is a label that does not exist in legal terms in Japan. Under Japanese laws relating to religion, religious organizations are entitled (though not obliged) to apply for registration as 'religious corporations' (*shūkyō hōjin*) with the Agency for Cultural Affairs (Bunkachō) as long as they fulfil certain criteria.[2] By successfully registering they gain legal protection under the constitutional guarantee of religious freedom, along with tax privileges. Most movements do apply for such reasons and under the registration laws there are various labels under which they can do so, including 'Shinto-lineage', 'Buddhist-lineage', 'Christian' and 'other'. There is no specific 'new' category. Agonshū identifies itself, via its registration with the Agency, under the label of 'Buddhist lineage' (*bukkyōkei*),[3] and this self-identification indicates how it has projected itself to the wider world.

At the same time, as we have mentioned above, it has commonly been viewed in Japan and in academic studies as a 'new religion'. This is a direct translation of *shinshūkyō*, the Japanese term that has become standard in academic circles to refer to religious movements that have emerged in Japan since the early nineteenth century. Nyoraikyō, established by a peasant woman, Kino Isson (1756–1826) in Nagoya in

1802, is often considered to be the first of these movements (Murakami 1975; Reid 1991: 13). In the past two centuries or so many hundreds of other religious movements with Japanese roots[4] have appeared in Japan and been included under the general rubric of 'new religions'. Because of this extensive time span, some movements included in the rubric may be 200 years old and others much younger; for that reason the Japanese term *shin shinshūkyō*, 'new new religion', was coined, initially by Nishiyama Shigeru (1979; 1986), to refer to a new wave of movements including Agonshū that emerged into widespread public view in the late 1970s and 1980s and that were initially seen as differing from earlier 'new' movements. The term briefly came into wider usage – including by scholars such as Shimazono Susumu (2004: 18) – and was used also with the English translation 'new new religion' (e.g. Reader 1988). However, it also was criticized by some scholars for adding confusion to the field (e.g. Inoue 1997). Subsequently, it has largely been dropped from academic discourse due to a growing recognition that it muddied rather than clarified matters, especially as many scholars felt that there was little that distinguished these apparently 'new new religions' from earlier ones.[5]

Overall several hundred movements ranging from those founded in the early nineteenth century to those only a decade or two old are commonly portrayed as 'new religions'.[6] As a collective phenomenon they are regarded as being one of the most significant developments in the Japanese religious world of the past two centuries. Although some scholars (see below) have raised questions about the viability of using such a blanket term to refer to such a large number of movements that also cover a wide variety of typologies, they have nonetheless commonly been discussed under a single label (i.e. new religions) in collaborative studies and overviews that identify what are seen as their common elements and portraying them as exhibiting enough commonalities to justify including them all under a single label (e.g. Thomsen 1963; Offner and Straelen 1963; McFarland 1967; Inoue et al. 1991; Shimazono 1992a). Studies of individual movements within this wider rubric also have usually discussed such groups as being representative of the wider phenomenon (e.g. Earhart 1989; Hardacre 1984, 1986). Helen Hardacre (1986: 3–36), for example, in a perceptive analysis of Kurozumikyō, a movement founded by a charismatic Shinto priest in the early nineteenth century, uses that movement to argue that the new religions as a whole express a unified worldview. Winston Davis (1980: 9), in his pioneering study of the uses of magic and exorcism in Mahikari, a group that first emerged in the late 1950s based around spiritual healing, emphasized his view of the commonality among new religions by claiming that Mahikari is 'typical of the lot'.

Their emergence has been closely associated with Japan's rapid changes, from a nineteenth-century feudal and predominantly rural society into a modern, urban, technological (and now postindustrial) one. As such, they have been associated with and are seen in some contexts as a response to issues of rapid modernization and the social changes that this may bring about. They have been seen as especially appealing to people unsettled by such changes, and as providing solace and hope, along with meaningful teachings and promises of salvation in a changing society. In so doing, what they are seen to be doing is offering ways for people to understand their position in the wider world while holding out promises of amelioration on individual and wider levels. This can include world transformation, through which injustices and inequalities will be eradicated. As such they have commonly had millennial orientations, especially in their early periods of development. Yet new movements also age, and as they do they have often moved away from an apparent radicalism and become more socially conservative while reaffirming traditional values. As will be seen below, in emerging from the broader Japanese religious environment they typically emphasize many themes and values found in the established religions, albeit at times in newer shapes and forms, and as such could be considered as reiterations of the old as much as they are new and modern developments.

The problem of the 'new'

We have already touched on a major disjuncture in the term 'new religions': that some of them are rather old. Many movements that are cited in academic studies of Japanese new religions have histories going back as much as two centuries and are made up primarily of a membership several generations old. While scholars examining new religions in other parts of the world have debated whether it is viable to continue to use the term 'new' after a movement has moved to its second generation of leaders and members,[7] in Japan this has hardly been the case. Movements are still incorporated under the banner of the 'new' even as they age, look increasingly as if they have been around for some while and consist almost wholly of people born into the movement – and born of parents and grandparents who themselves had been born into the movement. This is in part because the term 'new' does not straightforwardly equate to being very recently formed or new in a chronological sense. Rather, it serves as a contrast to the notion of 'established religions' (*kisei shūkyō*), a label commonly ascribed to the older Japanese religious traditions of Buddhism and Shinto that are generally viewed as the 'mainstream' in Japan and have been around for a millennium or more.[8]

Traditionally the primary avenues of religious affiliation in Japan have centred around these established traditions, through life cycle, household and community rituals and practices that build social bonds between individuals and families and the shrines and temples that serve their communities. Links to and affiliations with Buddhism in Japan are especially related to dealing with death, funerals and memorial rituals for the benefit of the spirits of the deceased of household lineages, while people have been associated with Shinto via rituals and festivals that tie households and individuals to the wider community and also, especially in the period from 1868 to 1945, to the nation. New religions are 'new' to the extent that they are nowhere near as old as the established traditions – but also because they are seen as providing a different focus of affiliation, based initially in individual volition and conversion rather than inherited tradition and social affiliation. This focus on individual conversion, rather than household, customary and cultural inheritance, however, wanes significantly after the first generation of members, with older new religions being increasingly reliant on inheritance from one generation to the next.

In other words, new religions are seen as alternative to the established traditions. They have commonly and historically been seen as offering something new, dynamic, exciting and attractive in contrast to the seeming social conventionalism of the established traditions – even if, as we indicate later, many new religions reiterate very traditional religious themes and manifest teachings and practices not dissimilar to, and often drawn from, Buddhism or Shinto. This dynamism, especially in early periods of formation, comes from charismatic founder-figures who claim new revelations and offer new practices that promise followers a path to salvation and/or allow followers a greater role in ritual participation than do the older traditions. By contrast, the older traditions have been seen by many to be centred on a priestly elite that dominates rituals and on a divide in which lay people are excluded from meaningful or leading ritual roles. Their image, too, to a degree, is of being somewhat mired in the past – or, as they have often been called, *furukusai* or 'smelling of age' – lacking in dynamism, not relevant in terms of the problems faced by people in the modern world and too closely associated with the status quo. Some (including clerics in the established traditions) have argued that a factor in the growth of new religions has been the weakness of the older traditions.[9] Agonshū is a good example of a movement that benefitted from being seen as new when it first attracted attention, and it played on this image by portraying itself not just as up to date and in tune with modern society and technology but ahead of the field in such areas. At the same time it also criticized established Buddhism and priestly hierarchies for being out of touch and for monopolizing ritual powers that could benefit and be participated in by ordinary people. These issues were certainly a factor in Agonshū's rise to popularity and in Chapters 2 and 3 we will look at them further.

Being new and alternative, however, has dualistic connotations. The dynamism of the new might attract people but it can also arouse hostility and suspicion, especially from the established traditions, from those who identify with the establishment and from those who see any new movement as a potential source of disruption and instability. New and emergent religions that, as is common in the Japanese context, have talked of world renewal and transformation may worry civil authorities and establishment groups including political agencies keen to protect the status quo. When they offer people a chance to change their religious affiliations or present an alternative to the services provided by the older traditions, they have often been seen as a threat and have faced hostility as a result. Nineteenth-century new movements such as Tenrikyō, Kurozumikyō and Konkōkyō faced hostile responses from Shugendō (a mountain religious tradition with links to Buddhism) because the healing rituals and teachings these movements provided offered an alternative to people who had previously relied on Shugendō for such things. As a result Shugendō practitioners, fearing a loss of their clienteles, reacted aggressively against such movements (Hardacre 1994). This has been a recurrent issue for new movements that have been attacked because they pose a threat to the religious services and monopolies previously held by the established religions. Agonshū, for example, has provoked reactions from some in the Shingon Buddhist tradition because its use of esoteric Buddhist practices appears to challenge an area that the Shingon tradition sees as its preserve.[10]

Attacks on the legitimacy of 'new religions' have been a recurrent feature of Japanese public and media life. In the earlier part of the twentieth century the Japanese media, along with people involved with the older traditions, and some academics (notably those involved in traditional Buddhist Studies, and with vested interests in preserving the elitist position of that tradition), used pejorative terms such as 'pseudo-religion' (*ruiji shūkyō*) and 'heresies' (*jakyō*) to refer to such movements, thereby implying that they were not proper and valid religions.[11] This hostility was often accompanied by suggestions that such movements were associated with fraud and manipulation, and that their leaders were not sincere and more akin to tricksters intent on making money by enticing misguided, uneducated people with false promises of worldly benefits and salvation.

The state, particularly from the first decades of the twentieth century until 1945, sought to regulate and restrict new movements, at times suppressing them and imprisoning their leaders for apparent crimes against the state. This happened, for example, when Honmichi, in 1928 and 1938, was accused of threatening social stability via its prophecies, while Oomoto faced oppression and the incarceration of its leaders in 1921 and 1935 for not affording adequate reverence to the Emperor.[12] After 1945 state interference in religion was blocked by a new constitution and guarantees of religious freedom, but new religions both as a collective group and individually still faced critical attacks, often spearheaded by a mass media that identified itself with the establishment and took on for itself a self-appointed role as a watchdog against potential social deviance (as the media saw it).[13] In the post-1945 era – a period in which there was rapid growth both in numbers of new movements and in their apparent popularity – the term *shinkō shūkyō*, which roughly translates as 'newly arisen religion' and contains nuances of transience, ephemerality and insubstantiality, became the common term used in the mass media and, initially, also in academic accounts.

Hostility has been a common element in mass media discussions of new movements in Japan. It is fair to say that when the mass media carries stories about new religions, they commonly centre on stories or rumours of malpractice, fraud, money, manipulation and sexual scandals (Dorman 2012; Baffelli 2016). By contrast, officials of new religions complain frequently that their positive contributions to society (e.g. in social welfare activities) rarely if ever get a mention in the media.[14] This negativity includes not simply reporting or alleging scandals but also attempts to produce critical exposés of new religions. The case of Jiu, a movement led by the charismatic female leader Jikōson that attracted a great deal of attention, and the support of some prominent celebrity figures including one of Japan's leading Sumō wrestlers, in the period immediately after 1945, is significant here. In part because it had attracted prominent celebrities who had been seen as Japanese cultural heroes, Jiu came under heavy attack from the media; its leader Jikōson was depicted as crazy and manipulative while its members (including the Sumō champion Futabayama) were portrayed as naive and as having been lured into a bizarre group through Jikōson's manipulations. The opprobrium directed at Jiu was such that the movement became destabilized, its celebrity followers were driven into leaving and eventually the movement faded away (Dorman 2012).

Another example of media hostility concerned Risshō Kōseikai, a Buddhist-oriented new religion with a strong focus on peace that rapidly became one of Japan's largest religious movements in the post-1945 era. In the mid-1950s it came under intensive attack from the *Yomiuri Shinbun*, Japan's largest newspaper, which has close associations with the Japanese establishment and mainstream conservative political forces. The *Yomiuri* waged an aggressive campaign and published numerous articles accusing Risshō Kōseikai of infringements, ranging from financial wrongdoings to manipulating its followers. The attacks were supported by Japanese politicians, who took up the accusations and conducted parliamentary hearings into the movement. This is not to say that such attacks were wholly unjustified, and subsequently Risshō Kōseikai instituted reforms to deal with some aspects (notably its recruitment methods) covered in the *Yomiuri* criticisms. Yet, as Morioka Kiyomi's (1994) study has shown, the Yomiuri Affair, as it was known, also damaged the newspaper and provided evidence of Risshō Kōseikai's depth of support; *Yomiuri*'s circulation dropped by 200,000 during its campaign. Moreover, the criticisms levelled at Risshō Kōseikai gave it the impetus to institute reforms and to develop new strategies of coping with external attacks, and in essence strengthened rather than weakened the movement.

We mention these just as examples of a recurrent situation in which the alternative and new have been attacked by a mass media that identifies itself with the establishment and has commonly assumed a negative stance towards any movement that appears to offer something different from the religious establishment. One should also note that there have been cases in which new movements have been clearly associated with malpractice, none more so than when Aum Shinrikyō committed a series of murderous crimes in the 1990s and in so doing caused severe repercussions for religious movements across the spectrum (Baffelli and Reader 2012; Inoue et al. 2011; Reader 2000a; Wilkinson 2009). Agonshū, as we mentioned in the Introduction and discuss further in Chapter 4, faced particular problems because Aum's founder, Asahara Shōkō, had once been a member of Agonshū and some of the teachings he developed in Aum were clearly derived from Agonshū. In the aftermath of the Aum attack new religions in general faced hostile media coverage, and were widely portrayed as potentially dangerous or even as a potential 'next Aum' – an accusation levelled at groups, from mass movements such as Sōka Gakkai, which had close ties to a political party that had been involved in government coalitions, to the small millennial group Panawave Laboratory, which was hounded aggressively by journalists and the police for sometime but which ultimately proved harmless albeit somewhat eccentric in nature.[15]

Hostility and negativity can (as with the case of Jiu) undermine a movement but, as the Risshō Kōseikai case suggests, it can also offer a means through which a movement can reorient itself and become stronger. As we will see in later chapters, Agonshū has experienced both sides of this coin; media revelations about an incident in Kiriyama's past that cast aspersions on his character were, as we show in Chapter 2, used to good effect by the movement to develop a core aspect of Agonshū's teaching and to enhance his status, while the backlash from the Aum Affair of 1995 (see Chapter 4) by contrast weakened the movement.

The 'new' as a category

As new generations of scholars, both Japanese and Western, have emerged, they have developed more nuanced studies of such movements rather than writing them off in the negative way evident in much of the earlier mass media. Such scholarship has illustrated the ways in which they provide viable and coherent teachings, doctrines and messages that resonate with the needs of people in modern Japan in ways that the older traditions appear incapable of doing. Moreover, there has been wider awareness that new religions in general often play an active role in social welfare activities and that they can contribute to the public good. Such factors have produced a generally less biased attitude towards these movements in the public and academic domains, and, since the 1970s, led to a shift in terminology, with *shinshūkyō*, a term lacking the negative connotations of being 'newly arisen' (as in *shinkō shūkyō*), coming into more general usage.[16]

Such studies have also refuted claims often put forward in earlier scholarship that presented new religions as having little substance in terms of doctrines and teachings, or dismissing them as merely borrowing their teachings from the established religions.[17] In a cogent argument that refutes the view that new religions lack doctrinal substance, Jamie Hubbard (1998) shows that Shinnyoen was firmly based in Buddhist doctrinal orthodoxies. Indeed Hubbard argues that if scholars examined new religions from the doctrinal perspective so commonly found in the academic field, and notably in Buddhist Studies, they would have found that new religions are actually similar to the older established traditions.[18] Monika Schrimpf (2011: 181) also emphasizes that Shinnyoen identifies itself as Buddhist. Studies of Risshō Kōseikai have drawn attention to its nature as a lay Buddhist movement emphasizing Buddhist concepts and teachings and seeking to incorporate them into an ethical framework relevant for modern life and families (Dehn 2011). Birgit Staemmler (2011b: 130–4) has similarly shown that Oomoto – a movement normally viewed as being Shinto-oriented – has a set of doctrines set out in the writings of its first and second founders, Deguchi Nao and Deguchi Ōnisaburō, that underpins the movement and guides the way its leaders and members act.

Such perspectives have shown that new religions are not the ephemeral phenomena depicted in earlier portrayals that referred to them as *nise* (false) or *shinkō* ('newly arisen/ephemeral'). As such the terms 'new religions' and *shinshūkyō* have now become the most commonly used terms in English and Japanese. However, and partly because of the recognition that such movements have doctrinally sound bases and may, as a result, share common ground with existing traditions, some recent studies have questioned whether using such blanket terms continues to be viable. Nancy Stalker (2008: 196), for example, considers that the label 'new religion' commonly affixed to Oomoto and other such groups means that it gets 'lumped together with disparate Buddhist and Christian groups'; as Stalker notes, the term 'new religion' sets them apart from the mainstream and emphasizes their marginality, rather than bringing out their continuities with established religions (196). Stephen Covell and Mark Rowe (2004: 246, n 6) have suggested similarly that new religions grounded in Buddhist teachings and interpretations of Buddhist texts might best be 'studied and interpreted' under a Buddhist label. In his study of Gedatsukai, a new religion founded by Okano Eizō in 1928 that had links with Shugendō and Shingon Buddhism, Byron Earhart discusses how membership of this movement appears to reinforce and strengthen adherence to what he sees as traditional practices and values. Indeed, Earhart (1989: 237) states, the more one studies Gedatsukai, the more it looks like an 'old' religion. As such he views it as a 'new tradition' – a reformulation of old themes in new ways, and considers that new religions in general 'are contemporary transformations of earlier Japanese religion' (240).

Such themes are also evident in Agonshū – a movement that was inaugurated some five decades after Gedatsukai but that, like it, drew on Shugendō and esoteric Buddhist elements, albeit with a more critical stance towards those traditions than Gedatsukai. In our study of Agonshū we show many areas in which this movement, officially founded in 1978, not only uses ritual practices drawn from esoteric Buddhism but has at the core of its doctrinal structure notions about ancestors and karma that are deeply embedded in traditional Japanese religious views and central to the structure of established Buddhism in Japan. Yet we also consider that placing it under one singular category such as 'Buddhist' would be problematic, notably because its teachings draw also from the Japanese folk world of beliefs about spirits, and because in the past decade or so in particular it has also manifested themes and notions from Shinto (see Chapter 4 in particular). Moreover, the terminology of the 'new' continues to have potentially underlying prejudicial connotations, but it also has implicit hints of dynamism that contrast with images of the old and established, and that relate to images that Agonshū and many other movements are keen to promote as evidence of why they are relevant and important in the modern day.

Revitalizations of enduring truths?

As the above suggests, the idea of the 'new' is highly ambivalent, invoking images of alternative and new ways of developing religious consciousness in a modern world in which the 'old' is out of step, but also arousing, among critics, accusations of ephemerality and a lack of serious depth. Some movements in the immediate postwar era did embrace the idea of the new by forming, in 1951, the Federation of New Religious Organizations of Japan (Shin Nihon Shūkyō Dantai), known, for short, as the Shinshūren. This collective body was set up to serve as a coordinating body to counter media hostility and negativity while promoting the common interests of new religious movements and developing a better public image for them. Yet only a small number of those movements commonly labelled as 'new religions' are members (currently some thirty-nine groups are affiliated) and many prominent ones (Sōka Gakkai and Agonshū, for example) are not.

It is common for movements to demonstrate their unease with the term, while some (e.g. Tenrikyō) object to being labelled as new religions (Staemmler and Dehn 2011: 5). Movements accept that they are organizationally new, keen to emphasize the idea of dynamism that goes with being new and like to portray themselves as in tune with the times and in their uses of technology. Yet few wholeheartedly embrace the idea and seek to depict themselves as wholly new in cosmological terms. The new truths, revelations and practices through which their followers can achieve salvation are rarely claimed to be totally new modern products. Rather, they are presented as ancient and enduring truths and practices that have been disregarded by others but are being brought to life anew by the movements concerned and by their leaders. In Tenrikyō, for example,

Nakayama Miki was designated as the messenger of God the Parent, a deity who, after creating the world, had receded into the background and been ignored by humanity. Because the world had thereafter fallen into chaos, according to Tenrikyō, God the Parent decided to return to restore order and build a new world. Nakayama Miki was the selected vehicle for this mission and her teaching was thus a re-articulation of the original truths of God the Parent, delivered through his chosen vehicle. Other new movements that focused on deities (often with a Shinto orientation) similarly have talked about the reappearance of an original deity who is returning to the world to reform it through the agency of a chosen figure. In Buddhist-inspired new religions, it is often the case that their founders claim to discover new or hidden truths in Buddhist sutras – something that, as we discuss in Chapter 2, was the case in Agonshū.

This point about being new and yet a manifestation of ancient and enduring truths – and the entire dilemma of the terminology of the new – was exemplified by an interview one of the authors had with a senior figure in a prominent religion focused on the Lotus Sutra and identifying itself as a lay movement in the Nichiren Buddhist tradition. The official – responding to a question that used the term *shinshūkyō* (new religion) to refer to his movement – denied that it was new. It might, he agreed, be new in terms of having been formed as a separate organization in the twentieth century. It was, however, he stressed, very much an ancient and historically grounded religion, dating back not just to Nichiren, the thirteenth-century Buddhist teacher, but through him to the very roots and origins of Buddhism. It was not so much new as a modern articulation of an ancient foundational truth. Yet, when the author concerned then commented that, given that the movement was therefore an ancient and traditional movement, he could not include it in his planned course on Japanese new religions, the official responded with shock. How could this movement – perhaps the largest new movement in Japan and certainly (in his view) the most important – be left out of such a course? In such terms, having denied he represented a new religion he almost simultaneously affirmed that he did. The movement was thus both an ancient one grounded in timeless universal truths and the origins of Buddhism and a new one of the modern era. While it should not be called a new religion, it clearly had to be included in a course on new religions.

There is, as such, a tension in the rhetoric and orientations of new religions, in which they emphasize their 'newness' as a form of dynamism not seen in other religions, yet stress that they are not really or merely new, but are articulating eternal truths that extend back even beyond those of the established traditions. This is something that we will see in later chapters as we examine Agonshū and note how it has proudly proclaimed itself as a modern movement in tune with the zeitgeist of the times (particularly during its first flush of growth in the 1980s) while simultaneously presenting itself as a movement offering unchanging truths that go back to the roots of Buddhism.

Continuities and characteristics

One of the factors behind the use of a singular term for a complex array of movements that have developed in Japan since the early nineteenth century is that they appear to exhibit a number of characteristics that (while not evident in every movement so labelled) seem to indicate a degree of commonality across the spectrum. Much of this is because they are products of the Japanese religious environment and thus draw on its basic themes and orientations – themes that indicate the degree to which such seemingly new movements are also extensions and continuities with the older traditions. They use and articulate many aspects of Japanese traditional cosmology, thought and practices, in ways that make them relevant to the needs and concerns of ordinary people in the present day. Thus, as we examine Agonshū we will note an emphasis on venerating the ancestors and performing rituals to pacify the spirits of the dead, along with a belief that misfortunes emanate from spiritual hindrances caused by unhappy spirits. Such views are embedded in Japanese folk religious traditions (Hori 1968) and play a significant role in the structure of Japanese temple Buddhism, which has a strong focus on rituals and memorial practices relating to the ancestors and to caring for the spirits of the dead (Covell 2005; Rowe 2011). Ritual practices, too, often demonstrate a continuity with older traditions; movements such as Tenrikyō and Kurozumikyō use ritual formats, along with architectural features in their centres of worship, that resemble those found in Shinto. Others draw extensively on Buddhist practices, texts and figures of worship, and view themselves as Buddhist movements. Sōka Gakkai, Risshō Kōseikai, Reiyūkai and Gedatsukai all come in this category, and see themselves as articulating Buddhist teachings in ways relevant for the modern day.

They are generally founded by a charismatic leader who claims to have discovered new truths and/or receives new revelations that form the basis of a new way forward, one that offers followers a path to salvation, often framed in this-worldly terms. Such charismatic leaders are perceived by those who follow them as conduits between this and other spiritual realms, as specially gifted teachers who have discovered hidden truths (sometimes within Buddhist texts and sometimes via the revelations of a deity) and/or who have been selected by deities to act as agents of change and to be their mouthpieces in this world. They have been the core around which nearly every new religion has formed and have served as their focus of inspiration and authority.

In Chapter 2 we examine this issue of charisma and charismatic leadership further through our examination of Kiriyama Seiyū and his development of a profile and image that inspires confidence and faith among followers and through which they can gain the means to deal with their problems and find salvation. We also note that this is an area in which the new replicates patterns already evident in the Japanese religious world. Popular charismatic movements existed in Japan before the rise of 'new religions'; the reverence accorded to founders in various established Buddhist sectarian traditions and the emphasis placed on their teachings and writings as canonical, indicates that founder-veneration and the role of individual inspirational figures has been a formative element in the structure of religious organizations in Japan for many centuries. This is something we discuss more in Chapter 6.

They are seen as offering followers a coherent view of their place in the world and a solution to their personal worries and problems. They emphasize notions such as self-cultivation as a means through which individuals can improve themselves, develop moral understandings of their situation and of the world around them and find salvation. The frameworks new religions offer in this context frequently emphasize very traditional concepts based in the folk religious world, for example, that illnesses and misfortunes are the result of spiritual impediments caused by malevolent or unhappy spirits, such as the spirits of dead kin who have not been properly cared for after death. Such interpretations in effect argue that there is a psychic (alongside or underpinning a physical) cause to illnesses and other misfortunes; it is a mode of interpretation that places the individual at the centre of any solutions to their problems. Illnesses may be seen as being caused not simply or primarily by physical factors such as germs, but due to underlying spiritual issues and impediments, such as past behaviour that has angered an ancestor spirit or led to the individual accruing negative karma that in turn produces maladies. In Tenrikyō, for example, illness is seen as a result of misdeeds that create a spiritual dust that clouds the mind and leads it astray. Illness may be a physical event but its roots are spiritual, serving as a warning and as a reminder of the need to lead a more moral life. Mahikari, for example, emphasizes that illness is a product of spiritual causes; while illness may be superficially caused by germs, the real issue was why those germs were ingested in the first place, something that is grounded in psychic factors (Davis 1980: 37). Dealing with such root spiritual causes is seen as an essential part of the recovery process. As we will discuss later, in Agonshū misfortunes and the problems of the world at large are grounded in the psychic world of unhappy spirits of the dead for whom the correct rituals of pacification have not been performed.

Such spiritual hindrances need not be a product simply of one's own actions but can include those inherited from other family members and ancestors; this indicates that people are not autonomous individuals so much as they are people living in a world of interdependence with their kin and ancestors. Here the concept of karma, drawn from Buddhism, is highly significant. Karma in Japanese folk contexts and in the view of many new religions can be both individual and shared or inherited from one's kin, and it can have negative connotations; one's deeds and those of one's ancestors can be a karmic impediment causing problems and serving as barriers to one's spiritual and material advancement in this life. Agonshū, as such, emphasizes the idea of 'cutting one's karma' (*karuma o kiru*) and thereby eradicating any negative impediments, through ritual practices and other actions designed to pacify the spirits of the dead and purify the practitioner's spirit.

Problem confrontation and solution – through which one can also achieve happiness, benefits and salvation in this life and beyond – is generally linked to practice, with adherents provided with accessible ritual processes and techniques to this end. For example, Mahikari's ritual practice of *okiyome* (spiritual purification) offers members a technique for dealing with spiritual impediments. In Mahikari's worldview, the creator deity Su-God emits pure spiritual light in order to purify the world. This pure light was initially mediated by and through Mahikari's founder, and Su-God's intermediary on earth, Okada Kōtama (1901–74), and he, in turn, created and blessed amulets that devotees could use as conduits for this pure light. Through wearing such amulets Mahikari devotees can channel Su-God's pure light onto others, transmitting it via their hands, which they hold over the person being treated, thus, according to Mahikari, purifying them spiritually, exorcising bad spirits and eradicating the causes of misfortune and illness. Mahikari thus enables devotees to become healers and ritual practitioners and, in so doing, it, according to Davis (1980: 302), democratizes magic and makes it available to and usable by all devotees. Mahikari is not alone in this but part of a wider tradition within the new religions of movements that use various techniques and practices of purification such as *okiyome*. Other movements may offer followers different techniques of purification and ritual practice (such as, e.g. chanting Buddhist sutras) that can empower the individual and make him/her into a healer. In general terms, new religions offer their adherents the means through which they can become ritual specialists and part of the process both of dealing with their own misfortunes and of helping heal those of others as well – and ultimately contribute to reforming and saving the whole world. Again, we will see this in action when we discuss how Agonshū enables followers to play roles in its major festivals and rituals.

This is an area where new religions tend to manifest differences with the traditional and established religions, which rely on and are based around formal priestly hierarchies. Agonshū has emphasized this point in its claims that it has liberated esoteric practices that were previously monopolized by the established Buddhist clergy in ways that enabled them to retain a hold over ordinary people, and made them accessible to ordinary devotees (Reader 1994). Other new religions have similarly developed practices that lay members can take part in as well as emphasizing the role of the laity as proselytizers of their faith – again something that has marked them out from the older traditions.

Communication and the importance of being accessible

Linked to this emphasis on the laity and ordinary members as a dynamic force in promoting the movement and in participating in the processes of problem solution and salvation has been a recognition that new religions have been adept at communicating their teachings in direct and accessible ways that ordinary people can understand. Often – and Agonshū is a striking case here, especially in its foundational era – they emphasize a sense of modernity in being able to use media such as mass produced leaflets and pamphlets and new technologies to spread their message. In such terms, too, the materials they produce – including leaflets, pamphlets, flyers and videos – serve as important texts for members and researchers alike. The use of such materials also indicates the capacity to articulate their messages in accessible terms that are readily understood, rather than in the often obscure and arcane language used in the established religions and that serves as a barrier to understanding for many people.

Kiriyama was a vocal critic of established Buddhism in this respect, accusing it of enhancing the control of priestly hierarchies through using obscure terminologies and texts that were inaccessible to ordinary people (Murō 1987: 54; Reader 1994). Similar criticisms have been made by other new movements such as Shinnyoen, which has accused established Buddhism of perpetuating the view that 'sutras belong to priests and these have little to do with common believers' (Shinnyoen 1977: 49).

By contrast it has been common for new religions to produce materials that can be easily read by followers along with accessible explanations of their teachings. Tenrikyō, for instance, has developed a canonical literature centred around the *Ofudesaki*, the writings of Nakayama Miki, and this is backed up with a tradition of study and interpretation that emphasizes the importance of doctrine and teaching in the movement, in which special lectures on core doctrines are available to members.[19] Glossaries and commentaries that provide explanations of terms and doctrines may also be widely available, especially when movements develop terminologies that have special resonance for their worldviews and doctrinal structures.[20] Kōfuku no Kagaku emphasizes textual study and reading as a means of conversion and of understanding the movement; members are expected to have read a number of the writings of its founder Ōkawa Ryūhō before joining, and attend seminars about them and continue reading his writings thereafter (Baffelli 2005). Members may send copies of Ōkawa's writings to those they seek to convert while frequently responding to questions about doctrines and the movement in general with the phrase *yomeba wakaru* (if you read (it) you will understand).[21]

Movements across the new religions' spectrum produce a vast amount of easily accessible materials designed to attract followers, to outline their teachings and practices, and to develop a sense of community and belonging among them. Pamphlets, flyers and newspapers were used fruitfully by Deguchi Ōnisaburō in the 1910s and 1920s to spread Oomoto's message in ways that ordinary people could understand and to help it develop into the largest new religion of its era (Stalker 2008; Staemmler 2011b). Others have similarly engaged in the production of a variety of materials for similar reasons. Leaders such as Kiriyama and Ōkawa, whose followers proudly proclaim that he has been mentioned the Guinness Book of Records because of his prolific production of books,[22] have published a stream of volumes to this effect. New movements in general have produced materials such as monthly magazines (sometimes directed at specific age or gender groups), booklets, pamphlets and simple volumes setting out core teachings, along with, as technologies have developed videos, CDs and DVDs (Baffelli 2016). This capacity to use various media forms to educate followers and spread teachings has at times been viewed with envy by older, established religious groups who have seen it as a reason why, in the modern era, they have struggled to retain followers and stop them moving away to the new religions, and have sought to follow the lead of new religions by producing similar forms of pamphlets and the like for their members, albeit not always successfully.[23]

This focus on accessibility and reaching out to as many people as possible should not be confused with a lack of sophistication, just as arcane language and texts accessible only to elite trained specialists should not be seen as meaning superior and higher levels of doctrinal sophistication. By using direct, straightforward language and media forms, new religions such as Agonshū get their messages across to a wide public audience in ways that cannot be achieved by texts written in premodern linguistic forms understood only by a handful of trained priests. This is an element in the comparative success of many new movements; by being readily understood, the language such materials use can have an empowering effect on members, who feel that they can fully understand the teachings and can take responsibility for their own spiritual path.

As such the pamphlets, leaflets, books, videos and DVDs that movements such as Agonshū put out are important research materials that need to be taken seriously as representations of their messages and teachings. They are as valid and meaningful as texts as are the various Buddhist sutras and texts that have been the focus of study and academic research in the Buddhist tradition, for they (like Buddhist sutras) convey teachings, meanings and views of the world that provide followers with assurance and guidance. They have been important items in researching this book, and in subsequent chapters we will refer frequently to Agonshū media productions, from books and videos to leaflets, CDs and pamphlets, as significant textual sources in the structure of the movement's belief and teaching systems, and as materials that shed light on the workings, nature, appeal and contemporary dynamics of the movement.

Entrepreneurship and the development of resources

This perceived ability to transmit messages and make use of modern technologies to do so is one manifestation of a broader capacity that new movements need to demonstrate if they are to develop a following and build the sorts of organizational and physical structures required by a mass movement. Building a movement from scratch requires the development of buildings, organizations and a viable financial structure to enable a movement to operate, carry out expansion projects, build and maintain centres and places of worship for followers to attend, proselytize and, if it grows in size, to have the people to run its operations. At the outset, when founders have their initial visions and seek to spread their teachings, they generally do not have access to the resources needed to develop a religious organization. They are unlike the older established traditions, with their shrines, temples, land and other resources that have been inherited from previous generations and from patronage and donations over many centuries. Nor are they able to draw on the social structures that have long provided economic sustenance for religious institutions, as is the case with Shinto and Buddhism in Japan, where the former has had community ties and the latter historical links with households and ancestral systems. Both Shinto and Buddhism have long had associations with political power structures and (at least in earlier eras) patronage. By contrast the new movements that emerged from the nineteenth century onwards had no such backing, historical resources or socially embedded support structures to call upon. They also, if they claim to have a reach and message beyond the localized Japanese context, may seek to develop an international profile, something that, as we will see, helps build their appeal further in Japan but that also requires resources. They have needed organizational skills, commercial and business acumen, entrepreneurship and ways of gathering resources in order to accomplish these tasks; religious visions and messages without the support mechanisms to project these to a growing audience and without the organizational abilities to create a movement that can further these aims are, like charisma itself without the relational support of followers (see Chapter 2), hardly likely to flourish.

New religions that have managed to successfully accomplish such tasks and to develop the organizational means to spread their messages have commonly relied on the voluntary support of devotees, who are the key providers of resources in money (via fees and the like) and services, including voluntary work, to help sustain the organization by giving some of their free time to helping at centres. Such voluntary activity is commonly seen as a form of religious practice and duty, and may be promoted as such, thereby serving as a spur to followers to aid their religion in such ways. Tenrikyō, for example, emphasizes the concept of *hinokishin*, voluntary service, as a form of religious devotion and practice for followers. At Agonshū centres one is likely to be greeted by devotees acting in a voluntary capacity to help the movement – something that has happened to both of us when we have visited Agonshū centres. As we discuss also, in Chapter 3, fund-raising and similar services are considered to be important tasks for members of Agonshū – tasks that also lead to individual rewards and recognition from the movement.

Beyond voluntary work, new religions rely on members for income and they do this via a variety of means, from regular membership fees to donations and payments for ritual services, to the purchase of ritual implements (something that members in Agonshū do in order to perform various practices essential to membership), books, videos, DVDs and other items of teaching. Paying for various services is not, of course, confined to new religions but is common to religious organizations in Japan and elsewhere. Established Buddhism in Japan, for example, relies heavily on fees for rituals and services associated with the memorialization of household ancestors (Murai 2010: 155),[24] while the sale of amulets and other ritual objects and services is commonplace among, and is often an important aspect of the economic support of, Buddhist temples and Shinto shrines (Reader and Tanabe 1998). As we will note in Chapter 1, when we look more closely at Kiriyama's life and activities, the founders of such movements often demonstrate a degree of commercial entrepreneurship in such contexts – an acumen that is requisite for the formation of successful groups.

At the same time, this is another area in which new religions have been criticized and attacked in Japan (more than, e.g. Buddhism and Shinto), and at times portrayed as little more than money-making enterprises.[25] As we discuss in Chapter 3, membership of Agonshū and engagement in its practices does cost money, and for some rituals it is not inconsiderable. Agonshū members have sometimes expressed concerns about the costs of membership yet at the same time, as Kiriyama reminded one such questioner (see Chapter 2), it remains up to the follower to determine what value they place on the services being offered. As will be seen in Chapter 3, there are those who feel that Agonshū offers them a message of hope, salvation and positivism through which to deal with their lives, and that the costs of membership and services it requires are therefore acceptable. We also note in Chapter 3 that some people find the demands excessive and may complain about it. In such terms we would suggest that new religions – certainly those like Agonshū that (see Chapter 2) incorporate a number of commercial arms from a publishing firm that markets Kiriyama's books, to a venture selling what the movement portrays as spiritually nourishing health foods – demonstrate a level of entrepreneurialism that fits well with the consumer capitalist orientations of modern society. The commercial acumen of such movements can also involve paying attention to the machinations of other groups and noting (and copying) activities that they use and that appear to be successful. As we note in the next chapter, various new movements of the 1980s established publishing enterprises to commercially market the writings of their founders, and some, including Agonshū, have engaged public relations firms to help them develop marketing strategies to heighten their appeal

(Baffelli 2016). The extent to which such movements may draw inspiration and ideas from other organizations – and their willingness to look beyond the immediate context of the Japanese religious milieu – was evident to us in the comments of the public relations director of one large Buddhist new religion during an interview in 2003, who said the movement had looked at a number of groups and organizations for ideas on how to develop its marketing strategies. These included the Catholic Church (which, apparently, had impressed this new religion with its use of multiple types of magazines aimed at different segments of the Catholic world) and Coca-Cola (whose use of eye-catching slogans and pamphlets had also proved inspirational).

World renewal and transformation

A recurrent theme among new religions is that of the need for world transformation (*yonaoshi*), in which the present state of affairs is overturned and a new spiritually oriented civilization takes its place. This is a potent message that incorporates a critique of the current state of the world – seen as overly materialistic and unfair. In some cases such millennial messages have been accompanied by the promise or implication that the present corrupt order needs to be swept aside in order for a better world to emerge. Oomoto, in its earlier period under Deguchi Nao, for example, spoke of *tatekai tatenaoshi*: the idea that the world was out of kilter because of the evils of materialism, and that this imbalance would cause calamities, destroy the old order and enable a new spiritual realm to emerge (Berthon 1985; Staemmler 2011a: 17; Shimazono 1992a: 42–7). Such aggressive millennial themes were evident in the earlier teachings of many new religions, including Tenrikyō and Oomoto, although very often, as movements became older, along with their first generation of leaders and followers, they have tended to tone down such forms of millennialism and to instead focus on improving the individual lives of followers rather than on changing the world as a whole. In late-twentieth-century Japan, worries about such things as nuclear warfare and environmental destruction – along with prophecies that saw 1999 and the end of the calendar millennium as potential turning points (see Chapter 2) – added a new impetus to such millennial concerns and played a part in the rise of Agonshū and several other new movements (Reader 2000a: 47–52).

Concerns about the problems the world is facing also feed into another key theme expressed by new religions: that they have a special mission for the world, usually via their charismatic leader who has discovered the truths needed to extricate the world from its problems. In Chapter 2 we will see how Kiriyama Seiyū's charismatic leadership in Agonshū articulated such themes. In setting out the idea of a special mission of world salvation, too, new religions have also developed new geographies that recalibrate the religious world, by building new sacred centres that express the teachings and centrality of the movement concerned – and in so doing shift the ground away from the traditional religions. Tenrikyō's sacred centre, where its founder Nakayama lived and is now venerated, is portrayed in its cosmology as the connecting point between the divine and human realms; it is the source of truth and the sacred centre, therefore, not just of Tenrikyō but of all humanity. Similar modes of building new sacred centres that form the focus of world missions and world renewal are found in Mahikari's centre at Takayama in Gifu prefecture and Agonshū's sacred centre outside Kyoto, which is portrayed as the epicentre of its mission to save the world by spreading the rediscovered truths of Buddhism to the world at large.

Japanese identity, nationalism and conservatism

Such new geographies and sacred centres not only imply that the centres of the older traditions are no longer really relevant, but often affirm a nationalistic message as well. For new religions in Japan that express messages of world transformation, Japan is the centre from which this will occur. Tenrikyō's conflation of the place of its founder's birth with the origins of humanity and the relationship between the human and divine worlds places Japan at the core of humanity's development. Byakkō Shinkōkai emphasizes a mission to spread peace from Japan to the rest of the world (Pye 1986). Agonshū's mission to spread Buddhism from Japan to the world at large, while seemingly espousing universal themes of world transformation, expresses the importance of Japan in this process. This helps develop an understanding of Japan's relationship with the wider world – an issue that relates to concepts of identity and that has been a recurrent element in Japanese social and cultural debates, with underlying nationalist tones, in recent decades.[26] While new religions preach messages about the world at large, a key element within such messages is an affirmation of Japan's centrality to the wider world. This can be seen as a form of religious nationalism (Cornille 1999; Reader 2002) and is a theme we will discuss in later chapters, where we show how nationalist themes have been present in Agonshū from its early days and how they have grown significantly as the movement has aged.

Such nationalist orientations – especially when allied to the use of traditional modes of interpreting problems (e.g. viewing them as related to the spirits of the dead) – also indicate that new religions, despite appearing on the surface to criticize the existing order and to express revolutionary views in talking about world renewal, tend towards conservatism in social terms. By placing an emphasis on the individual as an agent of self-transformation, new religions, Helen Hardacre (1986: 23) argues, tend to be politically uninterested. Concepts of morality, too, reinforce this orientation, as they commonly reinforce traditional family values and conservative views on gender. As Hardacre (1984) has demonstrated, Buddhist-oriented new religions such as Reiyūkai promote conservative gender ideologies that place women in a secondary position in society and reinforce cultural stereotypes in which the woman's place is in the home serving her husband and household. Kōfuku no Kagaku, which developed in 1980s Tokyo with a mission of world salvation, has emphasized a return to traditional forms of morality as the way to change society and become more conservative especially in the aftermath of the Aum Affair (Baffelli 2005; Baffelli and Reader 2011). The focus found in many new religions of placing the individual at the centre of problem-solution may on one level empower individuals but it also can serve to reinforce maintenance of the status quo, a point made aptly by Christal Whelan (2015) in her studies of GLA,[27] a spiritual healing movement established by Takahashi Shinji (1928–76) in 1970. As Whelan has commented:

> To seek the reason for any conflict within oneself and in this way to discover one's true self suggests an adaptation to the status quo rather than a more flexible and socially engaged dialogue. Withdrawal and finding the self always responsible rather than seeking changes where they might be most needed, in institutions or the society at large, ultimately represents a highly conservative response.

Similar patterns are seen in a host of other new movements as diverse as Agonshū, Kurozumikyō and Reiyūkai[28] that emphasize individual self-transformation, and in so doing negate the potential for political transformation in favour of personal self-development.

Capturing the spirit of the age

While new religions may speak about unchanging and inviolable truths, they are also products of specific eras and as such (if successful) reflect and resonate with the feelings of their era(s). This is an issue that has been especially highlighted in Japan through the now-abandoned epithet *shin shinshūkyō* and its English equivalent 'new new religion' that were used to describe movements that attracted attention in the 1980s. These terms implied that such movements shared common ground and were both products and reflections of the ethos of their era. Shimazono Susumu (2001: 18) has especially emphasized this point, arguing that 'new new religions' were a subcategory of the broader 'new religions' and were movements that reflected the spiritual circumstances of Japan of that period.

Among the movements so identified were Shinnyoen, Mahikari, Agonshū, Byakkō Shinkōkai and Kōfuku no Kagaku, as well as the now infamous Aum Shinrikyō. The first four of these had originated in earlier decades, but it was during the 1980s that they really appeared to attract major attention and grow rapidly; the 1980s was when Kōfuku no Kagaku and Aum Shinrikyō originated. This was a period when Japan was emerging as a leading world economic power and when pride in national achievements was at its zenith. This sense – strong in the 1980s – of Japan's emergent world position was manifest in the ways that movements of this era proclaimed (as did Agonshū and Kōfuku no Kagaku, for instance) that Japan was the epicentre of a new spiritual civilization. While Japan's economic success was a matter of national pride, the public mood was also tinged with a sense of cultural uncertainty as the processes of modernization, rationalization and globalization eroded Japanese traditional culture, changed peoples' lifestyles and raised questions about Japan's cultural identity. The new religions that grew in this period appeared to offer ways to deal with such tensions by simultaneously displaying a ready acceptance of modernity, an engagement with and reinforcement of themes of tradition and a reaffirmation of Japanese identity and cultural values. Their embrace of modern technologies (evident, for instance, in Agonshū's use of satellite broadcasting to transmit its rituals from the 1980s onwards) showed they were in tune with the modern world, while their emphasis on older Japanese religious concepts and practices such as the spirits of the dead, spiritual healing techniques and ancestor rituals showed they were equally rooted in and capable of reinforcing a sense of Japanese identity and tradition.

They also reflected a concern with the state of the world, manifest in various surveys and in popular culture, about potential chaos and apocalyptic scenarios at the end of the century (Nishiyama 1988: 221; Nishijima 1988: 156–65; Reader 2000a: 47–52) and thus had a particularly strong millennial orientation. This was intensified by the attention paid to the prophecies of Nostradamus that had been translated into Japanese in 1973. While these appeared to suggest a world crisis and final conflict by 1999 they also held out the promise of a saviour who would rectify matters. We look further at this issue in the next chapter, but suffice it to say here that such prophecies were interpreted by several leaders of new movements of the age (including Kiriyama in Agonshū, who was the first such leader to pay major attention to Nostradamus's prophecies) as a confirmation of their mission of salvation and world transformation (Kisala 1997).

A related theme in an age in which concerns about potential end-time scenarios were prevalent was an interest in prophecy and a tendency among the leaders of new movements to claim this as a special power. Interest in the potential acquisition of special powers (broadly under the label *chōnōryoku*, or superhuman powers), which included spiritual channelling and communicating with spirits from other realms, was another theme that attracted attention. This was especially so among urban educated young people who, after succeeding in Japan's competitive education system, wanted more than just materialistic lifestyles and steady career jobs and were attracted by promises of spiritual transcendence and the prospect of becoming part of a world mission of salvation.[29] Here Agonshū led the way in pronouncing that its leader had unlocked the key to such special powers through the rituals, practices and teaching Kiriyama had developed, while his publications emphasized themes related to esoteric practices (*mikkyō*) and the spiritual world (*seishin sekai*) that analysts identified as striking areas of interest at the time (Numata 1988; Shimazono 1996, 2001). We will discuss these issues, of the spirit world and the interest in esoteric practices, more in the next chapter. This emphasis on such powers (including spiritual healing) was, according to Shimazono (1992a, b) especially appealing as a counterweight to the increasing rationalization of society.

We should emphasize that none of these themes was particularly new or specific to the 1980s. Prophecy, an emphasis on spirits and communication with spirits, millennialism, notions of world salvation and interests in esoteric practices have all been evident in numerous new religions over the period since the early nineteenth century. They have been manifest in various forms and in different areas of the Japanese religious domain (and not just in the new religions) at numerous points in history. Nonetheless these themes, as Shimazono (2001), Nishiyama (1979, 1986, 1988), Reader (1988) and others have noted, were all very much at the forefront of popular religious consciousness in the 1980s and they were also to a great degree reflected in various areas of popular culture of the period (Shimada 1995: 106–7). It was this combination of themes and correlations to the popular religious zeitgeist of the times that marked out the movements emerging in this period and that led to them initially being described as 'new new religions'. Agonshū, as we have already noted, was one of these movements.

The importance of science in a modern religion

One area in which several of the new movements of the late twentieth century and beyond stood out was in their espousal of scientific themes – or, rather, their use of the image of science to project themselves as modern movements in tune with the times. While it was not uncommon for earlier movements to appear innately hostile to modernity,[30] later movements were keen to demonstrate that they were abreast of the modern world. By the latter part of the past century this was evident in the ways in which many of them portrayed themselves as 'scientific' in nature. While they claimed legitimacy from ancient sources such as Buddhist texts or revelations from deities, they combined this with assertions that what they were doing fitted into a modern, rational world and was based in science as well as religious themes. Many, to demonstrate the point, incorporated terms such as 'science' (*kagaku*) or 'research' (*kenkyū*) into their titles and/or their publications, and sought to portray their practices and interpretations of spiritual phenomena within a scientific framework.

An influential figure here was Takahashi Shinji, the charismatic founder of GLA, who influenced the development of several new movements from the 1970s onwards, including Kōfuku no Kagaku and Panawave Laboratory (Nishiyama 1988: 201; Numata 1987; 1988: 90–126; Whelan 2015). Takahashi was one of the first in the new wave of movements to make use of scientific terminologies; as Whelan (2015) states:

> Takahashi Shinji had a huge impact on the generation of new religions that arose in the seventies in Japan. Part of his appeal was the frequent use of scientific language and technological metaphors for articulating complex spiritual phenomena. One of his favorite metaphors for the reincarnating soul was 'the soul as a videotape' that a person could make contact with and replay.

The notion that spiritual phenomena could be incorporated within a scientific framework was taken up by groups such as Panawave Kenkyūjo (Panawave Research Laboratory) and ESP Kagaku Kenkyūjo (ESP Science Research Laboratory) that focused on prophecy (as was the case with Panawave) and paranormal spiritual powers (as with ESP) while incorporating terminologies that suggested that they were operating in a very modern framework framed around what, in their titles, appeared as modern scientific concepts. For example, Panawave – whose founder Chino Shōhō believed she was the spiritual successor of Takahashi (Whelan 2015) – prophesied world calamity and interpreted its root causes as being grounded in 'scientific' problems relating to magnetic waves that were afflicting the earth (Dorman 2005). Kōfuku no Kagaku, too, demonstrates its 'scientific' credentials and claims that it has a rational basis via both its Japanese name (which translates as 'the science of happiness') and by its official English title 'Happy Science'.

Kiriyama, too, claimed to have a scientific basis for his teachings about prophecy, karma, the resolution of problems and the influences of ancestors. He argued, for example, that his interpretations of Nostradamus's prophecies – and indeed the prophecies themselves – were scientifically verifiable (Kisala 1997: 53). He cited numerous Western sources related to psychoanalysis, psychiatry, psychology and neurology to support his own teachings, including Freud, Jung and Lipot Szondi. Kiriyama (2000a: 15) found Szondi's concept of the 'familial unconsciousness' particularly helpful in discussions about the role of ancestors in influencing the destinies of the living. He also sought to present Agonshū's Buddhism as a form of 'social science' (Kiriyama 1997) as well as giving lectures at various academic institutions (notably those to which Agonshū made donations),[31] and using invitations and awards (including honorary fellowships and professorships) from such places to present himself as a scholastic thinker. As such, while Agonshū, like the other movements cited here, presented itself as offering time-honoured ancient truths and emphasized the importance of spirits, it sought to repudiate any sense that it was anti-modern or 'superstitious' (an accusation that had commonly been directed at earlier new religions) by showing it was in tune with modernity, science and academic thinking. At the same time, it saw itself (as did the others cited above) not just as uniting religion and science by following teachings and practices related to spirits but grounded in science, but also as transcending the limitations of the scientific and augmenting it with religious insights. We will return to these points in Chapter 2 when we look more closely at Kiriyama's life and the various ways in which his movement has projected him as a figure of spiritual power.

Competing on common ground

In talking about science and seeking to present themselves as analytical rather than mired in superstition, the new movements cited above were reflecting the wider milieu in which they operated. They were influencing and being influenced also by the claims that other movements were making, and this, we consider, is an important element in the dynamics of new movements. The common themes that we have identified as pertinent to late-twentieth-century religions such as Agonshū, from talking about the prophecies of Nostradamus, to offering a path to salvation, to effecting a return to the roots of Buddhism (see Chapter 2 in particular), to proclaiming their ability to offer a scientifically grounded way of improving spiritual welfare and alleviating human problems, indicate just how much was shared between these movements. Yet sharing common ground also produces contest, for those who present themselves as holding the solution to the world's problems and portray themselves as having a mission of salvation are unlikely to accept the claims of rivals who assert similar things.

Winston Davis (1980: 73) has wryly commented that 'messiahs are seldom original thinkers'. Davis examines the teachings and 'gospel sources' of Mahikari developed by its founder Okada Kōtama, to show how they have been gleaned from a variety of sources, including other new movements and folk religious traditions. One can say something similar about other founders and messiahs in modern Japan, whether in the influences Kōfuku no Kagaku incorporated in its early days from GLA (Baffelli

2005; Whelan 2015) or in how Kiriyama incorporated esoteric Buddhist practices and elements of folk belief into his teaching. The recurrent use of Nostradamus's prophecies and the emphasis on apocalypse and millennial salvation among movements of the era also indicate how much they shared common ground and concerns.

Yet, even if messiahs are not always original in the themes they espouse or in the claims they make, they are in a real sense singular in nature, as are the religious movements through which they express their truth claims. Any messiah or world saviour with a message of world salvation is claiming that they – and they alone – have the truth, the capability to save the world and the solution to humanity's problems. Implicitly, by asserting such things, they are denying others who make similar claims. Kiriyama, by identifying with the saviour prophesied by Nostradamus, was in effect repudiating the claims of others who, when talking about the 'crisis' the world faced in the late twentieth century, proclaimed that they were the answer to that crisis. By incorporating esoteric ritual practices from established Buddhism and the Shugendō tradition while criticizing these traditions for making these practices the preserve of priestly castes, he was both attacking those traditions and proclaiming his movement as superior to theirs. Other religious leaders of the era who made similar claims about salvation, Nostradamus and so on, likewise, implicitly, and at times explicitly, were denouncing the claims of their rivals – including Kiriyama. In so doing they not only denounced other messiahs but also spurred competition between them over their rival truth claims.

This means that when one considers one leader or founder and movement as an exemplar of their era and the movements that have manifested in it, one has to also be aware of how interactions, rivalries and competition (often implicit more than explicit) may play a role in shaping how each founder and group operates, talks about themselves and develops their self-asserted claims of truth and spiritual superiority. We have discussed this, as we mentioned in the Introduction, in the context of Aum and Kōfuku no Kagaku in particular (Baffelli and Reader 2011), but we have also been aware, through various conversations and discussions with officials in a variety of new movements, that they know about, pay attention to and take heed of what others (viewed as rivals) might be saying and that this can shape how they present themselves in the public arena. Agonshū was keen to portray Kiriyama as a trendsetter who shaped the religious culture of his era, whether in being innovative in the use of media or in creating a renewed interest in esoteric practices, and this was an important part of the construction of his charismatic authority (see Chapter 2). Kiriyama claimed to be reviving 'original Buddhism' (*genshi bukkyō*) in Japan – again a claim expressed by other movements, including Aum Shinrikyō, whose founder Asahara Shōkō made similar claims for himself (Asahara 1988: 2; Reader 2000a: 79), and Kōfuku no Kagaku, which claimed that Ōkawa Ryūhō was not just re-establishing Buddhism but was actually the eternal Buddha (Baffelli 2005).

It was not, of course, just the founders of such movements that appeared to contest with each other for the mantle of messiah. The movements they led also offered their followers a similar singularity. Agonshū stated that only its followers were able to go to higher realms; in talking about the coming spiritual age, it said the world needed to develop a new, superior type of human with superhuman abilities – something that

Agonshū, because it combined wisdom and intelligence practice, alone could produce.[32] Asahara Shōkō (1992: 19–48; 1994: 154) proclaimed his followers to be bodhisattvas and spiritual warriors waging a battle to save the world and bring about world salvation, while Ōkawa (1995a: 19) similarly claimed his followers to be angels and bodhisattvas leading the world to a new age. In all these cases the leaders and their movements were not simply offering potential followers an exalted status in tune with the ambitions of the age and in which they could be world saviours, engaged in missions to save the world, or mountain ascetic practitioners taking on the tasks traditionally performed by priests to pacify the spirits of the dead and bring about peace and harmony. They were expressing a sense of competition with rival movements and emphasizing their special claims as a way of elevating their members above all others.

Such competition did not just involve claims about the status of leaders and followers but, at times, also the denigration of rival movements and of rival saviours and their disciples (Ōkawa 1995b). Aum and Kōfuku no Kagaku's leaders, in attacking each other, also insulted their rivals' followers (Baffelli and Reader 2011). When Agonshū received a Buddha relic from Sri Lanka, it announced that this was a true relic – unlike those held by other groups in Japan, which were portrayed as inauthentic (see Chapter 2). Agonshū thus not only asserted the authenticity of its own relic but also none too subtly (even though it did not name other movements that held these so-called false relics) denigrated other movements that possessed what they claimed to be Buddha relics.

Concluding remarks

One can discern a number of related themes that are found across the spectrum of movements that normally are included in the 'new' category but also, notably within movements operating in a similar era of development, areas of such common ground that they invariably produce competition and influence the ways in which such similar themes are expressed. We have only briefly outlined them in the context of the new movements that emerged in late-twentieth-century Japan, and they will resurface in the following chapters, as we look more specifically at Agonshū and its founder who, Agonshū claims, was very much in the vanguard of the times and who shaped the context in which religions operated in Japan. Such claims, of course, emphasize Kiriyama not simply as the founder of a religion but as a charismatic figure of authority for the age. Charisma and charismatic authority, as we have noted earlier, are regarded as key elements in the construction and nature of new religions, and they played a fundamental role in the formation and development of Agonshū. They are encapsulated in the life and activities of Kiriyama, and it is to his life and the themes that it manifests, especially as projected by Agonshū, that we turn next.

2

The Story of a Religious Founder: Kiriyama Seiyū, Turmoil, Charisma and Experience

Introduction: founders and their paths

In Chapter 1 we stated that a common characteristic of new religions was that they generally began with an inspirational founder who claimed to have found new truths and to offer followers new ways to confront the problems of the world and obtain worldly benefits. From Kino Isson of Nyoraikyō in the early nineteenth century, to later-nineteenth-century founders such as Nakayama Miki and Deguchi Nao, to more recent founder-figures such as Itō Shinjō of Shinnyoen and Ōkawa Ryūhō of Kōfuku no Kagaku, this has been a recurrent pattern in Japanese new religions. Such founders have also been highly practical in nature, with an ability to connect with ordinary people, providing them with teachings that are understandable and related to their needs and concerns. That practicality is evident, too, in their ability to create and implement the mechanisms and organizational dynamism needed to build a functioning tradition while inspiring devotion and commitment from followers. It is this combination of charismatic, innovative and spiritually charged powers and insights, along with the skill to operate in a worldly sense to implement such visions, galvanize supporters and create functioning mechanisms through which their teachings can operate that distinguishes such figures. Frequently, too, such founders – in some cases during his/her lifetime and in others at death – are transformed in the eyes of their followers and in the ways in which they project themselves into figures of worship on a spiritual realm above that of ordinary humans.

The extent to which any one founder can be viewed as an exemplar of the entire tradition of new religious movements in Japan is a matter of contention. Some, for example, Shimazono Susumu (1987: 17) have argued that there is no clear archetypal founder of a new religion, in that each one has his/her individual traits and qualities (and, we would note, also individual faults and problems). Benjamin Dorman (2012) supports Shimazono's argument through an examination of two female founders, Kitamura Sayo of Tenshō Kōtai Jingū Kyō and Jikōson of Jiu, who were active in the period after 1945. As Dorman shows, they differed in a number of respects that were integral to why Kitamura succeeded, using what was often negative publicity to good effect to establish a large-scale movement, while Jikōson was unable to overcome public and media opprobrium or establish anything other than a small movement that later fell apart. There is diversity in terms of the gender, social status and background of founders, too; many have been female and many others have come from poor rural and agricultural backgrounds. Some founders have had impoverished lives prior to following a religious path, while others have had an elite education – as in the case of Ōkawa Ryūhō, Kōfuku no Kagaku's founder, who graduated from Japan's most elite educational institute, Tokyo University, and worked in an international trading company in New York prior to founding his movement (Astley 1995).

At the same time, a number of recurrent themes are commonly seen in their lives and natures, and these provide a viable framework through which to gain an understanding of the general nature of religious leadership in modern Japanese religious terms. This is evident in the life and activities of Kiriyama Seiyū. His search for religious awakening, his problems in early life, the practices he undertook to confront such problems and the interpretations he later made of them, all form core elements in the movement's development, in its teachings and in the narrative it projects to followers. His charismatic personality, his communication skills via a variety of media, from sermons and public talks to books, pamphlets and visual materials, along with his entrepreneurial activities, and his ability to conduct dramatic and enticingly spectacular public rituals, have been a main source of attraction for followers. So too has his self-identification as a prophet and saviour who can resolve the world's problems, and this has incorporated claims and activities that seek to mark him out from other religious leaders who also might claim messiah-like and prophetic status within their movements.

Charisma and charismatic authority and leadership

Before we discuss Kiriyama in further detail we should briefly comment on the term 'charisma' and on related terms associated with it – 'charismatic authority' and 'charismatic leadership' – to explain what we mean by them. These are terms that are widely used in discussions about the founders and leaders of Japanese new religions,[1] as in studies of religion and religious founders in general. Max Weber's well-known definition is a general starting point for such discussions. Charisma, Weber (1968, 48) has stated, is

> [a] certain quality of an individual personality by virtue of which he [*sic*] is set apart from ordinary men [*sic*] and treated as endowed with supernatural, superhuman, or at least specifically exceptional powers or qualities. These are such are not accessible to the ordinary, but are regarded as of divine origin or as exemplary, and on the basis of them the individual concerned is treated as a leader.

We should note that while Weber uses gender-specific terms ('men' and 'he') the context in which we are talking goes beyond any gender-bound contexts. Many founders of Japanese new religions have been female – and one reason that has been mooted for this is that, until relatively recently, women were shut out of the political sphere in Japan and also out of the religious hierarchies of the established religions. There have been fewer gender-discriminatory orientations in the areas in which new movements have operated, and this offered scope for dynamic female figures to express themselves in this sphere.[2]

Weber's definition offers a reasonable starting point for our discussion of Kiriyama since, as our outline of his life indicates, he exhibited the themes identified by Weber, such as appearing to be set apart as specially charged with spiritual insight and power in ways that marked him out as a leader. We should add that at the same time Kiriyama's story and the persona constructed around him through his writings and sermons, and the teachings he espoused in Agonshū, go against one aspect of Weber's definition in that his powers could, he asserted at various times in his sermons and books, be accessed by his followers. However, as will also be noted later, at the same time the aura constructed around him mitigated against that notion, while the ways he has been portrayed in Agonshū rituals and pronouncements since his death (see Chapter 5) have now elevated him spiritually to a level beyond the reach of ordinary people.

Scholars such as Weber and Jean Comaroff (1994) have argued that charismatic figures tend to exist in tension with temporal power and the normative patterns of society, while offering religious solutions for ameliorating that society and its individuals, offering people the potential to change the world and giving them increased agency. Again these are elements found among Japanese new religious founders, who commonly stand apart from the established social and political structures and who have faced opprobrium as a result. As we mentioned in the previous chapter, the mass media, embedded as it is in Japan's normative sociopolitical structures, has tended to be antagonistic towards new religions in general, and its treatment of founders has been part of this hostility.

In standing apart from existing power structures founders often articulate critiques of that order along with promises of radically changing it. While such promises might appear to presage social and political revolution,[3] they rarely, however, operate in a political sphere. Rather, it has been common in Japan for charismatic founders to talk about an idealized notion of world transformation through individual spiritual reorientation, in which the founder serves as the role model for disciples and as an inspiration for the promise of world change through individual practice and religious communal performance, without suggesting that change might come about through direct political action.[4]

We do not propose a new definition or analysis of charisma as an abstract notion; our purpose is to draw attention to the point that in the context of Japanese new religions, founders have normatively claimed some form of special power, which is manifest in abilities that mark them out as singular figures who can accomplish feats such as prophesying the future, interpreting the causes of problems, building a dynamic organization and attracting followers who are convinced of the founder's special nature. This special nature that makes such figures stand out from the ordinary and manifest special potency in the eyes of those who are thereby attracted, falls under the broader rubric of charisma as discussed above. Importantly, though, it is important to recognize that charisma is not a quality universally felt or acclaimed; one person's charismatic leader may be another's anathema – as indeed the media attacks and broadsides aimed at founders and their movements indicate.[5] It and its concomitants, charismatic leadership and authority, are not simply self-proclaimed or the product of those who present themselves as having special powers, for example, by claiming to have received a special message from a deity or experienced new revelations and insights into Buddhist teachings that have given them a mission of world salvation.

Such figures – and charisma itself – are contingent on contexts and relationships. Claiming to be a saviour means little if one does not attract followers. Charisma is relational in that it is constructed between, and is a product of the interactions between, a leader, movement and followers (Tabor and Gallagher 1995: 142; Goosaert and Ownby 2008: 5; Feuchtwang 2008: 92; Ji 2008). The support of disciples who uphold and enhance the founder's status through their devotion and of a movement that coalesces around the founder and disciples are essential elements in the construction of charismatic leadership (Reader 2000a: 21, 237). As Ji (2008: 49) has argued:

> Charisma does not come from some mystic or mysterious, and therefore unfindable, place, but it is simply rooted in the effect of consecration of the interactions between a leader and his or her followers, between agency and structure, between individual and society. In such interactions, the ability of the (potential) charismatic leader to embody the collective consciousness may results in the continuous justification and even mystification of the leader's superiority.

Ji's argument builds on Feuchthwang and Wang's (2001) analysis of charisma in Chinese religious contexts as being the 'expectation of the extraordinary' (see also Feuchtwang 2008: 93–4; Ownby, Goosaert and Ji 2017: 16) in which the leader promises and appears to manifest abilities beyond the normal world, and followers, trusting in the efficacy and power of the leader, are able to believe in his/her capacity to perform extraordinary deeds, such as performing miracles, experiencing life-transforming events and/ or having epiphanies and revelations. As we will indicate here and in later chapters, this has certainly happened with Kiriyama, whose history of life-changing events, revelations and encounters with Buddhist figures of worship has produced an aura around him in the eyes of followers who, as a result, came to expect that extraordinary things would occur because of Kiriyama's activities. As this has happened, he has been raised to higher levels in life and, even more strikingly, in death, through the devotion of his disciples, so that he is now, as we will discuss further in Chapter 5, seen as an enlightened being who continues to watch over, guide and help disciples achieve liberation in this world and in the spiritual realms after death.

Charismatic entrepreneurship

Before we turn to the narrative that has been constructed (by him and his movement) around Kiriyama Seiyū, we should emphasize the point that charismatic leaders are not one-dimensionally focused on performing miraculous deeds or producing revelations. They need also, as Lorne Dawson (2006) has discussed, to be *bricoleurs* displaying a multiplicity of talents that range across a variety of domains, from the religious and ritualistic to the secular. As Victor Goosaert (2008: 26) has argued of Chinese charismatic religious leaders, they need to perform and bring together a variety of idioms including self-cultivation, scholarship and leadership. Moreover, they need to manage their dealings and interactions not just with followers but also with external agents and interests, such as, for example, other religious leaders, as well as secular agencies and political operators and authorities such as the state that in many contexts regulates the context in which religious movements operate (Ownby, Goossaert and Ji 2017: 18–19).

Critical to this multidimensional display of talents and skills is what Nancy Stalker (2008: 12–16) has described as 'charismatic entrepreneurship' – the skill of harnessing religious charisma in pragmatic this-worldly business-like ways to develop a religious organization and system, to mobilize followers and resources and to spread the word. Stalker argues that this entrepreneurial dimension is a key element in the development of charismatic leadership and a prime motivation for charismatic figures, who are driven not simply by religious visions but by the desire and ability to expand their following 'to realize and extend their religious view of the world' (14). She calls this ability the 'prophet motive' and, in so doing, illustrates the problematic nature of Weber's (1968: 52) notion that charismatics are in essence ascetic in nature, and that 'charisma is specifically foreign to economic considerations'. As Stalker notes, there are plentiful cases in modern times of charismatic religious figures who have led worldly lifestyles, while the building of religious organizations cannot be divorced from worldly needs.

New movements and leaders face many challenges in trying to develop a following and spread their messages. The avenues through which they can do this, from

Figure 2.1 Agonshū main temple in Yamashina (Kyoto prefecture). Photo by Ian Reader.

the construction of centres, temples (Figure 2.1) and the like, to the publication of information and printed, visual and online materials that can spread their word and attract followers, cost money. Yet generally such figures start with little more than their visions and a belief that they have been specially marked out to proclaim new truths. Initially they have neither followers nor the structures needed to spread the word. Nor, as we commented in the previous chapter, do they have the sorts of resources and organizational and economic support inherited from previous generations and embedded in social structures, as in the older established traditions such as Shinto and Buddhism in Japan. They therefore *need* to be outward looking, using organizational skills, business acumen and entrepreneurship to develop and build followings and institutions. Religious visions and messages without the support mechanisms to project these to a growing audience and without the organizational abilities to create a movement that can further these aims are, like charisma itself without the relational support of followers, hardly likely to flourish.

Charismatic entrepreneurship is thus not something that represents a disjunction with the needs and realities of new movements, but may be an essential and integral part of them. Stalker develops her discussion of charismatic entrepreneurship via the example of Deguchi Ōnisaburō, the son-in-law of Oomoto's founder Deguchi Nao. He became the movement's leader and expanded it rapidly in 1920s Japan, transforming it from a localized millenarian movement into a mass organization through a variety of activities, including mass publicity using broadsheets, pamphlets and other media forms. Ōnisaburō not only displayed organizational skills and the capacity to spread his messages but he was also a skilled publicist and exhibitionist, whose displays of art and publicity activities (including making movies in which he starred, along with newsreels) drew attention to Oomoto and served as examples of his entrepreneurship (Stalker 2008: 130–6).

Benjamin Dorman has developed this notion by showing how self-promotion is a critical element in the construction of charismatic leadership and in the entrepreneurship that successful new religious leaders manifest. This comes out particularly in contexts where leaders and founders are attacked in the media and face negative publicity. As Dorman shows, both Kitamura Sayo and Jikōson faced negative media publicity, but while Jikōson seemed unable to deal with this, Kitamura used the publicity, attention and notoriety accorded her by mass media exposure as a source of strength to heighten her movement's profile and public presence. Kitamura, as Dorman (2012: 7) shows, was a 'master of self-promotion' who saw media interest in her movement as part of 'god's strategy' in the 'promotional process for the establishment of "god's kingdom"' (192). While one cannot say that there is no such thing as bad publicity, since media hostility towards and public exposure of Jiu certainly damaged and virtually destroyed that group, cases such as Kitamura's show that skilled leaders can harness publicity and the media for their own ends.

We see Kiriyama as someone of a similar ilk to earlier charismatic entrepreneurs and self-publicists such as Deguchi Ōnisaburō and Kitamura Sayo. His leadership and role in Agonshū revolved not just around his claimed spiritual insights but also his abilities as a charismatic entrepreneur. He demonstrated during his lifetime that he was a skilled self-promoter and user of the mass media, one of the prime examples of this type in modern Japanese contexts. Besides constructing a religious narrative and set of teachings that are articulated via his life story, he founded a publishing company, used modern publicity mechanisms such as hiring in public relations agencies to bring his growing movement to public attention, produced dramatic ritual performances that served as important promotional materials for Agonshū and used what, in the 1980s, were viewed as cutting edge media technologies to expand his movement and give it an aura of dynamism, excitement and modernity (Reader 1991; Baffelli 2016). In the videos and, later, the CDs and DVDs that Agonshū produced, he also (like Deguchi Ōnisaburō in Oomoto) took a starring role, presiding over rituals, meeting world religious leaders, receiving spiritual messages from the Buddha, bestowing blessings on followers and accepting awards and honours from various international bodies such as universities.

We should note also that in its publicity and portrayals of the movement, Agonshū's achievements are invariably portrayed as the result of Kiriyama's own actions, visions and skills. Whatever work has been put in behind the scenes, for example, to set up a publishing firm and run it on a day-to-day basis, to organize a major ritual such as the Hoshi Matsuri, or to arrange a meeting with a significant religious leader such as the Pope or the Dalai Lama, and so on, is not mentioned in such movement-presented narratives and DVDs. The focus and resources of the movement have been centred on Kiriyama and on projecting him as the fount of all that Agonshū has done, and as the epicentre of its dynamic. Such projections and the resources devoted to them are thus in themselves a core element in the construction of his charisma and a manifestation of how those who produce Agonshū's publicity materials have served to shape and enhance his charismatic presence and public persona.

This is not just a manifestation of Kiriyama's self-promotional abilities but of a movement that has thoroughly shaped itself around a single figure. There is a hierarchic element to this, and one that also has, we consider, paternalistic dimensions. Kiriyama in life regularly assumed a stance of authority in front of his followers in which he referred to them in familiar terms as *kimi* (or as 'all of you' *shokun*), normally used in Japanese by someone in authority when talking to subordinates. In other words, Agonshū in its publications and projections of Kiriyama has devoted resources to reinforcing and enhancing his status while he, in speaking to followers, repeatedly reaffirmed that authority in hierarchic and paternalistic terms.

Reshaping narratives, soliciting positivity

While Kiriyama displayed little of the confrontational style of Kitamura (whose aggressive preaching was used to generate publicity) he certainly was able to transform negative stories about him in ways that strengthened his messages. As we discuss later, media revelations that Kiriyama had, prior to founding his first movement, been convicted and imprisoned as a result of illegal activities could have proved disastrous for the movement but they were transformed by Kiriyama into a message about the need to engage in spiritual practices in order to cut one's karma. Revelations that could have been fatal to his standing as a religious leader were thus turned into a source of strength in which criminality and personal failures became a teaching device infused with hope.

Kiriyama and Agonshū have also countered standard mass media negativity towards new movements by the simple act of advertising in the mass media. Each year, for example, mainstream Japanese newspapers carry reports on Agonshū's annual Hoshi Matsuri festival that are, in fact, paid-for articles commissioned by Agonshū. *The Japan Times*, for example, one of Japan's major English-language newspapers, publishes a report on the Hoshi Matsuri each year that is unfailingly highly positive in tone; if one looks carefully one will discern the word 'advertisement' in small letters in the top corner.[6] Similar items have appeared in other dailies in Japan. The phrase 'user-friendly religion' that appeared in one such newspaper article in 1987, and that presented Kiriyama as a modern interpreter of Buddhism and Agonshū as being in step with the needs of modern Japan, was in essence a product of Agonshū's own publicity machine.[7] Agonshū activities have continued to be reported in a positive light via such avenues after Kiriyama's death. Thus a ritual for the spirits of the war dead conducted in the seas to the north of Japan, which had been planned during Kiriyama's lifetime, went ahead after his demise. This was favourably reported on in a number of news media articles that have been uploaded to Agonshū's website, including one by the *Japan Times*, in similar ilk to their coverage of the Hoshi Matsuri, and in Japanese by the *Sankei* newspaper. The latter published an article by a journalist who had previously (see Chapter 5) given a lecture to Agonshū members and talked of his friendship with Kiriyama. To be able to do this, and to generate positive publicity, of course, requires money, and here again is an area where entrepreneurial skills are needed to generate the necessary means.

Life stories, hagiography and the problem of verification

Having outlined some broader themes related to Kiriyama, charismatic leadership and entrepreneurship, we next turn to an account of his life, religious awakening and development of Agonshū. Here we should also note the problems of discussing the lives of founders before they become famous or attract attention, since frequently there is little reliable material available about their early lives. Many founders appear – until their emergence into the public domain with claims of religious inspiration and messages of salvation – to have led ordinary and obscure lives that leave scant or bare bones narrative traces. It is only once they have achieved status as a founder with a movement that their narratives are written – usually by themselves and/or by people in the movements they lead. As such their biographies are constructs, written in ways designed to impart the images, meanings and, indeed, revisions of reality that the leader and movement would like to project. They are hagiographies rather than biographies. As such the lives of such founders prior to becoming publicly known figures may be revised to fit with themes of their teaching and to enhance the aura surrounding them. For example, Kitamura Sayo came from a peasant rural background; until she became known as a religious leader, there are few records of her life apart from those narrated by her movement. Yet her biography as constructed by her movement contains plentiful material about her younger life that clearly has been developed in light of her having become a religious founder. There may be times when a hint of historical reality breaks in, perhaps due to the investigations of external actors such as journalists who dig into a founder's past in the hope of finding something scandalous there, as happened with Kiriyama. Overall, however, it is more often the case that what we know about founders is predominantly what has been produced by them and their movements and is thus a manifestation of the ways in which the founder figure wishes to be known and have their past understood.

This does not mean we should disregard such hagiographic accounts. Indeed, rather than being a hindrance they are in fact valuable resources for understanding founders and their movements. Such life histories/hagiographies contain important moral teachings and motifs that provide models of behaviour for devotees to follow, and express how a movement wishes to project itself and its founder. As Ownby, Goosaert and Ji (2017: 16) have commented, hagiographies are not aimed simply at self-promotion or the glorification of a sacred figure but are 'an articulation between individual life and a general sacred moral order, thereby confirming . . . the reliability of religious teaching'.

Such hagiographic accounts serve to affirm the moral order founders and their movements seek to project as the truth, and are simultaneously evidence of their powerful, transcendent status – evidence that may lay the ground for later enshrinement. Such hagiographies, too, may be rewritten and amended to take account of the changing contexts in which leaders and movements operate, to readjust movements to later changes in teaching, and to reinforce the image of the leader as innately special. For example, the account of the life of Ōkawa Ryūhō is narrated in several Kōfuku no Kagaku publications. In particular, the final part of one of the movement's most important texts, *Shin taiyō no hō* (The New Laws of the Sun) initially published in 1994 (and republished again later) describes the leader's education, career and spiritual path. Compared to an older version of the same book, published in the late 1980s, the new version reconstructs Ōkawa's life in order to demonstrate that his life since childhood was marked by exceptional events caused by 'high spirits' (*kōkyūrei*) to prepare him for his future role as a spiritual leader. Even failures, such as the failure to be admitted to the postgraduate programme at Tokyo University, are reinterpreted as premonitions from the spirits to reveal his destiny as a future religious leader (Ōkawa 2001a: 171–2; Ōkawa 2001b).[8]

Another example of this process of re-narration is the way in which movements highlight themes of hardship and personal struggles in the early lives of founders while emphasizing how they managed to endure and overcome such suffering through discipline and dedicated practice. In such terms hardship may be portrayed as a natural facet of life sent to test them and help them attain deeper understandings and spiritual powers. This type of narrative is rather common in hagiographical accounts such as the life history produced by Tenshō Kōtai Jingū Kyō about Kitamura Sayo (Tenshō Kōtai Jingū Kyō 1954). This portrays her early life as one of intense hardship and difficulties. Her family was desperately poor and she was sent out at a young age to be married to a local farmer. The family into which she married had a history of exploiting poor young peasant women such as Kitamura, who were married off to escape the grinding poverty of their families. Each year, the account says, the farmer would take a new bride, and he and his mother would then ruthlessly exploit and overwork her while providing only the most meagre rations. Each year after the harvest, once she had been worked to exhaustion, the new bride would be rejected, divorced and sent back to her family. The next year a new bride would be taken in, and so on. Kitamura, just one more poor young country girl in this cycle of exploitation, however, was not bowed by the brutality of her mother-in-law or husband, or the arduous tasks allotted her. She was assiduous in her work, sincere in her manner and always ready to bear her heavy workload with good cheer; she strove her utmost and worked tirelessly despite only getting the barest scraps of food to subsist on. She was so dutiful, hard-working and able to accept her lot that at the end of the year, rather than send her away as had been the case of the others, she was accepted into the family, and subsequently raised children there and thus fulfilled the ideal of the dedicated hard-working wife and mother (Tenshō Kōtai Jingū Kyō 1954).

This account of her early life and the depictions of brutality, hardship and Kitamura's stentorian endurance and fortitude are certainly hagiographic, yet they also express clear messages about the virtue and value of dedication and working through one's problems rather than running away. Kitamura exemplifies, in Tenshō Kōtai Jingū Kyō's account, the importance of hard work, loyalty, discipline and of accepting and adjusting to one's circumstances. These themes serve as moral guidelines for devotees, and help reinforce the social conservatism, in which people accept their fates and work within them rather than rejecting them, that underpins Tenshō Kōtai Jingū Kyō's view of the world. Kitamura's spiritual breakthrough, the account tells us, came about because of her devotion even in the throes of hardship; rather than complaining, running away or being rejected as had happened with previous wives, she displayed the highly valued Japanese characteristics of *gaman* and *ganbaru* – terms that mean forbearance, dutiful dedication, sticking to one's task, and constant striving. The message is clear: do not run from your problems, externalize them or blame them on someone else, but face them, and, through your faith, overcome them.

Similar themes are found in other hagiographies produced by new movements in Japan about their founders. Themes of suffering, fortitude, endurance and overcoming appear regularly in the biographies of Deguchi Nao of Oomoto, who raised a large family through menial work while remaining loyal to her feckless wastrel of a husband even as he drank away whatever money Nao managed to get,[9] Nakayama Miki of Tenrikyō (Tenrikyo 2006 (1967)) and many others. Even Ōkawa Ryūhō of Kōfuku no Kagaku, who appeared to have achieved worldly success by getting into Tokyo University, had (in movement narratives) a back story of setbacks, from being a victim of bullying at school to an initial failure at his university entrance examinations (he had to wait a year and retake them, successfully), to being passed over after graduation when he sought to enter the elite level of the Japanese civil service (Akiya 2015: 35–8).

Kiriyama Seiyū's story as manifest in Agonshū, in books by Agonshū followers, in his experiences as projected to his followers and in the narratives we have heard from Agonshū officials, fits with these modes of hagiographic construction. While it does not contain the levels of poverty and exploitative hardship found in Kitamura's and Deguchi Nao's narratives (and which have a clear gender association), it does indicate a number of traumas and difficulties, including business failures, a suicide attempt and a criminal conviction, that are portrayed not as character deficiencies but as important stages in his religious development. In the following sections we outline a narrative of his life, particularly up to the 1980s, that, while it is drawn from a variety of sources, mainly emanates from Kiriyama's writings and sermons, from Agonshū publications, narratives told to us by officials in the movement and books by Agonshū followers.[10] Together they represent a construction of his life narrative that both gives rise to and fits with Agonshū's core teachings and its representations of Kiriyama as a spiritually powerful figure.

Kiriyama Seiyū: early life, trials and tribulations

Kiriyama was born in 1921 in Yokohama as Tsutsumi Masao, his official Japanese name; like many other Japanese religious figures, he later, in 1955, took on a new name (Kiriyama Seiyū) to signify his transformation as a religious figure. His early life was disrupted by the Great Kantō earthquake of 1923 that devastated the Tokyo region, and later he suffered from ill health, including, at the age of 19, tuberculosis, which caused him much pain and made him think for the first time about suicide. His poor health meant that he was unable to serve in the armed forces during the Second World War, unlike many in his age group and friends, who did go to war and were killed. He clearly at one time viewed his inability to go to war as fortunate, because, as he wrote in 1983, he still shuddered at the thought that if he had done so, he might have been involved in war crimes (Kiriyama 1983: 42–3). Yet, as we will see later, this view seems to have changed in later years, as Agonshū became increasingly focused on memorializing those associated with Japan's wartime activities, and visiting shrines associated with war and nationalism – issues we discuss in Chapter 5.

He sought to overcome his health problems through religious practices such as meditation, along with the development of a health-focused diet (Benod 2013: 166). Losses due to cancer in his family and his own record of illness gave him a premonition that he, too, would die of cancer by the time he reached his forties. As a result he began to visit numerous temples and shrines trying to find ways to change his fate (*unmei*) but without success. This led him to an early realization that priests in the established traditions lacked efficacy. Although the practices of esoteric Buddhism (*mikkyō*) were in theory supposed to be efficacious, they had, he realized, become formalistic in Japan and were devoid of power and spiritual value, while their priests' knowledge was merely superficial (Kiriyama 1983). Such criticisms of esoteric Buddhism were frequently reiterated in Agonshū tracts and were a theme of Kiriyama's life narrative broadcast during the enshrinement of his relics at the 2017 Hoshi Matsuri.

Kiriyama, according to Agonshū narratives, failed to secure any career or position that could provide economic stability and balance to his life. This story of personal problems and failures reached its apex in 1953 when he was arrested, charged, found guilty and sent to prison for his involvement in a scheme to illicitly manufacture and sell alcohol, in contravention of the tax laws. He spent several months in prison for this incident,[11] and this event and experience form a seminal point in his and his movement's trajectory.

There have been accusations that Kiriyama kept this aspect of his personal history hidden until it was discovered by journalists in the 1980s (Kakida 1984: 56–66). As such, the story was initially reported, in the media, as a scandal that seemed to imply that Kiriyama, far from being a religious leader, was really someone involved with deception and potential criminality. He was not the only founder to have had problems with the law; prior to founding Aum Shinrikyō Asahara Shōkō had been convicted and fined for the fraudulent manufacture and sale of herbal medicines (Reader 2000a: 53) while Itō Shinjō of Shinnyoen was found guilty and given a prison sentence (which was suspended) for striking a member of his movement in 1950. In Kiriyama's case it remains unclear as to whether the allegation that he had initially covered up the conviction is correct. What is clear is that, when details of this criminal conviction became public, the event became incorporated into the Kiriyama story alongside the tales of poor health, his business failures and thoughts of suicide, and was used to reinforce Agonshū's teachings.

Kiriyama's portrayal of the affair shows how these various misfortunes together served as an awakening and as a sign that he was afflicted by bad karmic forces. It has helped formulate a cardinal aspect of Kiriyama's teaching: that people are deeply affected by spiritual hindrances (*reishō*) from unhappy and malevolent spirits that will cause misfortunes and prevent them achieving happiness or realizing their goals. As such these hindrances (and the spirits that cause them) have to be quelled and pacified by religious rituals, practices and offerings – a perspective that lies at the heart of Agonshū's teaching about the importance of 'cutting one's karma' (*innen o kiru*).

Kiriyama regularly made use of this story of incarceration and of his past misfortunes as a teaching mechanism to tell followers that they too could overcome their problems and achieve what they wished for if they followed his path. By the late 1980s these messages featured prominently in his sermons. While drawing attention to his status as a religious teacher with the power to bring world salvation, he reminded followers that this was not always the case. Earlier in life he had been dragged down by misfortunes to the point of going to prison but had overcome these problems through his practice. He had been subjected to various karmic misfortunes, notably the karma of imprisonment (*keigoku no innen*), which in Agonshū is seen as one of twenty-two specific types of problematic karma that could afflict people (Benod 2013: 263–9). As such his life of misfortunes and his struggles to overcome them provided a model example to his disciples, informing them that anyone (even a potential religious founder) was subject to the laws of karma and the misfortunes they might bring, and that everyone had to try to eradicate such negative forces. It also showed that they could cut their own karma and be liberated just as he had done.[12] We will return to these issues in the next chapter when we discuss Agonshū's teachings, practices and rituals.

A suicide bid and a miraculous intervention

Yet if the incident illustrated the need to deal with his bad karma, Kiriyama remained caught in a cycle of unhappiness and was unable to find solace. Eventually he reached such a point of despair that he felt the only way left was suicide. Here the story reaches a climactic point, with Kiriyama throwing a rope across a beam to hang himself, only to be stopped in his tracks by seeing something lodged on the beam where he had thrown the rope. He reached up and found it was a copy of a Buddhist text, the *Kannongyō* or Kannon Sutra. The *Kannongyō* is actually the twenty-fifth chapter of the Lotus Sutra (*Hokekyō*), one of the most significant texts in the Mahāyāna Buddhist canon, but in East Asia it has been popular as a self-standing text of praise to Kannon, the bodhisattva of compassion who promises to save all who reach out to her. Kiriyama read the text and its contents changed his life; he was inspired by the text's affirmation of Kannon's compassion and her wish to protect all from danger. He sensed that finding the text in this dramatic way was no chance event, but something preordained, showing that he had a special connection with Kannon. Rather than killing himself, he was instead saved by her mercy. This story of absolute despair and dramatic salvation through the discovery of the text – and through it Kiriyama's realization that he had a special bond with Kannon – serves as a miracle story and foundation legend for Agonshū and the starting point of Kiriyama's path as a religious leader (Kiriyama 1983: 76–7; Yajima 1985: 43).

Kannon's miraculous intervention showed Kiriyama that he henceforth should devote himself to a religious path and help others embrace Kannon's mercy. He thus, in 1954, established a religious group, the Kannon Jikeikai, with Juntei Kannon (one of the many manifestations of Kannon in Buddhist cosmology) as its main image of worship. His name change from Tsutsumi Masao to Kiriyama Seiyū in 1955 represented a rite of passage as he embarked on a new life as a religious seeker guided by Kannon. Around the same time he began to engage in Buddhist ascetic practices and studies; according to his narrative and subsequent Agonshū history, he also received a Shingon Buddhist ordination. While some in the media have questioned the validity of this ordination, it appears that he did undergo some Shingon training, and the ordination provided him with the legitimacy to conduct and engage in Buddhist and related esoteric ceremonies, practices and rituals such as the *goma* fire rituals that have become Agonshū's main public events.[13] He also, in 1956, developed links to a Jōdo Shinshū temple, Yōgenin, in Kyoto; this temple had a particular focus on Kannon and Kiriyama claims to have been invited to deliver sermons there on a number of occasions (Kiriyama 1983: 102; Benod 2013: 165–6). Later he established the Kannon Jikeikai's first centre close to Yōgenin.[14] These connections to different sectarian temples and traditions enabled him to claim he had studied across the breadth of Buddhism (rather than, as is common in Japan, only within the confines of one sectarian tradition and its texts and practices) in his search for the essential teachings of Buddhism. Later he was to expand his connections by developing links with various Buddhist figures and traditions beyond Japan, as he sought, according to Agonshū, to formulate a Buddhism that transcended any sectarian boundaries.

From 1954 until 1970 he also undertook various ascetic practices associated with Shingon Buddhism and with Shugendō, the mountain religious tradition. These included studying the *goma* fire rituals of the esoteric tradition, engaging in meditation and cold-water ablutions such as standing under waterfalls, and performing other ascetic and ritual practices carried out by the *yamabushi* (mountain ascetic religious practitioners) of Shugendō. Claiming mastery of such practices, he began to project himself as a teacher of them as *goma* rituals became a staple element in his movement. In 1957 he published his first book, *Kōfuku e no genri* (The principles of happiness) although it appears to have had little impact. He also started to attract some followers to the Kannon Jikeikai, although it remained a very small group.[15]

From searcher to leader

In 1970 there was a new turning point in Kiriyama's life when Juntei Kannon appeared to him in a dream to say that, through his ascetic practice and training, he had 'cut his karma' and that henceforth he was no longer a seeker but a leader with a mission to guide others to salvation. Juntei Kannon also told Kiriyama that the way to liberate others from their bad karma and to pacify the spirits of the dead that were causes of unhappiness was via the *goma* fire ritual.[16] It was because of Kiriyama's training in, and mastery of, the esoteric Buddhist and *yamabushi* traditions that he was able to do this.[17]

From 1970 the Kannon Jikeikai instituted public *goma* rituals; its first Hoshi Matsuri – the main annual ritual event in Agonshū's calendar – took place in that year in the region of Mount Fuji with around two hundred people in attendance. It thereafter was held in Kanazawa until 1974 and from 1975 onwards at Yamashina near Kyoto (Figure 2.1). Kiriyama also began to travel extensively, visiting the United States, where he met with figures such as the Tibetan Buddhist lama Chogyam Trungpa, who had developed a following of mostly younger American seekers, and India where he encountered various Indian gurus. Agonshū portrays such encounters as highly significant, implying that they represented widespread international recognition of Kiriyama's spiritual powers (Murō 1987: 67). He subsequently met some even more prominent religious figures, notably the Dalai Lama in 1983 and 1984, and Pope John Paul II in Rome in 1985. Such encounters serve in Agonshū narratives to enhance his authority and mark him out as an internationally known religious leader.

In 1971 Kiriyama published a second book, *Henshin no genri* (The principles of transformation (of the body)) in which he talked about five supernatural powers (*chōnōryoku*) that he had acquired through his practices in *mikkyō* (esoteric Buddhism), and about how he could guide others to achieve those powers. The five powers were the power of prophecy and divination; the power of high levels of activity; the power to alter oneself and one's environment via one's thoughts; the possession of great physical and spiritual strength; and the awesome power (*nenriki*) to enable oneself and others to realize their wishes (Kiriyama 1971; Numata 1988: 61). This book occupies a seminal place in Agonshū's history: according to movement rhetoric it was this book that started what became known in Japan as the '*mikkyō* boom' (*mikkyō būmu*)[18] – a 'boom' or rise in popular (and media) interest in esoteric Buddhism and its rituals, practices, art and iconography. This was frequently mentioned by Japanese scholars and in the media from the late 1970s onwards and into the 1980s as an element in the popular religious culture of the era (Numata 1988). Whether Kiriyama really did start this 'boom' is neither clear nor the point; in Agonshū's narrative, he did and this forms part of its image construction of Kiriyama as someone who shaped the religious culture of the age. It also emphasized and enhanced his status as a religious leader. In the years that followed, and notably among the new movements that became the focus of media attention in the 1980s, interest in supernatural powers and esoteric practices were recurrent elements of popular religious culture (Reader 2000a: 47–52). For example, for Asahara Shōkō, who founded Aum after leaving Agonshū, superhuman powers were an important part of the religious system he established; indeed his first book was titled *Chōnōryoku* (Asahara 1986).

Rediscovering the truths of Buddhism

During the 1970s Kiriyama, according to Agonshū, studied Buddhist texts extensively, and came to the realization that while sutras such as the Heart Sutra (*Hannya Shingyō*) and Lotus Sutra that were prevalent in Japanese Buddhism offered spiritual insights, they did not provide the ultimate teachings about how to attain *jōbutsu*, or liberation. The term *jōbutsu* has a dual or overlapping meaning in Japanese contexts – a dual usage also evident in Agonshū. While it means liberation, enlightenment and 'becoming a Buddha' it also is used to refer to the spirits of the dead who become pacified and benevolent ancestors through the performance of Buddhist rituals after death. Liberated through such rituals, they become buddhas (*jōbutsu*). Essentially Kiriyama was saying that Japanese Buddhism and the texts it used could neither help people achieve spiritual liberation nor aid the spirits of the dead to achieve peace and become benevolent protectors and ancestors after death. He was in effect accusing the whole tradition of failure and, in his dissatisfaction with it, he had decided to go back to earlier parts of the Buddhist canon rather than continuing to focus on the Mahāyāna sutras prevalent in the Japanese Buddhist tradition. This led him to the Āgama sutras, which are among the earliest texts of Buddhism and part of the Pali Canon. It was here that he made his next spiritual breakthrough; it was in the Āgamas that he 'discovered' the essence of Buddhism and the way to properly liberate spirits.

For Kiriyama the inner meanings of the Āgamas – which, he proclaimed, taught the laws of causation (i.e. karma) and the ways to attain liberation from one's karma and become enlightened – had been missed by generations of Buddhists in East Asia. They had misguidedly overlooked the early Buddhist tradition (dismissively referred to as the Hinayāna or 'lesser vehicle') and its sutras, in favour of the historically later Mahāyāna tradition and its sutras that took root in East Asia. According to the bilingual Agonshū booklet *Agonshū to wa* (which includes also an English-language text and title *The Agon-shū* and is given to potential members as a core description of the movement), Kiriyama 'discovered that the only real records that accurately reflect Laud (*sic*) Buddha's teachings while he was alive are found in the Agon Sutras' (Agonshū ed., nd.: 2).[19] It was, Agonshū stated, because of Kiriyama's immense experience in, and long engagement with, various austerities and ritual practices such as the *goma* that he was able to develop the insight and power to discern the true inner meaning of the Āgama texts. After the demise of Shakyamuni, Buddhism had split into factions, with the result that any focus on correct practices became dissipated until

Kiriyama emerged to bring them together again by combining the insights he had gained from practices in the Mahāyāna and esoteric traditions with the revelations of the true essence and path of liberation he had discovered in the Āgamas. He was not just reuniting Buddhism but returning it to its origins and essence. As such, Agonshū was not just a modern Japanese movement promising the acquisition of esoteric and superhuman powers; it was the essence of original Buddhism (*genshi bukkyō*), which it was bringing back to the world. In reuniting all the disparate traditions of Buddhism into one, Agonshū was, in fact, 'complete Buddhism' (*kanzen bukkyō*), a term that has been incorporated into Agonshū rhetoric along with *genshi bukkyō* to indicate the movement's self-perception. It is also a term used in Agonshū's evocations of praise for Kiriyama who, as the narrative broadcast over loudspeakers at the 2017 Hoshi Matsuri told listeners, revived *kanzen bukkyō* in his mission to bring about world peace. Agonshū pronouncements since his death have also claimed that, while the historical Buddha initially proclaimed the Āgamas, it was Kiriyama who actually taught their inner meaning (see Chapter 5).

Convinced, via his insights from the Āgamas, that he had a special mission to bring original Buddhism back to the world Kiriyama established a new movement. On 8 April 1978 he dissolved the Kannon Jikeikai and in its place founded Agonshū. The date itself is a significant marker of the movement's identification, for 8 April is the date, according to Japanese Buddhists, of the Buddha's birthday. On this day every year the *hanamatsuri* festival commemorating Buddha's birth is celebrated at Buddhist temples. The foundation of the new movement thus implies the birth (or, rather, the rebirth) of Buddhism; just as Shakyamuni's birth, celebrated in Japan on 8 April, marks the beginnings of Buddhism so the foundation of Agonshū on 8 April marks the establishment of a renewed Buddhism for the present day. The term used to translate Āgama into Japanese is 'Agon' and it was from these sutras that his movement acquired a new name: Agonshū. The dual imagery here – founding the movement on the Buddha's birthday and taking its name from ancient Buddhist scriptures – thus indicates Agonshū's sense of identity as a Buddhist movement and its self-image as a rebirth of, and return to the roots of, Buddhism.

Buddhist Studies textual scholars might be sceptical about Kiriyama's claims regarding the Āgamas and about whether they contain the core teachings that Kiriyama has discerned. They might also doubt whether it is possible to unite all forms of Buddhism under the aegis of one movement and set of texts. However, this is not (from the perspective of Agonshū or from our point of analysis) relevant. The importance for Agonshū is grounded in the narrative and belief that Kiriyama was able to discern truths that others (including the entire Buddhist establishment) had missed because they did not have the depth of spiritual awareness he had gained through his ascetic practice. Both sectarian Buddhist and academic dismissals of his statements about the Āgamas would merely, from the Agonshū perspective, underline Kiriyama's point about the failures of the Buddhist establishment, rather than disprove the validity of his claims.

In claiming that he had found the essence of Buddhism in a particular text, Kiriyama was doing nothing new. As we stated in Chapter 1, the rediscovery of ancient truths and the mission to bring them back centre-stage and spread them to the wider world are common characteristics of new religions and their founders. They are elements in the construction of charismatic status, something that in Agonshū heightened Kiriyama's standing not just as a skilled practitioner and ritual specialist but also as an interpreter of texts. Stephen Feuchtwang (2008: 93) has argued that charisma is 'new-old', by which he means that while charisma may be something associated with new visions and revelations, it is also derivative in that it draws on something that already is viewed as authoritative. Drawing on ancient texts or revelations from potent deities is one way of affirming the potency of new visions and of substantiating the new with the affirmations of the old. In Japanese contexts, this may be through drawing on existing and established traditions, for example, by claiming that a founder's revelations derive from an ancient (albeit previously hidden) deity, as with the revelations of Nakayama Miki in Tenrikyō, or through reinterpretations of Buddhist texts. This latter path has a long history in Japan, not just in Buddhist-oriented new religions but also in the established Buddhist tradition. As Jay Sakashita (1998: 54) has suggested, adopting a Buddhist sutra as a core canonical element provides a mode of legitimation for a new movement, and such legitimation may be more important than the sutra itself. Shinnyoen's founder Itō Shinjō, for example, discovered the essential truths of Buddhism in the Nehan (Nirvana) Sutra and built his religion around that view. Nichiren, the founding inspiration for the Nichirenist tradition in Japan, saw the Lotus Sutra as the apex and essence of all Buddhist teaching and various Nichiren-oriented new Buddhist movements such as Sōka Gakkai, Reiyūkai and Risshō Kōseikai emerged in twentieth-century Japan affirming (albeit with differing interpretations of the sutra) this view.

Kiriyama, in turning to the Āgamas and claiming new insights in these ancient texts, was thus operating within the framework of the 'new-old' matrix outlined by Feuchtwang. This dynamic was evident too in Agonshū's claim, as a newly emerged movement, to be restoring 'original Buddhism' – something again not unique to Agonshū. Several other movements that came to the fore in the last decades of the twentieth century similarly spoke of restoring, rediscovering and returning to 'original Buddhism' (*genshi bukkyō*) and/or of developing a higher form of Buddhism for the modern age. Such themes were expressed also by Aum Shinrikyō and Kōfuku no Kagaku, both of which were growing in the 1980s and were in many respects seen as rivals competing with Agonshū. Aum Shinrikyō devoted efforts to studying early Buddhist sutras and talked of restoring 'original Buddhism' (Reader 2000a: 79; Asahara 1988). Kōfuku no Kagaku went further by focusing on the writings of its founder, Ōkawa, as its canonical source while Ōkawa declared that he was the historical Buddha in a previous life, and is the eternal Buddha incarnate. As such Kōfuku no Kagaku's claims of being the source of original Buddhism have been grounded not in claims about new readings of preexisting sutras but in the claim that their leader is the source of Buddhism.[20] While Kiriyama and Asahara both assert themselves as being the spiritual descendants of the Buddha, Ōkawa has implicitly subverted their claims by presenting himself not just as someone seeking to revitalize original Buddhism but as its founder.

Millennialism, the prophesied saviour and the affirmation of sanctity

Such truth claims in which Kiriyama alone has discerned the inner essence of Buddhism lead on to other assertions that shape the aura that Agonshū has built around its founder: that he has been chosen to spread Buddhism to the world, and that he is a saviour with a mission to bring about world peace. These are themes that we will discuss further in Chapter 3 in the context of Agonshū's teaching and ritual practices. Integral to these visions of a restoration of original truths are notions of individual salvation and world renewal, and the idea of the world in chaos and in need of transformation. Such millennial themes, as we noted in Chapter 1, have been a recurrent feature of Japanese religious history, notably in the development of Japanese new religions, which have commonly spoken of world renewal (*yonaoshi*), wherein the materialism and inequities of the world would be replaced by a more spiritually aware age in which all would live harmoniously in peace. Such ideals have commonly been focused also on the notion of individual transformation, in which the individual is a microcosm of the world and must be the starting point of any renewal (Hardacre 1986: 3–36), rather than through a social process of political change.

A recurrent strand in millennialism, and evident in the perspectives of many new religions, is that the world is in need of transformation. In Oomoto, for example, as we mentioned in Chapter 1, Deguchi Nao used the term *tatekae tatenaoshi* (demolition and reconstruction) to claim that the current material world and society needed to be overturned and transformed. Deguchi Nao, coming from an agrarian background, yearned for a return to an idealized rural idyll in which materialism was eradicated, and she was hostile to modern forces, materialism and influences from outside Japan. Her millennialism was anti-modern, nationalistic and xenophobic. Kitamura Sayo in Tenshō Kōtai Jingū Kyō in the immediate period after the end of the Second World War also preached millennial visions in which she prophesied the collapse of the modern material world that she denounced as corrupt, and emphasized the need for radical change. In both cases, as is common in millennial movements, this early religious radicalism yielded to a more conservative vision in which calls for a dramatic transformation of society and the restoration of an imagined and idealized spiritual realm gave way to an emphasis on individual transformation and to less vituperative critiques of society.[21]

The millennialism of movements such as Agonshū that came to the fore in the 1980s was also conditioned by a number of circumstances particular to the epoch. The Cold War and fears of nuclear oblivion were still present, intensified by Japan's experience as the only country to have suffered the atomic bomb – a memory that indicated that nuclear weaponry was not an abstract fear but a destructive reality (Miyamoto 2011). Alongside this were increasing fears about the environment. Crucially, too, worries about the end of the second calendar millennium[22] and associated fears such as the so-called Y2K bug, further served to heighten fears that the world was facing chaos and needed transformation. This situation was exacerbated by the prophecies of the French medieval writer Nostradamus, which suggested that a world crisis and impending doom would arise by 1999. Nostradamus's prophecies were first translated into Japanese in 1973 and they had a major impact on popular culture, in manga and television shows. These prophecies added to a popular religious culture in which notions of disaster and cataclysm either as a prelude to the end of the world, or as a mechanism to destroy the current material civilization and give rise to a new spiritual realm were prevalent. At the same time, the translation (or perhaps a somewhat loose translation) of Nostradamus's prophecies also suggested that a saviour would arise from the East to avert such disaster (Kisala 1997; Reader 2000a: 50–2). Such prophecies fed into the narratives of those religions that espoused millennial themes and saw themselves as offering hope for the future.[23]

Kiriyama was one of several Japanese religious leaders of the period (including Ōkawa Ryūhō of Kōfuku no Kagaku and Asahara Shōkō of Aum Shinrikyō) who made prophecies about the dangers the world faced at the end of the millennium and about potential wars, disasters and calamities that threatened human existence. They also claimed to have prophetic powers to foresee the cataclysmic events that were about to unfold – and to see how to deal with them. Their claims to such powers naturally also served as an area of contention. Asahara and Ōkawa, for example, engaged in claims and counterclaims on this score, as each asserted the primacy of his prophecies and powers over the other in ways that caused them both to intensify their emphasis on millennial themes and possible destructive scenarios (Baffelli and Reader 2011). Kiriyama, too, asserted his powers and superiority in such areas, for example, in *Henshin no genri*, where he identified prophecy as one of the powers imparted by his system of teaching. In various publications he drew attention to Nostradamus's prophecies and articulated his own reading of them and of the crisis the world faced. His 1981 book *1999 nen karuma to reishō kara no dasshutsu* (Escape from Harmful Spirits and the Karma of 1999), for example, is generally considered to be the first time a religious leader in Japan engaged with Nostradamus's prophecies (others were to follow, including Asahara and Ōkawa) and is indicative of a recurrent pattern of Kiriyama being in the vanguard of the religious field of that era (Kisala 1997: 48, 53). It set a benchmark that other rival claimants sought to meet and surpass. In *1999 nen karuma to reishō kara no dasshutsu* Kiriyama focused on prophecies about the potential destruction the world faced, argued that there was a scientific underpinning to these prophecies and claimed he had a solution to the problem. Using a line of argument that occurs repeatedly in Japanese discourses, he attributed the root cause of the problems to an overweening focus on materialism, which he saw as a cultural influence of Western civilization, and offered a solution via the spiritual culture of the East.[24] He also emphasized a recurrent point in Agonshū's teaching: that unhappy spirits of the dead were a prime cause of such unease and that performing the appropriate ritual services to pacify them was a vital element in the process of world salvation (Kiriyama 1981; Reader 1991: 215). Millennial destruction and salvation were thus fused with traditional Japanese notions of the spirits of the dead, their influences on the living and the rituals traditionally performed in Japan to pacify them.

The solution to this looming problem was, of course, Agonshū, whose rituals along with Kiriyama's 'discovery' of new truths that enabled him to revitalize original Buddhism gave it the power to save humanity. He utilized what Robert Kisala (1997: 53) has called a 'rather elaborate transposition of letters' to interpret Nostradamus's phrase *Roy d'Angolmois*,[25] which appeared to signify a saviour King from the East who would arise to resolve the looming millennial scenario. Kiriyama's interpretation indicated that he and Agonshū fitted this designation as the agents of salvation prophesied by Nostradamus. One should note that Kiriyama was using the 1973 Japanese translation of Nostradamus by Gōtō Ben, a rendition regarded as being more akin to Gōtō's interpretations of Nostradamus than to literal translations (Kisala 1997: 50). Kiriyama also claimed to have had personal revelations from Nostradamus that confirmed his reading of the text – again affirming (in the eyes of followers) his powers of spiritual communication. Subsequently other religious founders such as Asahara and Ōkawa, each of whom unsurprisingly identified himself as the prophesied saviour, produced texts claiming that they had had direct spiritual communications with the medieval French sage (Asahara 1991; Ōkawa 1988). Unsurprisingly none recognized the revelations of their rivals as valid.

While one could understandably see Kiriyama's self-identification with the saviour apparently prophesied by Nostradamus as somewhat arcane and speculative in nature, it has its own internalized logic. If Nostradamus were right in foreseeing a crisis at the end of the millennium and in saying that a saviour figure would arise to avert it, it made 'sense' to recognize that Nostradamus must have been talking about Kiriyama, a religious leader who was already aware of his own destiny and mission, who had already discovered the inner truths of Buddhism and who was ready to spread them anew to the world. It served (along with his earlier reading of the Āgamas) as a message to potential and existing followers that here was someone with immense spiritual power who could 'see' beyond the surface of texts to discover deep hidden and inner truths within them, and who had even been spoken to by Nostradamus to confirm this. It also served as a repudiation of others who claimed (falsely, in the eyes of Agonshū) to be the saviour prophesied by Nostradamus and who asserted that they were restoring original Buddhism. Through such readings of Nostradamus, Kiriyama thus went from being the modern discoverer and reviver of the ancient truths of Buddhism, to being a messiah at a time of world crisis with a mission of world salvation. It was a further step in the elevation of the teacher and founder to a level of spiritual authority that transcended normal human realms and enhanced his charisma in the eyes of followers.

Competing to be in the vanguard

Kiriyama, as we previously mentioned, was portrayed in Agonshū as a trendsetter, the leader who started the '*mikkyō* boom'. In the 1980s he was clearly, like Deguchi Ōnisaburō in an earlier era, someone who was aware of the underlying concerns and trends of the time and who was able to bring them into the framework of his movement. As Kisala (1997: 53) commented, Kiriyama 'has consistently shown a sensitivity to popular culture', and Kisala backs this comment up by identifying various themes, including interests in early Buddhism, esoteric Buddhism, psychic powers and Nostradamus's prophecies, that were manifest in popular culture from the 1970s onwards and that Kiriyama picked up on.

For Agonshū he was not just in the vanguard of such interests but the person who shaped the religious culture of the age. According to Agonshū, Kiriyama was also one of the first religious leaders (if not the first) to talk about the *seishin sekai* (spiritual world), a term that became popular in Japan from the late 1970s onwards and was used by scholars to refer to groups of practices and teaching developed around loosely organized networks. According to Shimazono, the term started to be used in 1978 in a bookstore in Tokyo, where a section devoted to the 'Spiritual World' was set up (Shimazono 2004: 275), including books about healing, meditation, channelling, reincarnation and, more generally, the idea of a spirit world and of practices associated with self-development. Shimazono (1996, 2004) sees the *seishin sekai*, together with the 'New Age' in the United States, as part of what he calls 'new spirituality movements' (*shinreisei undō*) – and, more recently, 'new spirituality culture' *shinreisei bunka* (Shimazono 2007) – that represent a 'new global religious culture' (Shimazono 2004: 276). Involvement in the *seishin sekai* is not conditioned by formal affiliation to specific religious groups but is more akin to a postmodern individualized agenda of self-selected practices that require no commitment to or membership of religious organizations.[26] It refers also to the idea that Japanese society is becoming more individualized and moving away from a traditional focus on the household as the key social building block (a focus that has been central to the structure of established Buddhism, for example). Agonshū has been one such movement that in the 1980s framed its teaching and practices in the context of the *seishin sekai*, in particular regarding topics such as reincarnation, meditation, healing, the coming of a new age and the idea of connections between science and religion. The group, for example, frequently used the word *seishin sekai* in its publications, published a ranking of the top 100 books on the 'spiritual world' (Shimazono 2007: 168) in the Agonshū magazine *Za Meditēshon* (The Meditation) and in 1982 devoted a special issue on the topic in its magazine *Meisō Meditation* (Baffelli 2016: 21).

Whether the idea of a growth in interest in spiritual matters, as indicated by the notion of the *seishin sekai*, has any validity is not the point here. Rather, it is that Agonshū has laid claims to the idea as its own and, in so doing, further asserted the position of its founder as an innovator shaping the religious contours of the age. It also, like the claim that Kiriyama invented the *mikkyō* boom, contains an implicit critique of other groups. The 'invention' of the *mikkyō* boom and the concomitant rise in interest in esoteric Buddhist practices that appeared to follow it, contained a criticism of the older esoteric sects who were not just accused, by Agonshū, of keeping the powers of esotericism for their priestly hierarchies rather than enabling ordinary people to engage in it, but of failing to arouse enthusiasm for their basic teachings. Asserting his invention of the *seishin sekai* not only places Agonshū and Kiriyama, again, in the vanguard of the age (i.e. not just as a 'new' religion, but also as a 'modern' religion) but implicitly suggests all those who drew in any way on notions related to the *seishin sekai* were simply aping Agonshū and, lacking innovative ideas of their own, following in Kiriyama's footsteps.

Although Agonshū did not overtly attack its rivals in this context, its espousal of millennial thoughts, its prophecies of potential upheaval and its use of Nostradamus in ways that emphasized Kiriyama's mission played a significant role in highlighting these issues. As was mentioned earlier, Kiriyama was the first such leader to directly address the prophecies of Nostradamus. His first book on the topic was in 1981, and he later published another book on the topic (Kiriyama 1995a), which reiterated many of the themes of this first book and in which he talked of the prophesied cataclysm to come while claiming to have received a personal revelation on this matter and identifying Agonshū as the salvific vehicle identified by Nostradamus to avert this crisis and transform the world. As Kisala (1997: 53–4) notes, Kiriyama's reading and revelations relating to Nostradamus in effect validated his own prophecies.

Spiritual manifestations and miraculous events

Kiriyama's status as a leader along with affirmations of Agonshū's standing came through a variety of manifestations and messages from the spiritual realms. As the Hoshi Matsuri grew in size year on year from the late 1970s onwards (see Chapter 3 for a description) a variety of figures from Buddhist and Japanese cosmologies manifested themselves (according to Agonshū) at the event. In 1978 Nanda, the Dragon King mentioned in the Lotus Sutra, appeared in the *goma* pyre flames at the Hoshi Matsuri; in 1979 the Buddha Shakyamuni, Juntei Kannon and Dainichi Nyorai (the Cosmic Buddha of the Shingon tradition) appeared. In 1980 Shakyamuni along with myriad Buddhas and *kami* (Shinto deities) manifested themselves. These apparitions served in Agonshū's constructed narrative to validate the ritual and to confirm that the celestial and spiritual worlds supported and were present at it.

In 1980 perhaps the most important recognition of all occurred. While visiting India, Kiriyama went to Sahet Mahet, the site of the first ever Buddhist monastery (Sravasti) set up by the Buddha himself. While observing the historical ruins there Kiriyama felt a vibration; it was a message spiritually communicated directly to him from the Buddha. This communication is depicted in an Agonshū video of the visit in which Kiriyama is shown to react as he 'hears' Shakyamuni's message. The communication served to further enhance his position as the revitalizer and unifier of Buddhism in the modern day. The vibration received from Buddha (whom Kiriyama addresses familiarly in the video as '*anata*' [you]) was a signal to Kiriyama that not only did he have a mission to unify Buddhism again but this mission was sanctified by the Buddha, and it involved building a new sacred land in Japan, a Buddhist temple that would symbolically be the 'new Sahet Mahet' from which Agonshū's 'complete' and 'original' Buddhism would be spread to the rest of the world. The message thus not only conferred on Kiriyama the approval of Buddha and made him the Buddha's successor but also affirmed two important dimensions to Agonshū's teaching, namely, the mission of world salvation prophesied by Nostradamus and the centrality of Japan in this mission. While Agonshū's message that Kiriyama was a saviour restoring original Buddhism to the world had universalist dimensions, it also had a very clear national orientation, placing Japan at the epicentre of the world in spiritual terms, the nation from which peace and salvation would spread. This perspective was not unique to Agonshū, as we commented in Chapter 1, but was found among other movements of the 1980s as well, and is a recurrent theme in other new religions as well (Pye 1986;

Young 1988). Subsequently the 'miracle of Sahet Mahet', as Agonshū later dubbed it, has assumed ever-greater significance in the aftermath of Kiriyama's demise, and serves as manifestation of the transmission of the 'true law' (*shōbō*) of Buddhism from Shakyamuni to Kiriyama and, with it, in effect, Kiriyama's position as the Buddha of the current era (see Chapter 5).

Other seminal events included the bestowal of Buddha relics on the movement. Agonshū claims to been given a number of such relics, starting in 1974, but with two particularly significant ones – the first by the Dalai Lama in 1983 and the second by then-President Jayawardene of Sri Lanka in 1986.[27] The factors behind the latter event are unclear.[28] Agonshū had certainly developed links with Sri Lankan Buddhist organizations in the period beforehand, and there has been a long tradition within the Buddhist tradition of the acquisition, exchange and dissemination of Buddha relics, usually for the purpose of spreading influence and the enhancement of good relations between Buddhist associations and regions (Strong 2004; Trainor 2007). There are a number of other Buddha relics in Japan, from a relic in the non-sectarian temple Nittaiji in Nagoya, given in 1904 by the King of Thailand to Japan, to relics in the possession of individual Buddhist temples and of Buddhist-oriented movements such as Shinnyoen, which received relics from Thailand in 1965. Yet for Agonshū the relics from the Dalai Lama and President Jayawardene are special; they are the only 'authentic' relics, apart from the one donated to Nittaiji.[29]

This assertion simultaneously implies that other movements (including Shinnyoen) that claim to possess Buddha relics are merely worshipping false items, or 'pieces of stone or sand' (Agonshū 1986: 28–31; Reader 1988: 243), while affirming Agonshū's authenticity and superiority in Buddhist terms. As Kiriyama informed an interviewer, the relic was given to him because the representatives of a Buddhist country, Sri Lanka, recognized his unique position as the modern-day leader who had discovered the true essence of Buddhism and was spreading it across the world (Murō 1987: 230). The Sri Lankan relic, known in Agonshū as the *shinsei busshari* (true relic of the Buddha), was, thereafter, enshrined as Agonshū's main focus of worship, leading to a change in Agonshū practice (see Chapter 3) and serving as the central focus of its rituals from 1987 until February 2017 when another important set of relics – of Kiriyama himself – joined it.

These events and examples of international recognition, or rather Agonshū's interpretations of them, serve as a continuing narrative that demonstrates, from its perspective, the spiritual potency and standing of its founder, and hence, through him of Agonshū itself and of its members. This construction and enhancement of charismatic authority is not a one-way process; as the founder is exalted, and as events purportedly affirming his charismatic powers occur, they also enhance the status, self-worth and spiritual power of his followers. For members of Agonshū, the revelations and spiritual communications from Nostradamus and the Buddha, the bestowal of the 'genuine' relics of Buddha and the appearance of various deities and Buddhist figures at Agonshū rituals not only validate their leader and movement but affirm their own status as followers of the spiritual leader charged with restoring original Buddhism and saving the world. They, as such, contribute to a continuing process of affirming Kiriyama's charisma and spiritual authority because it in turn reinforces their own standing.

Titles, talents – and yet human

Many new movements in Japan have portrayed their leaders in life as something beyond the human realm. Ōkawa Ryūhō of Kōfuku no Kagaku, for example, as we mentioned above, declared himself to be the eternal Buddha and El Cantāre, the founder of the universe, while many new religions have declared their founders to be *ikigami* (living deities) or *ikibotoke* (living buddhas) during their lifetimes. Konkō Daijin, the founder of Konkōkyō, was an *ikigami*, for example, and Naganuma Myōkō of Risshō Kōseikai was viewed by followers as an *ikibotoke*, while Nakayama Miki of Tenrikyō was *Oyasama*, the 'parent of all humanity'.[30]

By contrast, in life Kiriyama continued to be portrayed in the movement as a human figure. Nonetheless he was clearly accorded levels of respect and devotion that placed him in a special category and that sowed the seeds for his later posthumous elevation. He held exalted titles in Agonshū; officially he was the *kanchō geika* (literally, Reverend Holiness) and he also took on other accolades, such as the title *Ajari* (an exalted rank of Buddhist practitioner), to affirm his enhanced status in Buddhist terms. Agonshū accounts accorded him numerous splendid accomplishments and abilities in various fields. He was, for example, portrayed as a high-level Go master and a scholar who had achieved various academic honours (Benod 2013: 158). He was so revered that, as Benod reports, followers were supposed to kneel down when he entered Agonshū's training centres (312). Disciples spoke reverently of him, attributed various spiritual benefits and protective powers to him, and gave thanks to him for such things. For example, in the aftermath of the terrible Tōhoku tsunami tragedy of March 2011, Agonshū made the spirits of those who had perished there and the revival of the damaged region a key focus of its memorial rituals, including its December 2011 *Meitokusai* festival and the 11 February 2012 Hoshi Matsuri. The latter was dedicated to praying for the revival of Japan after the tragedy and numerous *goma* sticks were incinerated to pray for the spirits of the deceased. In reporting these events Agonshū's Japanese language members' magazine carried a series of testimonies and accounts by disciples who had participated in the festivals, including several from the regions affected by the disaster (*Agon Magazine* 2012). They told of losing their homes and other tribulations, but of being helped by fellow members elsewhere – and of the emotional and spiritual support that the *kanchō geika* (i.e. Kiriyama) gave them as they strove to overcome their difficulties. They referred to the importance of taking part in the rituals to pray for the dead – and the importance of continuing their practice in Agonshū as a key element in their recovery. Running through the accounts are continued references to the grace of Kiriyama and thanks for his spiritual protection.

Thus, for example, a male devotee from Ishinomaki (one of the places badly hit during the tsunami) in Miyagi prefecture spoke of how his house had been swept away, although he – at home at the time – somehow survived. People from Agonshū quickly got in contact to help him and do rituals for his health and safety, while he expressed his thanks to the Buddha and the *kanchō geika* (Kiriyama) for their spiritual protection (*Agon Magazine* 2012: 68). A female member from Saitama spoke of a Kiriyama sermon after the tsunami in which he warned of other potential earthquakes that might hit Japan in the coming year or so. In order to protect members of her family she had then given an Agonshū altar to her sister (who at the time was about to undergo surgery). Although her sister's family had previously been hostile to Agonshū, after the sister's safe recovery from surgery, they realized they had been protected by Agonshū and changed their attitude; as such the woman concerned expressed her thanks to the *kanchō geika* and Buddha for their protection. Other accounts in the magazine express similar themes of thanks to Kiriyama for his protection even though a massive disaster had occurred; all the accounts in the magazine use the same mechanism of thanks, referring to *hotoke sama, kanchō geika* Buddha and the leader (Kiriyama) (*Agon Magazine* 2012: 64–83).

Given that such accounts, published in Agonshū's magazine, use a repeated format in which the same modes of address and thanks are uniform throughout, one could well suspect that a formulaic mode of narration is at work here. This is something that has been discussed by various scholars who have examined narratives in new religions. Tsuneo Kawakami (2008: 272–340), for example, has drawn attention to the ways in which conversion stories have been constructed in a number of new movements, via group meetings, revised narratives and editorial input from the movements concerned. Shimazono (1993) has discussed how this process operates in Reiyūkai, Myōchikai and Risshō Kōseikai, through which followers initially articulate their conversion stories orally in small meetings. These then are developed into written accounts and a select few are then published (often with help from senior officials in the movement) in movement publications. Such accounts are thus mediated by the needs, processes and orientations of the movement concerned; Kawakami (2008: 301), for example, notes that accounts by members of Kōfuku no Kagaku almost invariably refer to Ōkawa Ryūhō's writings and quote extensively from them. Judging by its production of members' accounts as outlined above, we consider that Agonshū is operating in similar manner in presenting followers' stories and narratives in ways that emphasize their founder and leader.

This is not to say that the stories of those whose experiences and views are being published in Agonshū magazines are either being falsified or invented; in discussions with Agonshū members we have heard enough accounts of gratitude and devotion to Kiriyama to be aware of the regard in which he has been held by them. Agonshū as a movement has been formed around Kiriyama, so it is unsurprising that those who join the movement tend to have strong feelings of devotion towards him. Those feelings feed into the mediatizing processes operative in Agonshū, as in other new movements, and are then expressed via its publications in ways that can impact on and inspire other followers and heighten their devotion. As Kawakami (2008) has also noted, the ways in which such stories and experiences are narrated can in their turn shape the way that subsequent members' accounts are produced.

In such ways, members contribute to the continuing process of the construction and reinforcement of the founder's charismatic presence and authority. One of the striking points in Agonshū devotees' accounts of the aftermath of the tsunami is that even those who had been terribly affected by the disaster – such as the man whose house had been destroyed – gave thanks to Kiriyama for his protection (perhaps from having suffered the fate of the many thousands who died in the tragedy) while others, shaken by the events, thanked him for his spiritual protection because subsequent earthquakes had not occurred. Besides showing how members and their stories – mediated through the frameworks of the movement's publicity mechanisms and its magazines – are thus an intrinsic and relational element in the framing of Kiriyama's charisma and authority, they also indicate how, even in his lifetime, the dynamic towards elevating him above the human realm was in operation, with Kiriyama and the Buddha being thanked for their spiritual protection and grace in the same sentence. In this we can see further the seeds of his subsequent post-death spiritual elevation.

A Buddhist leader and a scientist

As we have already discussed, the claim to have rediscovered original Buddhism and adapted it to a modern context was a central element in the construction of Kiriyama's charismatic leadership. However, there is also another important aspect that, according to Kiriyama, marks him out from previous leaders and shapes his image as someone fitting the developments of charismatic founders in the late twentieth century. Feuchtwang (2008: 94) argues that modern charisma is also based on a leadership capable of bringing change via a repertoire that mixes secular, scientific and transcendental vision. In other words, modern charisma does not only refer to previous religious traditions and practices, but also claims the authority of science. We noted, in Chapter 1, that many new movements of the late twentieth century sought to portray themselves as being 'scientific' in nature. Agonshū certainly used this notion as part of its exaltation of Kiriyama and in order to support its teachings. As we will discuss in Chapter 3, purportedly rational explanations of teaching based on cause-effect logic have been used by Agonshū to support the validity of its doctrines and practices. Similarly, in emphasizing Kiriyama's charismatic standing, Agonshū narratives portray him as someone who is not just a Buddhist leader but a scientist as well. This is shown in one of Agonshū's main texts, *Kimi wa dare no umarekawari ka* (Kiriyama 1993) and its English version produced in 2000, *You Have Been Here Before: Reincarnation* (Kiriyama 2000a).[31]

In this book Kiriyama discusses his theories regarding reincarnation and possession and locates them within what is portrayed as a scientific framework. He provides several examples of people who visited him for help because of misfortunes, unhappiness and family problems (such as having a violent son/daughter). According to Kiriyama's account, his abilities allow him to understand the causes of his clients' unhappiness. After having identified the 'unhappy spirit(s)' that had been incarnated, he would perform pacifying rituals for them and give them a posthumous Buddhist name. His abilities, Kiriyama (2000a: 26) states, are based on the knowledge of special esoteric principles and techniques from the Tibetan tradition that he mastered, as a result of which he obtained the title of lama from a monastery of the Nyingma Buddhist sect.[32]

While quoting several Buddhist texts to support his theories, he also discusses scientific ideas in ways that associate science with Agonshū thought, but that also portray it as incomplete. For example, Kiriyama (2000a: 136) criticizes scientists who think that mind is solely a function of the brain, and goes on to deem this theory as unsatisfactory:

> It didn't matter to me whether the brain is composed of physical matter or of a non-matter. It was irrelevant to me whether the mind is a component of the brain or the other way round. Either way, there is *something* that transmigrates. I wanted to know more where this *something* is located. It exists, so it has to be located somewhere. I only wanted to pin down where that somewhere is. And that is why I began, as a lay person, to study neurophysiology. (151)

Kiriyama continues by arguing that his scientific interests helped him in his Buddhist training, and declares that he is the first Buddhist leader (particularly in the esoteric tradition) to have conducted studies in neuroanatomy. This scientific training allowed him to overcome the limitations he found in Shingon Buddhist practice, as well as enabling him to make his practice perfect: '[N]ow I saw that in order to master the method of attaining Buddhahood one had to develop powers that went beyond the brain's ordinary functions. These are powers that come from the awakening and perfecting of one's spirituality' (153–4). Kiriyama claims that his discovery about the brain are the results of his spiritual practice, combining Indian Kundalini yoga and Tibetan Vajrāyana Buddhism, and that 'neurophysiology hasn't come this far yet' (162). In doing this Kiriyama places himself beyond both Buddhism and science, while asserting that he had reached a deeper understanding of both of them. This self-proclaimed scientific ability and knowledge is another strand in the make-up of his authority and contributes to his self-representation as a figure of multiple talents – a theme we return to later in this chapter. It also represents a recurrent pattern in which Kiriyama claims to use an awareness developed from one set of activities and practices to enhance his understanding of another sphere, and to transcend the limitations of such spheres. We saw this in his claims to have discovered the true meanings of the Āgamas because of his esoteric training (i.e. combining esoteric practice with textual studies of early Buddhism) and to thereby bring together different strands of Buddhism into a transcendent whole that supersedes the individual parts of the tradition. In claiming that his spiritual practices in Buddhism have enabled him to develop deeper insights into scientific understandings of the mind and to overcome the current limitations of science, Kiriyama is again presenting himself as a transcendent figure opening up new paths for humanity.

The charismatic performer and entrepreneur

We will say more about the latter period of his life in Chapters 4 and 5 where we deal with how Agonshū dealt with his physical ageing and death. Here we turn to an element in the nature of Kiriyama's leadership that has been touched on earlier and that also features in Agonshū's narrative, namely, his organizational and entrepreneurial activities. These will also be encountered again in later chapters, as they play a role in Agonshū's expansion in the 1980s and in its subsequent operations. They include the rituals he developed, including ritual practices traditionally confined to the ordained elite of established religious traditions that he opened up to ordinary members, the striking mass ritual of the Hoshi Matsuri that drew audiences of half a million or more people in the late 1980s, and the adoption of various means of publicity, including mass publications, public relations companies and the use of the latest cutting-edge technologies of the era to bring Agonshū to wider attention.

Kiriyama's performative abilities are an innate part of his charismatic status and authority, and are equally a manifestation of his entrepreneurship, just as they were with Deguchi Ōnisaburō and his appearances in films and ritual activities (Stalker 2008: 108–41). We have, for example, noted how Kiriyama has been the focus of numerous Agonshū videos that depict him in various guises such as 'receiving' the communication from the Buddha at Sahet Mahet, and presiding over Agonshū rituals. In the various events and rituals Agonshū has developed under his guidance – and which, like the Hoshi Matsuri, have served as major publicity and recruitment vehicles and sources of income for the movement (Reader 1988: 241) – Kiriyama's presence was, until his demise, central. In descriptions of the Hoshi Matsuri and the monthly fire ritual held at Agonshū centres, observers have commented on the authoritative way in which Kiriyama presided over proceedings, combining dramatic ritual performances with warm and engaging sermons, and displaying magisterial command of his devotees as he marched around the precincts of the Hoshi Matsuri ritual fire arena (Reader 1988, 1991, 1994). Devotees, by following his lead and showing reverence for their leader as he engages in such displays, themselves engage with and contribute to the construction of him as a charismatic performer.[33]

In later periods, as he aged and was no longer able to walk for any period or to deliver sermons, he continued to be a central focus of attention and devotion in Agonshū ritual performances. We will look further at these issues in Chapter 3, as well as examining, in Chapters 4 and 5, how he continued to be portrayed and remain key in rituals in later life. Here the point to note is that his authority and status as a charismatic leader were reinforced through his performances and sermons at Agonshū's ritual and festive events, which to a great degree could be seen as events showcasing his charisma and projecting it as a prime selling point of Agonshū (Figure 2.2).

Expansion and the necessity of publicity and finance

Earlier we noted that new movements cannot draw on inherited resources and memberships to support them and that building a movement from the ground up involves not just attracting followers but the development of buildings, organizations and a viable financial structure to enable a movement to operate. It also needs people to run various aspects of its operations. Certainly many (perhaps all) new religions can call on the voluntary service of devotees who might give some of their free time to helping at centres, and such voluntary activity, as we stated in Chapter 1, is commonly seen as a form of religious practice and duty. Visitors to Agonshū centres are likely to be greeted by volunteers keen to talk to them about Agonshū activities, while Agonshū is able to put on mass events such as the Hoshi Matsuri because large numbers of

Figure 2.2 Kiriyama Seiyū performing at the Hoshi Matsuri. Photo by Ian Reader. From the Photo Archives of the Nanzan Institute for Religion and Culture, Nagoya, Japan.

members give their time to help organize the crowds, direct traffic, assist at the ritual events and look after the stalls at the site. Agonshū magazines encourage such practices by carrying reports by members who have served in such ways and who uniformly present positive accounts of their experiences while giving thanks to Kiriyama for caring for them and giving them the opportunity to do such things (*Agon Magazine* 2012: 35–83). Such reports in themselves serve as internal Agonshū mechanisms heightening the founder's charisma; not only do members celebrate their participation in rituals but they view it as the result of the benevolence of their founder, who thus is even more exalted because of this generosity.

Yet it takes more than voluntary service to ensure a movement can operate at nationwide levels in the scope that Agonshū does – and here the dynamic leadership of Kiriyama has been central. Besides energizing followers who are keen to offer their services, he has built (or, at least, he has overseen the building of) an organizational structure, a publicity machine aimed at bringing his teachings and news about Agonshū to as wide an audience as possible, and the development of Agonshū sites and centres in various parts of Japan, from its Tokyo temple and centre to its complex at Yamashina, just outside Kyoto, where its main temple is located. The site at Yamashina that was acquired in the 1970s clearly required significant outlays of money. It has been the site of the Hoshi Matsuri since 1976. It was developed further over the years, with a temple (the 'new Sahet Mahet' for the modern age) being built there and opened in 1988. Numerous other buildings, including shrines dedicated to Shinto deities, statues (including a Lion of Jerusalem statue to commemorate the links Agonshū developed with Israel and the rituals it has conducted there), a Bhutanese Buddhist

Service hall devoted to Buddhist art and intended also to celebrate Agonshū's close links with Bhutanese Buddhist orders, have been added to the complex. Such things clearly require funding and in the following sections we outline a few of these areas to illustrate the dimensions of entrepreneurship in Agonshū – something that emanates initially from Kiriyama himself.

Publicity, development and commerce

One of the most significant publicity activities the movement has engaged in has been Kiriyama's establishment, in 1971, of a commercial publishing firm, Hirakawa Shuppan, to act as the main gateway for his writings and Agonshū publications. Like the leaders of many other new movements in Japan, Kiriyama has published prodigiously over the years and the Hirakawa Shuppan website (as of May 2017) lists sixty-six books by Kiriyama that it publishes.[34] However, it is not simply a vehicle for Kiriyama, for it is a commercial venture tapping into a wider market of interest in esoteric and religious matters. As such it publishes a variety of books not related to Agonshū but covering topics that have some association with the likely interests of its members, such as works about esotericism, prophecy, superhuman powers, yoga and Tibetan Buddhism. It also produces Japanese translations of books about these subjects initially written in other languages. By using Hirakawa Shuppan, ostensibly a commercial publisher, as his vehicle of proselytization, Kiriyama and Agonshū have been able to place their books in major bookshops – and nowadays also online stores such as Amazon – and thereby gain access to wider markets.

Kiriyama was adept at increasing Agonshū's profile and visibility through a variety of means including hiring a public relations agency – during the 1980s this was Dentsū, one of the largest in Japan – to organize and promote the movement nationally. Agonshū became known in Japan during the 1980s for its use of mass media technologies, an area where it claimed to be ahead of the field. It was the first in Japan to use satellite broadcasting, through which its rituals were simultaneously broadcast to Agonshū centres throughout the country. It even developed a monthly ritual that fitted into the thirty-minute satellite broadcasting time that a broadcasting company (at the time seeking to develop a market in the new technology) allocated to the organization, allowing members to participate in rituals with the leader at a distance (Baffelli 2016: 68–87). Its advertising spreads in newspapers such as the *Japan Times* drew attention to this use of technology to portray Agonshū as a religion that, while it emphasized Buddhism and morality, was in tune with modern times and with the flow of modern life. Kiriyama, as founder and leader, was the driving force in such matters, and such activities enhanced his reputation – underlined by Agonshū claims that the group was the 'the religion of the new media age' and the Japanese response to American televangelists[35] – of leading the way and shaping the contours of the religious field of 1980s Japan.

Via Agonshū Kiriyama has established a variety of other enterprises, such as the production and sale of special health foods and the use of traditional Chinese medicines (*kanpōyaku*). Such items and services can be acquired through Agonshū centres and are also available at its public events such as the Hoshi Matsuri, where numerous stalls sell Agonshū health foods (advertised as *mikkyō shoku* or 'esoteric food') and offer a variety of spiritual services from traditional medicines to divination. While such services and goods are meant to publicize and promote Agonshū's messages and to improve the lives and health of those who acquire them, they are also, of course, a source of income for the movement and a sign of its engagement in business activities.

This attention to health and organic food, combined with Kiriyama's interest in religious and spiritual trends in the United States, including televangelists such as Billy Graham and psychics such as Edgar Cayce, resulted, according to Christal Whelan (2007: 404), in the creation of a 'total care system' in the movement. Visitors to Agonshū centres and to the Hoshi Matsuri will see on display a variety of goods commonly associated with religious institutions – amulets (*omamori*) and other such items – that can be purchased for a fee and that are seen (as they are in the wider Japanese religious context) as ways of seeking and expressing concerns for practical benefits. At the Hoshi Matsuri, the commercial dynamic is very clearly evident to visitors, with groups of Agonshū devotees walking around with trays of amulets that can be purchased, and – like street traders – calling out to visitors about the goods they are offering (Figure 2.3).

Such activities – along with the fees members pay for membership and to have various rituals performed (see also Chapter 3) – are nothing special to Agonshū as they are found widely at Buddhist temples, Shinto shrines and many other new religions as well. They are a reflection of the wider importance of economic activity in the support structures of religious movements and institutions. Yet, at the same time, the extent to which Agonshū has used such means and engaged in commercial activities, and combined them with others such as publicity and proselytization, clearly indicates an

Figure 2.3 Stall at Hoshi Matsuri selling *omamori* and other amulets. Photo by Ian Reader.

orientation and perhaps even at times a preoccupation with entrepreneurialism that has been fostered in Agonshū under Kiriyama's tutelage.

The movement not only encourages members to volunteer their services but to contribute membership fees and pay for ritual services that can cut their karma and bring happiness. These are messages and attitudes that Kiriyama assiduously articulated and reiterated in life, as can be seen by his reply to a concerned member given in a Question and Answer session reported in the Agonshū members' magazine in 2012. The member concerned was unsure whether she could continue to afford the monthly fees of 2,000 yen and mentioned how other members had had similar problems and that some had left the movement because of the financial strains they faced. In his reply Kiriyama outlined the value of sacrifice in the search for salvation and happiness, noted his disciples were directly connected to Shakyamuni the Buddha through him, reminded the disciple that he, Kiriyama, had made sacrifices in his pursuit of the truth, and suggested that surely anyone wishing to receive the true teachings and gain salvation would find ways to get the wherewithal to do so (*Agon Magazine* 2012: 13–18).

His answer demonstrated his skilful manner in engaging with followers while promoting his movement and expressing a commercial motive at the same time. While to outsiders this could appear to be sales pitch almost of a snake-oil salesman variety, it also has its rationale from within the context of Agonshū. Like all religions, Agonshū is in effect selling goods of an intangible variety, such as salvation and personal ease, while Kiriyama is engaging in a rhetoric in which he emphasizes the value of those goods – goods that are not simply intangible but beyond material calculation. By emphasizing that members are directly linked to Buddha through him, reminding them of his mission (and implicitly making them feel they would be letting him down if they left) and linking their situation and his own (he chose to make sacrifices for the truth) he not only emphasizes the value of what Agonshū offers members, but also creates a sense of continuing obligation for them. And the 'product' he is offering, salvation, is surely worth such a minimal amount of money. Within his response there were also subtle further sales pitches, for he also encouraged members who still had doubts to read more of his books (something that might, of course, require purchasing them). He added that, while there might be members who felt they could not afford the fees, they should reflect that, for the sake of a small amount they might be sacrificing their entire future and that of their ancestors. His reply, in other words, was an example of the economic aspects of religious belonging, of charismatic entrepreneurialism in action and a reminder that what he offered was something that was beyond the boundaries of such a trivial thing as money.

The multitalented founder and player on the international stage

Another area where Kiriyama has displayed an entrepreneurial drive, and in which he has clearly directed Agonshū so as to heighten his stature, is in developing an international profile that has strengthened his image in the eyes of his followers. We have earlier mentioned his meetings with the Pope and the Dalai Lama, and Agonshū has used these in multiple ways to promote the standing of its leader and founder, with photographs of these meetings being prominently displayed in its publications and centres. Kiriyama has also gained other forms of legitimacy and status enhancement in the eyes of his followers by receiving various honours and accolades from foreign institutions, notably academic ones, including honorary degrees, academic positions and invitations from universities in countries such as Mongolia, China and the United Kingdom.

Such academic honours and invitations, often related to endowments and donations that Agonshū has made to academic institutions, add to his list of accomplishments and also complement (in the eyes of the movement) his scientific prowess while serving to further enhance Kiriyama's status as a multitalented figure whose awareness of Buddhism is backed not just by spiritual insights but by academic as well as scientific knowledge. Some of the books he has published relating to Buddhism demonstrate this by indicating, on their covers, that he is writing them in his capacity as an academic based on the honorary positions and invitations he has received. Thus, for example, Agonshū published an English translation of Kiriyama's book comparing Greek and Buddhist wisdom 'in conjunction with the author's invited visit on 8 June 2000 to the School of Oriental and African Studies, University of London',[36] thereby drawing on the prestige of an invitation to a leading academic institution to which Agonshū had previously given large sums, to validate the book itself. His book portraying Agon Buddhism as 'social science' (Kiriyama 1997) is based, according to the Agonshū website, on a lecture that he was invited to deliver at Sun-Yat Sen University (Chinese: Zhōngshān Dàxué) in China, in his capacity as emeritus professor (*meiyō kyōju*) there, a position that may have some connection to Agonshū's activities in providing funds for academic institutions. Such honours and recognition by famed academic institutions affirm, for Agonshū members (who of course are the financial source of the resources that are utilized in such contexts), Kiriyama's eminence as a Buddhist scholar and teacher. They thereby reinforce his claims to have understood Buddhist sutras and discerned the essence of Buddhism in the Āgamas. For devotees it is a further sign that their founder is not just a localized Japanese teacher but a player on the world stage, not simply an inspiring leader but a multidimensionally talented figure recognized by world religious leaders and academic institutions alike. His status in turn reflects well on their self-perception as followers of this august spiritual leader.

Such projections of the leader as a multitalented person are not special to Agonshū but represent a trait found among many new movements in Japan, one that serves to enhance the charismatic status of founders and leaders and shows that they can combine a variety of skills of the sort that Goosaert (2008: 26) has identified as important elements in the make-up of charismatic leaders. Many of Kiriyama's contemporaries have been portrayed (and have portrayed themselves) in similar ways. As Kawakami Tsuneo (2008) has noted, Fukami Tōshū, the founder of World Mate, a religious movement that developed in the latter decades of the past century in Japan, is portrayed within that movement as a multiskilled individual with artistic achievements such as being an opera singer, actor and scholar. Indeed, Fukami is not averse to telling people about his apparently wide-ranging array of talents, as one of the authors of this book learned when he was invited to a conference at Columbia University in the United States in 2002.[37] Fukami gave a talk there during which he informed the audience of his widespread talents in the arts and academia, and of his skills as an opera singer and Noh actor (and many other qualities and artistic skills besides). He also informed his listeners that he was a magnificent philanthropist and mentioned various academic achievements and invitations that he portrayed as recognition by international universities of his prowess in such fields.

Founders such as Ōkawa Ryūhō are likewise portrayed in their movements in similar terms, as figures blessed not just with spiritual powers and insights but a multiplicity of other skills and artistic abilities. Kōfuku no Kagaku's English-language web page, for instance, boasts of his numerous skills and achievements, from producing films to authoring vast numbers of books and teachings that 'provide concrete proposals for resolving worldwide political and economic situations'. At the same time he has developed educational institutions, founded a political party and established charitable foundations through which to aid those who are oppressed, poor and suffering racial and other forms of discrimination. Indeed, as the website states, he is not just a religious leader but the 'Founder and CEO of the Happy Science Group' – a label clearly designed to emphasize his entrepreneurial skills and to show how the movement is highly modern and able to fit in with contemporary business culture. His abilities do not end there for he is also, as the website indicates, modest and 'never boasted about his God-given intelligence'.[38]

Sōka Gakkai's Honorary President (and de facto leader since 1960) Ikeda Daisaku is, according to that movement, a skilled photographer while, as Clark Chilson (2014: 67) has indicated, Sōka Gakkai has enhanced his status by attributing to him the founding of research institutes, an Art Museum, concert associations and universities, and portraying him as a writer, poet, novelist and recipient of numerous honorary degrees and awards from around the world. Shinnyoen emphasizes the skills of its founder, Itō Shinjō, as a sculptor of Buddhist images. In previous eras, as Nancy Stalker (2008) has demonstrated, Deguchi Ōnisaburō's status in Oomoto was built not just around his spiritual insights but his artistic activities in areas such as pottery and poetry. In such terms, charismatic status is enhanced in the eyes of followers through an emphasis on the founder/leader's accomplishments across a variety of fields, and is not confined just to solving disciples' problems, offering paths to salvation or providing inspirational teachings. It also appears, in our view, that talking about a multiplicity of talents in this way has become almost de rigueur for modern charismatic founders in Japan, and that the emphasis on acquiring recognition (whether through being seen with the Pope or the Dalai Lama or getting awards from foreign universities) may also be spurred by the sight of other founders and leaders who have done such things.

The life story as charismatic construction and core teaching

Charisma and charismatic leadership thus are also linked to and are in part a product of image creation by founders and their movements. The Kiriyama story is not so much a work of fiction as an embellished account of his life constructed by the leader and his movement in ways that create meanings for his followers while augmenting his charismatic standing. The suicide and salvation story, his dream initiation from Juntei Kannon, the message from Shakyamuni at Sahet Mahet and so on are all grounded in Kiriyama's words rather than in any verifiable or documented empirical evidence. Nonetheless they together constitute, alongside his other activities and achievements (for instance, setting up a movement and expanding it rapidly, developing a set of teachings and rituals and so on), a meaningful framework for the movement that, by enhancing his standing, reflects well on his followers. Members who follow Agonshū contribute to the construction of this charismatic profile and status through their engagement with this narrative and through their enthusiastic reaffirmations of it, evident, for example, in the thanks they give, in the Agonshū magazine accounts, to Kiriyama. The founder and his life story as articulated in Agonshū thus serve as a core teaching, a form of morality play that sets out the movement's world view while providing evidence for followers of the value and practicality of Kiriyama's teaching and reinforcing their self-worth as his followers. It is a practicality grounded also in the rituals, worship and related practices of Agonshū, which operate together as an entity in which teaching and practice are conjoined. It is to such matters that we turn next in Chapter 3.

3

Teaching as Practice: Ritual, Benefits and the Costs of Devotion

Introduction: the complementarity of teaching and practice

In this chapter we examine Agonshū's teachings and practices, along with the expectations the movement has of its followers. These themes cannot be separated. Agonshū's basic teachings centre on karma and the necessary of 'cutting' or eradicating it, and its practices are meant to do just that. From the actions and rituals carried out by individuals in their homes and at the movement's centres, to its public services and the Hoshi Matsuri, Agonshū's practices are an articulation in ritual form of those teachings and a means of enacting them. They are also innately linked to Kiriyama's life. As the previous chapter showed, the issue of karma and how it affects individual lives was very central to Kiriyama's own life course and his understanding of why he faced so many problems before embarking on a religious path – and why, according to Agonshū, he was able to become a transcendent religious leader through cutting his karma.

Teaching and practice in Agonshū are highly founder-centric, devised by Kiriyama, linked to important issues in his life and experiences, and grounded in the ritual processes he knew and developed. He was the key focus and leader of Agonshū rituals and practices until late in his life. When he became too frail to conduct the rituals himself he continued to serve as a symbolically powerful ritual presence – something that has continued after his death. The practices he instigated in Agonshū – notably the *goma* fire ritual – have, especially since his death, been portrayed as particular ritual forms developed by him alone. They have also been highly visible in nature; Agonshū has sought to attract outsiders through its use of spectacular ritual performances, notably the Hoshi Matsuri. It is a religion that seeks to attract attention and to be 'seen' so as to attract more members, and its spectacular public rituals are viewed in the movement as recruiting mechanisms[1] that propagate its teachings and enable non-members to take part in its events. Members have important roles in such contexts, for Agonshū makes significant demands on them. They are expected to perform practices in order to cut their karma, to take part in helping the movement operate successfully, to publicize the movement via its ritual and festival events and make these a success and to assist the movement financially. Such activities contribute to the nature of Agonshū as a spectacular religion while enacting its teachings in the lives of its followers.

Before turning more directly to Agonshū, we will return to the comments we made in Chapter 1 about how media – and even some academic – depictions have portrayed new religions as lacking in serious doctrine and depth. These depictions attribute their success to a lack of doctrinal sophistication, suggesting that it has occurred because they offer simplistic and easy to understand promises focused on this-worldly benefits and worldly advancement. This perspective not only implies that new religions are lightweight and superficial but implicitly dismisses their followers as gullible and concerned merely with material rewards. If we can distil these negative portrayals down to three basic points, they are that new religions focus primarily on promises of worldly benefits and thereby lack any coherent moral framework, they have little in the way of serious doctrines or a canon and followers, seduced by the hopes of material rewards, lack any real doctrinal awareness, and rely wholly on their leaders for such things.

None of these assumptions carries much weight in our view. Any criticism that new religions focus on 'this-worldly benefits' (*genze riyaku*) is particularly disingenuous because all this does is recognize that they are therefore highly normative in Japanese religious contexts, rather than being somehow deviant or superficial. This-worldly benefits are legitimated in Buddhist texts, manifest themes of morality, express the underlying belief that Shinto deities and Buddhist figures of worship are there and ready to aid humans in this world and that humans should benefit from the graces of the spiritual realm. All of these concepts are evident in the ways Buddhism and Shinto operate in Japan, while *genze riyaku* is a core theme in the dynamics of Japanese religious culture both historically and in the present day (Reader and Tanabe 1998). New religions have certainly developed themes of this-worldly benefits as part of their appeal, but in so doing they are following a pattern established by the older traditions rather than diverging from them. They have often, indeed, done it better, and this has been a factor in their ability to attract followers away from the older traditions, and in the hostility that they have faced as a result – a point evident in the attacks on earlier new religions in the nineteenth century mentioned in Chapter 1.

Moreover, a religion such as Agonshū, which views receiving benefits (material, spiritual and emotional) in this life to be inextricably linked to dealing with spiritual problems, pacifying the spirits of the dead and 'cutting one's karma', is not outlining a simplistically beguiling promise of 'this-worldly benefits'. It is setting out a worldview with a moral foundation that shows followers a way of dealing with the world around them and offers them the hope of attaining happiness and a sense of belonging. In doing these things it draws on some of the basic patterns of Japanese religious thought while expressing a doctrinal framework that is allied to practices designed to put those teachings into action.

The importance of teachings and texts

As we commented in Chapter 1, an element in the appeal of new movements in general has been their ability to produce a variety of materials that enable potential and existing followers to find out for themselves what the movement is saying. Agonshū fits into this context well and encourages followers to engage with its teachings and develop an understanding of them. Kiriyama's writings form a central element in this, along with a variety of other materials produced by the movement. These include various magazines as well as videos – and later, as the technology has moved on, CDs and DVDs – for members that set out core teachings in visual form accompanied by soundtracks narrating Kiriyama's words. Such videos and DVDs can also be watched by interested parties at Agonshū centres – something that both authors have done at various times during their research (Reader 1991; Baffelli 2016). Often such materials reproduce the content of Kiriyama's books and reiterate visually the messages within them. Thus, for example, Agonshū produced a video to set out in visual form the themes of Kiriyama's 1981 book *1999 nen karuma to reishō kara no gedatsu*, including the film of Kiriyama's 'encounter' with and reception of a message from Shakyamuni at Sahet Mahet in India that forms such an important position in Agonshū's history. The production of such materials has not stopped with Kiriyama's death for subsequently new texts have developed; these are the *kaiso reiyu* spiritual messages said to be relayed by Kiriyama's spirit. Furthermore Agonshū representatives have started offering interpretations of Kiriyama's teaching and developing new strands to it, largely connected with his post-death status – issues we discuss at length in Chapter 5.

For those who want to know more about Agonshū's teachings, there are plentiful opportunities to do so via the large number of publications and aural and visual materials Agonshū produces. Kiriyama encouraged followers to read such publications and listen to recordings of his sermons to deepen their understandings and to resolve any questions they had. In a Question and Answer session reported in Agonshū's membership magazine in 2012, for example, a member expressed doubts about the efficacy of her practice and asked whether it was worth continuing. Kiriyama's reply not only stressed the importance of continuing the practice but also emphasized that anyone with doubts could visit Agonshū centres and have things explained to them there, and they could also listen again to his dharma talks (*hōwa*) and read his books (*Agon Magazine* 2012, 3–4: 16). Agonshū offers counselling services to followers not just so that they can seek advice on personal matters but also so that they can get clarifications about its teaching. As Kiriyama also indicated, those with queries and doubts can contact the head Agonshū office and get detailed replies to their concerns (*Agon Magazine* 2012, 3–4: 16). Knowing that one can or should be aware of the teachings, and that avenues for understanding it are widely available, thus is an important part of being a member.

Teachings, practices, changes and continuities

Agonshū's teachings and practices work in tandem to provide followers with an understanding of the right way to live in this world, and to give them a sense of hope and a feeling that they can manage their problems and attain something better for themselves in this realm and beyond. Together they express themes of moral behaviour, self-development and advancement, along with a positive unified world view through which members can understand their place, as Japanese people, in the wider world and their sense of identity as such. To that extent, we suggest that while Agonshū portrays itself as a Buddhist movement with universal aims and messages, it is at core predominantly concerned with issues pertinent to 'Japanese people' – a theme that we see becoming stronger as the movement has aged (see below, especially Chapter 4).

While teachings and practices operate together as a coherent whole rather than as separate spheres in Agonshū, this does not mean that they have remained constant throughout the movement's short history. Changes and turns of direction are neither uncommon nor surprising in newly formed movements, where an inspirational founder can frequently produce new revelations, while the contextual circumstances in which movements operate can necessitate or encourage shifts in practice and teaching. Part of the appeal of the new will always be in the excitement and sense of dynamism that it can bring – and such dynamism often means and produces changes, new ideas and new practices. Kōfuku no Kagaku provides a good recent example here. It started in the mid-1980s as a small study group focusing on discussion on happiness and truth but then grew comparatively quickly into a larger organization in the early 1990s and became more overtly oriented towards Buddhism as it did so. Texts from the early period were reprinted in 1994, replacing the word *kami* (deity/god) with *butsu* (Buddha) and *shinri* (god's truth) with *buppō shinri* (the truth of Buddha's teachings) (Baffelli 2016: 94). Over the years Kōfuku no Kagaku has included new teachings and practices, but the core teachings, based on the four 'Principles of Happiness' (*Kōfuku no genri*), that is, love (*ai*), wisdom (*chi*), self-reflection (*hansei*) and development (*hatten*), have remained constant, as has the central concept of the 'creation of Utopia' (*yūtopia kensetsu*). These core teachings have allowed the group to continue adding and experimenting with new practices, while at the same time expanding their range of influence into secular domains such as politics (the group established a political party in 2009) and education (Kōfuku no Kagaku opened a boarding school in 2010 and an unaccredited university in 2015) (Baffelli 2017).

Agonshū likewise has undergone many developments, shifts of focus, changes and additions to its teachings and practices during its lifetime. We saw this in Chapter 2, when various revelations received by Kiriyama led to new developments in the movements he headed, from the focus on Juntei Kannon in the Kannon Jikeikai to the formation of Agonshū, and the emphasis on original Buddhism that emerged after the revelation he claimed to have received from Shakyamuni in India. The acquisition of a Buddha relic from Sri Lanka in 1986 also brought changes, as the *shinsei busshari* became Agonshū's main focus of worship. Kiriyama's death has led to more changes, which will be discussed in Chapter 5. Agonshū thus epitomizes the tendency of new movements to amend, change and develop their orientations especially during their formative periods in the first-generation of leadership, not just in terms of teachings and focuses of worship but in practices. As Agonshū grew, for example, it developed more rituals and events through which the founder could be seen by audiences across Japan and beyond, and as it grew it began to perform rituals overseas that became central to its identity.

Such changes do not mean that Agonshū is merely transient and with no fixed grounding. At its core from its earliest days it has had a stable core of teachings that provide the movement with a firm grounding upon which to build and add new ideas, practices and rituals. Early studies of Agonshū (e.g. Reader 1988; Numata 1988) identified the centrality of teachings about ancestors and the spirits of the dead, which were seen as the source of benevolence if properly cared for and of unhappiness, misfortunes and dangers if neglected. The importance of rituals to pacify and liberate such spirits was central to Agonshū, manifest in one of the pyres at the Hoshi Matsuri, while various practices to be conducted both at home and in Agonshū centres were needed to achieve the core doctrinal goal of cutting one's karma in order to be free of past impediments and achieve happiness and liberation. Liberation (*gedatsu*) and cutting one's karma and thereby achieving Buddhahood (*jōbutsu*) were intricately linked. So were beliefs in the ability to acquire special powers to make one's life better in the here and now and in the thereafter, both through cutting karma and pacifying and transforming the spirits of the dead into benevolent entities, and through acquiring merit by performing ritual practices associated with the acquisition of benefits. The idea that membership of Agonshū was not just about individual issues but, through them, translated into a movement, led by Kiriyama, with a mission to save the world, along with an emphasis on affirming the significance of being a Japanese movement asserting notions of Japanese identity, was also embedded in the movement from the early days. Such themes evident in early Agonshū have remained central until the present day, as shown by Alexandre Benod's (2013) study and by the interviews and studies of recent Agonshū materials we have done in the past few years.

They are manifest also in the various publications and media outputs that Agonshū has produced. For example, a short booklet by Kiriyama titled *Hito wa donna innen o motsu ka* (an English translation of the would be 'What sort of karma do people have?' or more colloquially, 'What's your karma?') that sets out his core views on karma and its manifestations, was initially published in 1965 (in the era of the Kannon Jikeikai) but has remained in circulation ever since; it has been reprinted numerous times (the most recent we have is from 2013) and remains a core Agonshū text. Similarly, Kiriyama instituted a series of five chants at the end of his sermons and at ritual events to emphasize the message of positivity and optimism that Agonshū sought to instil in followers. These five phrases are as follows: *Sā yaruzō! kanarazu seikō suru! watakushi wa totemo un ga ii no da! kanarazu umaku iku! zettai ni katsu!* and basically translate as 'Let's do it! I will certainly succeed! I am blessed with very good luck! I will certainly do well! I will definitely win!'[2] Kiriyama got followers to chant these five phrases at the end of Agonshū's first *tsuitachi engi hōshō goma* (first of the month fire ritual) in April 1987 and they have been key chants in the movement ever since. As reiterations and expressions of the message Kiriyama repeatedly emphasized in his writings and sermons, of how a positive attitude is key to overcoming problems and living a fruitful life, the five phrases have, in a real sense, become a canonical text and practice for Agonshū members. They were still chanted, for example, after each speech given by Kiriyama at the end of monthly or annual ceremonies, such as the Agonshū's *Hatsu goma* (first fire ritual of the year ceremony) on 3 January 2014, an occasion one of us attended. This practice has continued since his death, with members being exhorted by Agonshū priests to end ritual events with the chants just as Kiriyama would have done (see also Chapter 5). This is particularly interesting because it demonstrates how a form of language, intended to enhance the interaction between the leaders and members, when the membership was smaller and direct interactions with Kiriyama was more possible, gradually became ritualized as part of its canon. Agonshū has also published a twelve-volume set of Kiriyama's talks under the series title '*Sā, yaruzō kanarazu katsu*' that focuses on how to realize their aspirations. Yet core ritual chants can also be amended or expanded; little more than a year after Kiriyama's death the movement had added a sixth phrase to this canonical core, one that affirmed the continuing association between disciples and the founder who had instigated the core five chants (see Chapter 5).

Retaining a core set of teachings and practices helps a group develop a coherent sense of identity and provides it with a sense of stability even at periods of rapid change and growth. It enables members who joined early on to feel at home and act as guides who, familiar with core teachings, are able to provide information and assistance to new recruits seeking to adapt to the movement.[3] They form a stable core around which to build as new events and revelations occur and as a movement expands. In Agonshū as this has happened new teachings and ritual practices have been added around that enduring core, and these then form part of its dynamic of novelty and innovation – as, for example, with Kiriyama's revelation at Sahet Mahet that led to the building of a new temple and world mission and the acquisition of the Buddha relic that brought in a new focus of veneration and a shift in practices.

Karma, the dead, liberation and happiness

Cutting karma, dealing with the spirits of the dead, living a happy life and achieving liberation in this life and in the next realms form the most central elements in Agonshū's teachings. Cutting karma and pacifying the unhappy spirits of the dead operate on personal, individual and global levels. The dead do not terminate their relationship with this world or with their kin at death, for their spirits continue to exist and retain a link to this world. They need to be cared for via appropriate rituals to ensure that they are pacified, attain peace and become full ancestor spirits and realized buddhas (*jōbutsu*) after death, so that they can bestow benevolence on this world and find peace and move on in the next realm. Failure to do this will leave the dead as unhappy spirits who remain tied to this world with the potential to cause misfortune both in personal and wider contexts. Individuals are subject to various unhappy karmic fates and misfortunes if the spirits of the dead of their ancestry (going back generations) are not properly cared for, while the accumulated unhappy spirits (notably, in contexts where large numbers have died prematurely and violently, as in war) can have negative effects on the wider society and world. In all Agonshū lists, in the aforementioned text *Hito wa donna innen o motsu ka*, twenty-two such types of negative karma, including, unsurprisingly, the karma of imprisonment (*keigoku no innen*) (Kiriyama 2013 [1965]). Unhappy spirits are believed to cause misfortunes, but also to reincarnate in people and determine the course of their lives.[4]

Although the terms 'karma' (*karuma*) and '*innen*' (commonly translated as karma) appear to be used somewhat interchangeably in Agonshū, Kiriyama has indicated that they manifest differences. *Innen*, in Agonshū, refers to 'the fundamental set of karmic causes and conditions that determines a person's fate . . . *Innen* are conditions that determine a person's fate, whereas karma is the generative force that drives these conditions, or *innen*' (Kiriyama 2000a: 92). As such, Agonshū's focus is on determining the *innen*, or conditions affecting and shaping the fate of individuals, and it identifies two sets of influences to this effect: horizontal (*yoko*) and vertical (*tate*). The horizontal forces relate to the karmic repercussions of our previous lives and impediments carried over from them, and the vertical to those inherited from our ancestors (Agonshū 1992: 2–3; Kiriyama 2000a: 99).

Karma and *innen* are negative forces. Unlike in older new religions (and in traditional Buddhism), in which karma could be either good, bringing merit or bad (Hardacre 1986: 31) movements such as Agonshū that attracted attention in the 1980s have viewed karma and *innen* very much as negative forces. Both Agonshū and Aum Shinrikyō, for instance, saw karma as something that had to be eradicated lest it produce further misfortunes. Aum was particularly pessimistic in this respect, viewing karma as a dark and foreboding force that permeated the phenomenal world, affected everyone who lived in it and required incessant ascetic practice to stem its negative pull. For Aum, karma, unless counteracted via ascetic practice, would inevitably lead the living, at death, to the Buddhist hells (Reader 2000a: 12–13). Agonshū was more optimistic in that it saw salvation and happiness in this world as viable and did not regard asceticism as a necessity simply to keep the forces of karma at bay. Nonetheless karma remained essentially negative, and was associated, in Agonshū, with the idea of *reishō* or spiritual hindrances. The term '*reishō*', according to Numata (1988: 63), became widespread among new movements and in popular culture in the 1980s, with Kiriyama playing an important role in arousing interest in the concept. In Agonshū *reishō* refers to hindrances from the spiritual world (such as unhappy spirits of the dead) that afflict the living and cause misfortunes. They are hindrances of the vertical variety, inherited by individuals from their familial ancestors.

Negative karma also impacts on what happens after death; Agonshū adheres to notions of transmigration (*rinne*) and says that at death spirits may fall into the (Buddhist) hells at death and certainly will have to confront their bad deeds in life. At the same time, according to Kiriyama, being a member of Agonshū serves to ameliorate these after-death fates. Compared to non-members, for whom the hellish realms after death are highly likely, Agonshū followers have the possibility of ascending to higher spiritual realms.[5] They are offered solutions to the problems of karma and spiritual hindrances. The first step in this process is to identify what type of karmic problem is being suffered and which spirits are causing it, and this can be done via various services provided by Agonshū. Through his ascetic practices and insight Kiriyama had acquired *reishi* (clairvoyant powers) that enabled him to 'see' such spirits and identify which ones were causing specific problems. Through doing this, he (and those to whom he transmitted such spiritual skills and teachings so that they could serve as counsellors) could also determine the ritual practices and memorial services needed to pacify these spirits and remove their negative influences.

Kiriyama claimed the ability to discern the causes of his followers' unhappiness (see Kiriyama 1993 and 2000a), for instance, identifying the unhappy spirits behind familial problems. After this he was able to perform pacifying rituals for them and gave the spirits a posthumous Buddhist name. According to Kiriyama he possesses two types of clairvoyance skills. One, which is called *gedatsu* clairvoyance, or clairvoyance of liberation, is used to identify and pacify ancestors' spirits who may be causing problems in someone's life. The second, called *meitoku* clairvoyance, is used to identify other unhappy spirits that may be the cause of unhappiness, but that are not immediately identifiable in the family line of the person affected (Kiriyama 2000a: 88).

Since karmic hindrances are the source of problems, cutting one's karma is the way to achieve *gedatsu*, liberation, and thus happiness and salvation. This is done through practices that also can help unhappy spirits attain salvation and peace (conflated in Agonshū under the term '*jōbutsu*' – becoming a Buddha, becoming a pacified/ realized ancestral spirit). The first step in such contexts – at least in individual terms – is to identify the spiritual causes of one's misfortunes, and to this end Agonshū has established counselling and divination services that are available at its centres. The counselling process offers people an avenue through which they can articulate what they feel is going wrong in their lives, and it can be used not just by followers but also by members of the general public. While neither of us are members of Agonshū, we have been invited to undergo counselling on various occasions over the years when visiting the movement's centres. On one visit to an Agonshū centre in November 2005, for example, an invitation was extended to meet one of the *sensei* ('teacher' – as people at the centre referred to those who were credited with the ability to offer counselling). To do this required filling in a form about the 'problems' being faced (the form included several topics, such as health, work relationships, family) after which a discussion with the teacher would be set up. Although we have not gone any further than asking about the process and although neither of us has been assessed to divine whatever misfortunes might be afflicting us, or to identify what (in the eyes of Agonshū) are the root causes thereof, the process itself indicates how the movement works. The visitor or member has to take the first step in identifying the issues, after which counsellors can start to divine and ascertain the spiritual causes and sources of such misfortune and then prescribe the appropriate ritual actions that should be taken.

While the focus is certainly on individuals, who are at the core of problem solution, this does not mean that such individuals are necessarily held to be blameworthy for their problems or made to repent. Unlike in some movements, where problems may be 'brought upon oneself' (Hardacre 1986: 22), in Agonshū misfortune need not be a result of one's own failures but because of unfortunate prior conditions, such as the presence of unhappy spirits, one is not aware of. Kiriyama's imprisonment provides a good example here. Subject to the karma of imprisonment due to unhappy spirits he had inherited but was unaware of, it would appear that in Agonshū terms he was not directly morally responsible for the crime, even as he had to take steps to deal with those unhappy spirits in order to move on. This stance in itself might heighten the attraction of Agonshū, since it offers explanations of problems that are within the remit of the individual without placing blame on those individuals.

While this appears to indicate that individuals are susceptible to malevolent spiritual forces it does not mean they are helpless. Far from it; Agonshū's emphasis on cutting karma is grounded in the view that karma can be eradicated and unhappy spirits liberated through practices and rituals. And here the individual holds the answer to his/her problems simply by going to an Agonshū centre, undergoing counselling and identification of the causes of their problems, and engaging in practices and rituals – some performed by the individuals, others by Agonshū specialists on their behalf – that are designed to eradicate the karma affecting them. Practices – including morally rightful behaviour and good deeds – eradicate karma by pacifying the spirits that are an impediment to happiness, and by creating spiritual merit that counteracts negative influences and helps the individual improve his/her own mind and being. The chants of Agonshū disciples that they will 'certainly succeed' (*kanarazu seikō suru*) and that emphasize a positive mindset are externalized manifestations of the need to cut karma and free oneself from the hindrances of the past.

Liberation – *gedatsu* – pacifies the unhappy spirits, removes their impediments and produces happiness in this world; liberation, in other words, is a this-worldly accomplishment even as it involves dealing with the spirits of the dead. Liberation is important not just for the living individual but also for the spirits, which are also suffering and can finally achieve liberation from the 'pain of death' and be reborn (Kiriyama 2000a: 238). Cutting karma leads to happiness and to success – the latter of which need not be materially based but can include leading a happy life, being optimistic and content, and having self-respect. Agonshū's view of this-worldly benefits and success, as such, appears to be much the same as is found in the general Japanese religious context, in which 'this-worldly' need not mean 'material' but can include less tangible issues such as peace of mind and the like (Reader and Tanabe 1998).

Living a happy life is central to Agonshū. This reflects themes found repeatedly among the movements that have developed in Japan since the nineteenth century. Tenrikyō (1984, 2002), for example, speaks of *yōkigurashi* (living a joyous life). Happiness is, unsurprisingly, also one of the central elements of Kōfuku no Kagaku (Happy Science), whose definition of happiness in this life includes realization of one's own potential, success and economic wealth. This-worldly positivism and the idea that one can attain salvation and happiness in the present life are not just recurrent characteristics of Japanese new religions but are, in the view of scholars such as Shimazono Susumu (e.g. 1992a), a defining marker of them. Agonshū certainly (as its canonical chants indicate) exudes a this-worldly positivism. At the same time, this is tinged with negative undertones and the recognition that the world is not ideal but an arena where negative forces that can cause misfortunes both individually and collectively exist. In recognizing such problems it exhibits the millennial themes that, as discussed in Chapters 1 and 2, have been a recurrent theme of Japanese religious traditions, and notably among the movements that emerged since the early nineteenth century. Agonshū's millennialism attributes the turmoil and travails of the world to unhappy spirits (notably the war dead) that collectively pose an existential threat to humanity. Eradicating karma and performing rituals for the unhappy dead thus can be a collective as well as an individual practice; as such, Agonshū places great emphasis on public rituals and festivals – usually carried out on a grand scale and with spectacular effects – to this end.

This could certainly be seen as an example of social conservatism and a lack of overt political interest in changing society. By emphasizing individual transformation and collective rituals as the mechanism to change the world, Agonshū certainly eschews any idea of seeking a change in the social structure by means of protests and politically oriented action. For Agonshū, any transformations in the phenomenal world or in the way society might operate are viewed in spiritual rather than political, social and economic terms.

Gender and female equality of attainment and practice

Despite Agonshū's apparent conservatism, lack of political engagement and eschewing of any means of transforming society other than by internalized individual spiritual change and ritual performances, Agonshū demonstrates a progressive orientation in the context of gender. Kiriyama (2001: 73) has stated that ultimately everybody has the potential to become a buddha (*daredemo budda ni nareru no da. Anata mo, anata mo, soshite anata mo*).[6] In its discussions of karma and spiritual hindrances Agonshū maintains a clear neutrality in gender terms. This is a significant attraction in the movement, and an area in which it differs significantly from what is found in much of established Buddhism and in many new religions. These have reinforced a conservative bias that places women in an inferior position in society and views them as having such deeply negative karmic forces that they can only attain enlightenment after being reborn as a man.[7] Helen Hardacre (1984) has discussed how Reiyūkai, for example, views women as having such karmic afflictions that place them in a subservient position. The narratives of movements such as Tenshō Kōtai Jingū Kyō that elevate the sufferings and dutiful behaviour of Kitamura Sayo, a young oppressed housewife who stoically accepted her lot and worked devotedly for a husband and mother-in-law who mistreated her, reflect a recurrent theme of placing women in the subservient role they have long endured in Japan.

By contrast some of the so-called new new religions that became popular in the 1980s had a different and, we suggest, more modern view on gender, either according women the same status as men or viewing each as having differing yet complementary roles, without necessarily considering one more important than the other.[8] In Aum Shinrikyō female practitioners could achieve similar and higher status to males, although that movement retained a traditional Buddhist view that women had 'bad karma' that needed to be overcome (Munakata 2010: 105–8). In Agonshū what mattered was how one dealt with one's vertical and horizontal karmic influences, not what one's gender was. As Kiriyama's statement that everyone has the potential to become enlightened indicates, Agonshū does not say that women have greater karmic hindrances or need to do more practice than men in order to achieve similar levels of spiritual development. Female informants in Agonshū have told us that woman can reach the higher levels of Agonshū just as can men, and they have contrasted what they find in Agonshū on this point with their perceptions of established traditions such as Shugendō. For example, in an interview conducted with a long-term female member in 2005, she explained the training necessary to become an Agonshū *shugenja* (ascetic practitioner) was the same for male and female members and both of them could perform at the Hoshi Matsuri. Her comments appeared to contain an implicit criticism of the restrictions placed on women in traditional Shugendō, for example, on female access to sacred mountains.[9]

Figure 3.1 A female *Yamabushi* performing during the Hoshi Matsuri. Photo by Ian Reader.

This made Agonshū attractive to women who wanted to develop themselves in spiritual terms and who were put off by the apparent gender prejudices of established Buddhism and some of the older new religions. Agonshū's own statistics indicate that more women than men are officially designated as *kyōshi*, teachers in service of the movement. In 1996 Agonshū reported that it had 259 such teachers of whom 113 were male and 146 female (Bunkachō 1997: 96). In 2016 there were 133 male and 173 female *kyōshi* (Bunkachō 2017: 97). In events such as the Hoshi Matsuri, female participants are highly visible at important points in the ritual process; it is a female *yamabushi* who shoots a series of symbolic arrows into the air to drive out evil spirits as a precursor to the ritual lighting of the *goma* pyres (Figure 3.1). The administrative chief (*rijichō*) of Agonshū has for many years been a female, Wada Naoko, and she has played a significant role in Agonshū, and especially in the period since Kiriyama's death, she has delivered talks and overseen major ritual occasions (see Chapter 5). Her status, along with the visible presence of female practitioners at Agonshū events and centres, serves to demonstrate that Agonshū does not discriminate between males and females. All are subject to karma and all are equally able to cut themselves free of it.

Morality and performance

Agonshū links efficacy (solving problems), positive outcomes (succeeding in one's life and living a happy life individually and collectively), practices (e.g. rituals to care for the spirits of the dead) and morality (in which people have a moral duty to care for the deceased, even those not directly associated with them, and have a duty to act in rightful ways) together. As such it could be seen as an example of the argument developed by Shimazono (1992a) that Japanese new religions contradict the Weberian notion that as societies undergo modernizing and rationalizing processes they become less oriented towards practices and notions related to magical and spiritual interventions in the world. In Shimazono's view new religions combine magic and morality. Their teachings have moral bases but they also incorporate the use of rituals and techniques that, underpinned by doctrinal interpretations of misfortune and its cures, enable people to better themselves and deal with their problems in this world. To that extent teachings tend to be this-worldly – and they are very much bound up with, reinforced by and articulated via practices.

Winston Davis (1980: 299), too, has associated the appeal of new religions with their seeming ability to offer emotional responses to problems; Davis uses the term 'magic' in this respect, drawing on Weber's use of the term as an 'ad hoc and emotional way of responding to human need'. Focusing on Mahikari, in which members can learn the spiritual purification and healing technique of *okiyome*, which is meant to control spirits believed to be afflicting a person, and use them to bring benefits to the person concerned, Davis argues that this 'magical response to the world' is a key feature of new religions, in which there is a 'democratization of magic' that enables followers to face life's challenges and participate in and perform rituals and techniques such as *okiyome* (302).

Davis and Shimazono have both, in such terms, drawn attention to the ways in which new religions offer people the potential to be masters of their own fates and to be active ritual practitioners. Agonshū, in offering members the means to identify and deal with the issues that cause them misfortunes and to develop a sense of positivity through which they might achieve liberation and happiness, certainly democratizes the idea of practice, and most specifically that of engagement in esoteric rituals that had otherwise been the preserve of priestly classes. However, we consider it highly problematic to speak of 'magic' in the context of Agonshū. It is, for a start, not a term that we have found appearing in its Japanese-language[10] or English-language publications. Spiritual powers – such as the clairvoyance that Kiriyama claimed as an attribute – are not seen as some form of emotional or ad hoc response to the world but as the product of his long path of practice, which combined religious and scientific training, involved ascetic practices, meditation and ritual studies. As we noted in Chapter 2, Agonshū views such powers as having a basis in science as well as religion, even as they transcend both. In *Henshin no genri* Kiriyama set out the five powers that could be attained through Agonshū practice, but these are not portrayed as magical in nature.

Davis actually uses 'magic' as a translation of the Japanese word *kiseki* used by Mahikari; *kiseki* is commonly translated as 'miracle' and this is how Mahikari views the term. Davis (1980: 11) conflates miracles and magic by asking, 'What are miracles if not the bridge between religion and magic?' However, movements such as Mahikari and Agonshū would reject this because they see magic as a mechanistic process that has no moral dimension whereas a miracle has a moral underpinning. Agonshū, like many religious movements in Japan, uses the idea of miracle (*kiseki*) to speak about beneficial events (e.g. healing or life improvement) that happen because of practice and counselling but it does not conceive it as something associated with magic.

Moreover, the notion of ritual as a moral action is prevalent in Agonshū, while spiritual potency is produced by ritual because of its essence as a moral act. Thus performing a memorial service or ritual for the spirits of the dead and venerating the *shinsei busshari* and calling on Buddha's grace can cancel out a bad deed or force, such as an unhappy spirit. This, in Agonshū's view, is a logical process, a 'mechanism' (*mekanizumu*) as Kiriyama has referred to it,[11] through which unhappy spirits who are causing hindrances are transformed via rituals into realized buddhas. For those who believe that the spirits of the dead continue to exist after death and that they have a continuing relationship with this world, and who consider that praying and caring for those spirits is as vital a task after their death as it is to care for people in life, the rituals are a means of caring, not of magic. As such there is no sense of magic within the Agonshū framework of interpretation; spiritual powers may appear to be beyond the normative human compass but they can be attained through training and the moral force of ritual practice. They are therefore *earned*, and are not in any way ad hoc, emotional and acquired as a result of magic.

Besides considering the idea of 'magic' to be something of a misnomer in the Agonshū context, there are also some caveats to be made about the idea of 'democratization'. Certainly Agonshū enables its followers to perform a variety of practices and rituals; they can serve as *yamabushi* and conduct the *goma* fire rituals that have normally been the preserve of esoteric Buddhism and Shugendō, for instance, and they perform their own memorial rituals at home before their own replica of Agonshū's *shinsei busshari* casket. Anyone who wishes to do so can engage in such practices and share in their efficacy; ordinary people are masters of their fates and can achieve liberation both for their ancestors and for themselves, thereby attaining happiness and special powers in this life, and ascent into higher spiritual realms thereafter. Nor, as we have noted, is gender an issue.

However, 'democratization' comes at a price in terms of time, commitment and money. Being able to assume some roles, such as being a *yamabushi* and conducting *goma* rituals, for example, requires training, while ordinary membership requires monthly fees and a commitment to daily practice. For some people this can be a problem, a point made by the questioner cited in Chapter 2, who stated that some people had left the movement for such reasons. She, too, was worried about whether she could continue as a member, since that required training and extensive commitments to the movement in terms of time and money, especially for those who wished to take part in the Hoshi Matsuri as a *yamabushi* or be able to conduct *goma* rites. Even individuals who do not undergo such training and who simply wish to perform personal rituals for the departed at home have to take on board an array of obligations and membership fees.

Practices, duties and the costs of membership

Agonshū in effect offers potential followers a trade between what the movement promises to do for them and what they need to do for the movement. In such respects it is no different from any other religious movement that promises rewards and expects devotion and support (the latter invariably including a financial dimension) in return – or, rather, expects devotion and support and offers rewards in return. This transactional dimension is common in religious terms, and Agonshū offers a good example of this phenomenon. It also is indicative of the wider religious consumer culture in Japan, where religious adherence and action are rarely cheap. This is not, as we emphasized in Chapter 1, something special to new movements but inherent in the established traditions, which have numerous inherited resources and which also make financial demands – often quite high ones – on members.

Participatory religion, which is what movements such as Agonshū are, can be demanding in such respects, and like many other movements, Agonshū charges monthly membership fees – according to the female member cited earlier, normally 2,000 yen per month.[12] Members might also be expected to buy at least some of the movement's books, magazines, videos, DVDs and so on, and pay for various ritual services. They are also, as in many other movements, expected to spread the word – not simply by telling others about Agonshū but by encouraging them to contribute to the movement by purchasing and writing requests on *goma* sticks to be burnt at events such as the Hoshi Matsuri. They are also expected to purchase a set of ritual implements that includes a replica of the *shinsei busshari* Buddha relic casket, which serves as a form of household altar, a rosary, a sutra book, incense and other items that are used in home prayers and ceremonies for the spirits of the dead. According to Benod (2013: 229) and Yamada (2012: 161), the collective cost of these items is 38,500 yen.[13] Members are given a membership card valid for three years, which entitles them to use Agonshū facilities and attend and participate in rituals at its centres, although if one fails to pay one's monthly subscription for three months in a row this right may be withdrawn (Benod 2013: 236–7).[14] They are expected also to follow a morally correct path by, for example, observing Buddhist precepts set out in Buddhism's eightfold path of right thoughts and actions.[15]

Members are expected and encouraged to perform *shugyō*, a term that literally alludes to ascetic practices, although in the ways it is used in many Japanese religious contexts – and certainly in Agonshū – it can be best considered as simply 'practice' without necessarily any ascetic dimensions.[16] Agonshū describes all members who take part in its events and rituals as practitioners (*shugyōsha*).[17] *Shugyō*, in effect, is any form of activity related to the movement – as can be seen by the basic list of members' practices listed by Agonshū. This cites four main types of practice (*shugyō*) for ordinary members. One is the daily practice of reciting sutras before one's personal *shinsei busshari* casket. Another is meditation, which can be learnt at major Agonshū centres, where a special room may be set aside for the practice. A third is participation in rituals in public places in Japan (*tochi jōreihō*), in order to pacify unhappy spirits there, and a fourth is the practice of cleaning (*seisō shugyō*). This can be done at Agonshū centres (members have an obligation to assist in ensuring the movement's centres operate smoothly and look tidy) but also in public places such as parks.[18] Performing such public acts is not just a gesture of goodwill and public service but of promoting the movement and enhancing its public image. It is an act of proselytization. Members are expected to actively spread Agonshū's message and such public acts serve as a way of doing this. Agonshū differs little from other new religions, in which proselytizing one's faith is part and parcel of being a devotee. Nor is the practice of cleaning and tidying public spaces special to Agonshū; it is a common activity in several new religions, through which devotees wearing clothing identifying themselves as devotees of a particular group seek to demonstrate the social caring nature of the movement concerned. It is also seen – as is any form of *shugyō* – as a spiritually enhancing activity in which the practical cleaning of a public space equates to the symbolic cleaning of the spirit and mind.[19]

The first mentioned of these forms of *shugyō* – the daily home ritual of veneration before the *shinsei busshari* casket – is the one that members are expected to do on a regular basis. It is also an indication of how practices can change in a new movement. Until 1986 the core practice for members was one known as the *senza gyō*, a daily practice extending over a period of 1,000 days in which disciples chanted Buddhist sutras before a home Agonshū altar (Reader 1988: 253; Benod 2013: 234). This individual practice along with communal fire rituals performed by Kiriyama would, according to Kiriyama (1981: 113–18) remove all negative karmic forces (*reishō*) from one's entire familial line and lead to liberation. Performing the *senza gyō* was also a way to acquire higher status within Agonshū. Because it involved an extended series of actions, it was considered to be demanding – and to that extent could have been seen as a barrier to some potential members. However, when the *shinsei busshari* was acquired in 1986, Kiriyama declared that the *senza gyō* was no longer essential to the process of cutting karma; venerating the powerful Buddha relic and receiving the spiritual power emanating from it would take its place and be more efficacious (Agonshū 1986: 26). It was from that time on that miniature replica *shinsei busshari* caskets were made and acquired (for a fee) by members, whose practice turned to worship in which veneration and belief in the salvific powers of the *shinsei busshari* took precedence over notions of ascetic practice. According to Agonshū and members we have spoken to, the *shinsei busshari* enhanced the understandings and abilities of followers and speeded up their spiritual development compared to the practices they performed prior to its acquisition.[20]

Higher ranks and the performance of rituals

As various commentators have noted, new religions tend to make it easy for people to join – and usually also their basic membership fees are low enough to make them attractive. However, as Christal Whelan (2015) puts it in her discussion of GLA: 'Joining GLA is easy to do, but becoming a member merely lets one through the door. Once inside, the novice cannot easily be passive without obtrusively drawing attention. There is considerable pressure to become more actively involved, which requires a continuing, and not small, investment of both time and money'. As Whelan notes, members also need to do a training course to learn the basics of the movement, and also attend other seminars and show willingness to volunteer at GLA centres in order to progress further. Participation in such training seminars requires fees (around 30,000 yen for the two-part training course required) as well as emotional commitments and time spent on volunteer work. The same is true in many other new movements. For instance, to progress to higher ranks of membership in World Mate – ranks that enable the member to perform special forms of ritual practice and learn World Mate's arts of divination – requires substantial sums of money that might amount to several million yen (GBP £10,000 or more) (Kawakami 2008: 121–2).

Agonshū is no different in that entry may be easy but progression and higher status may require additional effort, time and expense. Beyond basic membership, followers can also take part in training sessions and other activities that enhance their status; these also require additional payment, either (or both) for the appropriate accoutrements that go with higher ranks, and the training sessions required.[21] Agonshū lists a number of additional practices and training modes that can be attained. Two involve training sessions, the *Agon bukkyō denpōkai* (literally, the Agon Buddhism Transmission of the Law meeting/seminar) and the *Rennōjuku* (literally, 'brain-refining school'). In each of these members are taught various rituals and techniques (including fire ritual practices and sutra recitation) associated with Agonshū's way of pacifying and liberating spirits. At these training events, too, members can undergo the cold water austerity of standing under a waterfall (*takigyō*), an austerity widely found in Shugendō and other Japanese ascetic and shamanic traditions, and one that, according to Agonshū, disciplines the mind and body.[22] Those who complete the above *Agon bukkyō denpōkai* training meetings five times qualify for permission to perform the esoteric *goma* fire ritual that has traditionally been the preserve of esoteric Buddhist priests and Shugendō initiates, but that, via Kiriyama's training, is accessible to Agonshū members (Agonshū 2014).

Those who undergo such forms of training can also acquire the rank and status of *yamabushi*, mountain ascetic practitioners, and gain a distinctive set of clothing that marks the person out as (in the words of Agonshū) 'lay ascetics devoted to mental and physical self-discipline in the mountains' (Agon Shu 2017: 13). There appears to be no restriction on becoming a *yamabushi*; anyone who joins the movement can do so, it would appear, as long as they fulfil the obligations of practice, pay membership fees, attend appropriate training courses and acquire the appropriate ritual accoutrements. Between us we have attended a number of performances of the Hoshi Matsuri and talked to Agonshū practitioners wearing traditional *yamabushi* robes and participating in the fire rituals there; while a small number have been full-time Agonshū officials, most have held ordinary jobs and serve as *yamabushi* primarily at the Hoshi Matsuri and other Agonshū public fire rituals.

There are different levels of ranks in Agonshū's system of *yamabushi*, depending on experience and service, and indicated by different colours of robes (Benod 2013: 222); the highest ranks (including the movement's official leader, Fukada Seia) wear purple robes, and those at other levels wearing orange, green or white. Orange depicts a higher rank than white, while female practitioners normally wear green or white.[23] Besides *yamabushi* lay practitioners, Agonshū also has a small number of priests who have had Buddhist ordinations,[24] who oversee the movement's rituals and ceremonies, including funerals and the bestowal of posthumous names (*kaimyō*) on members, give sermons and (especially since Kiriyama's death in 2016) provide interpretations of his teachings (see Chapter 5). Agonshū's performance of funerals and bestowing of posthumous names replicate standard practices and patterns in established Japanese Buddhist sects. In developing a priesthood Agonshū is in effect reiterating its argument that it is a Buddhist movement, since Buddhism has in Japan and elsewhere been framed around an ordained clerical structure. In its system of ritual ranks for *yamabushi* and its development of a priesthood Agonshū thus appears to be replicating a hierarchic pattern found in the established Buddhist tradition. This again is not uncommon in new movements that, as they develop, accord greater status to longer-term members and those who contribute most to the movement in terms of engagement, service and fees. At the same time, however, Agonshū continues to offer followers more scope in terms of ritual participation than is normally the case in Buddhist sects dominated by their priesthoods, and while it has hierarchic dimensions, it offers anyone who wishes to progress up that hierarchic framework the opportunity to do so, as long as they are prepared to contribute and participate accordingly.

Kanjin: the practice of alms solicitation

There is one more area of practice and duty for members that we need to draw attention to before we outline some of the movement's main ritual events. This is the practice of *kanjin*, alms solicitation. It is especially prominent in the period leading up to the Hoshi Matsuri every February, when members are encouraged to engage in what Agonshū terms '*gomagi kanjin*', soliciting the purchase and writing of *gomagi* – the wooden sticks on which prayers are written, and that will be incinerated at the festival.[25] Although rarely mentioned in materials about Agonshū or, indeed, on its website,[26] *kanjin* plays an important role both in what Agonshū requires of followers and in how followers can achieve advancement and status within the movement. It represents a key element in the growth and success of the Hoshi Matsuri and in Agonshū's economy, and is evidence of the ways in which ordinary members contribute to the public face of the movement.

Kanjin is a term found in early Japanese Buddhism, relating to soliciting alms for the purpose of religious activities. Janet Goodwin (1994), for example, has detailed how early and medieval Japanese Buddhist mendicants known as *hijiri* went around the country preaching popular modes of Buddhism and soliciting alms to be used in the promotion of Buddhism and the construction of Buddhist statues and temples. Donations for such purposes brought merit to the donors that could aid them in their future life or lives. Such alms-solicitation was a key activity of Buddhist ascetics and it played a role, too, as Yoshii Toshiyuki (1996) has shown, in the promotion of Japanese pilgrimage sites and circuits.

Kanjin is thus a term associated with traditional Japanese Buddhism, and a way of acquiring the resources necessary to promote Buddhism and Buddhist institutions. By using the term Agonshū is thus identifying itself within a Buddhist framework, while legitimating its solicitation of donations by using the label of traditional Buddhist alms-collection. The practice of *gomagi kanjin*, according to Agonshū parlance, enables the wider public to take part in the festival alongside devotees and to participate in Agonshū's mission of world peace, while also benefitting from its methods of resolving personal problems, achieving goals and happiness, and caring for the spirits of the dead. Many of the *gomagi* burnt at the Hoshi Matsuri come from people outside the movement; visitors on the day may well decide to purchase and write on *gomagi*, while large numbers have been solicited in advance through the *kanjin* activities of Agonshū members.

Agonshū's concept of *kanjin* appears to have been developed by Kiriyama during the early 1980s, the period when the movement expanded rapidly and when the Hoshi Matsuri grew from a small ritual event into a huge mass affair. In the early 1980s Kiriyama referred to *kanjin* in various sermons, and Agonshū produced a booklet of some thirty pages about the practice, drawing mainly on Kiriyama's talks coupled with advice about how to go about it. This booklet – the *Gomagi kanjin shugyō tokuhon* (Manual for the practice of *gomagi* alms-solicitation) has been circulated to members inside the movement, rather than being publicly available, although a copy has been put online on a website about Agonshū that is not run by or connected to the movement.[27]

The title of the booklet clearly identifies alms solicitation as a religious practice (*shugyō*). The booklet reproduces Kiriyama's sermons about the practice, in which he identifies the *goma* ritual and its *goma* sticks through a standard esoteric Buddhist lens as a symbolic means of burning away evil passions and desires (*bonnō*) and thereby liberating oneself. Without eradicating such passions and the negative karma associated with them one cannot attain happiness (p. 3). Alms solicitation, Kiriyama states, is one of the highest activities possible; it is both practice (*shugyō*) and almsgiving (*fuse*) (pp. 7–8). The *goma* stick is a microcosm of the world and of the wider path of Buddhism; by writing just one *goma* stick one creates a karmic link to the world of the Buddhas and to the provision of good fortune (p. 8). Shakyamuni himself preached the importance of almsgiving as a key element in Buddhism and by this, Kiriyama argues, he was indicating the practice of *gomagi kanjin* (p. 9). Kiriyama emphasizes that devotion (to Agonshū) is not just about doing one's own practice but spreading the word to others, through such things as distributing leaflets and soliciting alms through the sale of *gomagi* (*gomagi kanjin*).

He refutes firmly the notion that this is in any way a business or sales activity (*shōbai de wa nai* 'it is not commerce!'). Indeed, it is totally the reverse – it is an almsgiving act of spreading the (Buddhist) law (*hō o fuse shite*; p. 9) and of understanding Buddhist teaching. Such activities are in no way commercial, he proclaims, for we (i.e. Agonshū members) are not sales people but representatives of Shakyamuni engaged in the sacred practice of spreading his teaching (pp. 9–11). He recognizes that people might feel apprehensive and uneasy about accosting non-members and asking them to pay for and write on *gomagi*, but he exhorts them to remember that they are disciples of the Buddha with an obligation to spread the teaching (p. 11). This is not just a religious activity but also a social one aimed at human salvation at a time when society and the world in general are in a precarious state (p. 13). Even getting just one person to purchase a *gomagi* is both an act of proselytization and of social welfare; if a person writes just one *gomagi*, then that person will be connected to the Buddha and Buddhist teachings, and to the good karmic connections (*en*) associated with them. This will spread Agonshū's teaching and method of enabling unhappy spirits to be pacified and become realized buddhas (*jōbutsu hō*) and thus improve the state of a world threatened by destruction and unease (pp. 15–16).

Kiriyama states that *gomagi kanjin* is also a practice of spiritual/mental liberation (*kokoro gedatsugyō*) through which one can counter and confront one's own pride.

Feeling embarrassed about approaching people for alms, he says, is a matter of pride and this needs to be dispensed with if one is to follow the Buddhist path. Here he draws attention to traditional monastic practices of alms solicitation such as the Zen Buddhist monastic begging round (*takuhatsu*) and argues that what Agonshū members do in their *gomagi kanjin* practice is the same. The aim is not to acquire money but to spread the word and to enable other people to become involved and gain the merit of giving alms (as with donating to begging monks) (pp. 18–19). Interestingly Kiriyama also notes that it does not matter if one is unable to vend a single *gomagi* because what is truly important is the practice itself (p. 20). However, he then offers advice on the best ways to sell the *gomagi*, and the booklet provides further suggestions for this. On should start by writing one's own *gomagi* with a prayer for successful alms solicitation and by making lists of one's contacts. After talking to people one knows about Agonshū, one can branch out by attending local events and talking to people there about the Hoshi Matsuri, and so on (pp. 22–9). At all times one should carry Agonshū pamphlets as well as copies of newspaper articles about the event that can be handed out to anyone interested. In such contexts, Agonshū's practice of commissioning paid newspaper articles about the Hoshi Matsuri (see Chapter 2) serves an added purpose, as a means through which to potentially sell more *gomagi*.

One can also use the telephone or write to people, explaining what Agonshū does, telling them about the 'amazing' (*fushigi*) events that happen at the Hoshi Matsuri and how they can be part of it simply by purchasing and writing a *gomagi*, and how one can do *senzo kuyō* (memorial services for ancestors) through the medium of the *gomagi*. Given that doing such services is a common practice in Japanese religious contexts – and one that when normally done at Buddhist temples can be costly – the suggestion that one can fulfil obligations to one's ancestors through the purchase of just a few *goma* sticks costing 100 yen each could serve as a striking sales pitch. One should also check whether those one approaches have particular needs or worries at the time; for example, grandparents who have grandchildren about to undergo important examinations might be interested in the potential of Agonshū prayers for education success that can be written on *gomagi* and so on (pp. 29–30). One should also afterwards call or contact people one has persuaded to purchase *gomagi*, to check on their well-being. The booklet also contains a sample experience, of *gomagi kanjin* experiences, in which a member talks of how s/he went about the whole process, including giving *gomagi* to other people as a way of making connections with them, and of how this helped improve his/her own situation (p. 31).

Members who collect sizeable numbers of *gomagi* through this process are offered rewards in the shape of spiritual goods such as Buddhist pictures, mandalas, amulets and pendants related to Agonshū. We will see this in more detail in Chapter 5. *Kanjin* activities are a way to acquire greater status in the movement, and are strongly encouraged by the movement, whose website contains numerous examples of *kanjin* activities. Among recent ones are a fire ceremony held in Osaka in November 2016, when 400,000 *gomagi* were collected and incinerated for the protection of the Osaka region,[28] and a regular monthly event in the area around the Hiroshima Peace Park, in which Agonshū rituals for world peace and related *gomagi kanjin* activities are carried out.[29] To that extent, while *kanjin* is particularly focused on the Hoshi Matsuri, a point that recurs throughout the above-mentioned booklet, it is also a widespread practice related to the movement's other ritual activities.

A number of points are evident in the context of *kanjin* in Agonshū. It has been a significant element in the development and expansion of the Hoshi Matsuri, and as a source of finance within Agonshū. One pays 100 yen for a standard *gomagi* on which to write a prayer for success or for the spirits of the dead; when one considers that some thirty million *gomagi* have been burnt in some years at the Hoshi Matsuri (Reader 1988) this represents a considerable sum for the movement, even allowing for the costs of producing and bringing the *gomagi* to Yamashina and the expense of putting on the ceremony. If the numbers being collected, written on and burnt may be less than in earlier times (see next chapter), they still are counted in their millions.

Besides being a major financial resource for Agonshū, the practice and concept of *kanjin*, especially in the ways in which it has been portrayed in Kiriyama's sermons, emphasizes the extent to which Agonshū seeks to identify itself within a Buddhist framework and to present its activities as Buddhist. This is evident in how soliciting the purchase of *gomagi* is associated with the Zen monastic begging round, and in Agonshū's use of Buddhist terms such as *kanjin* and *fuse*. It also is a means whereby Agonshū can engage with people beyond the movement; one can be part of an Agonshū ritual and make a contribution (if one is so persuaded by Agonshū's rhetoric about world peace and the like) to its causes.[30] At the same time, of course, the wider emphasis on *kanjin* can be viewed as another example of the entrepreneurial dimensions of the movement and of Kiriyama. It fits well with Kiriyama's sales talk, cited in Chapter 2, in that he sought to convince a concerned disciple that paying a monthly fee was worth it. The rewards offered for managing to sell plentiful *gomagi* – and the suggestions that one should initially buy and write one's own for the success of the venture and perhaps give out a few as gifts – also have a clearly entrepreneurial dimension to them.

Kanjin can also clearly be viewed in a negative light, as an example of what critics claim new religions in general do – namely, exploit followers and seek money. While all religions, as we have previously noted, rely on donations and funding from followers, the extent to which Agonshū encourages *kanjin* could be seen as adding fuel to such criticisms.[31] Sometimes complaints about such matters may be voiced online by disgruntled members or ex-members[32] while the woman concerned about monthly fees, who referred to people leaving the movement because of financial concerns, also indicates that this can be a worry for devotees. The insistence in Agonshū's booklet and in Kiriyama's sermons that this is not *shōbai* (business, commerce) seems to show, too, that Agonshū is well aware of the ways critics (and worried members) might view things, and of the extent to which its activities to finance itself and to make its rituals successful could be tinged with the odour of commercialism and the potential criticisms associated with it.

Major rituals and public events

There are a number of ritual and festive events in Agonshū's annual calendar and in this it is little different from any other Japanese religious organization or institution. In

Agonshū there are two important monthly events. One is the *Tsuitachi engi hōshō goma* (first of the month fire ritual) held on the first of each month. It consists of a fire ritual followed by a sermon and lasts half an hour – a time determined initially by television arrangements Agonshū negotiated with broadcasting firms to transmit live broadcasts of the event to members across the country (Baffelli 2016: 73–4). The fire ritual and sermon were both done by Kiriyama until quite late in his life. This ritual focuses on seeking practical benefits, such as happiness, prosperity and dealing with life problems, and the sermons deal with overcoming problems and encouraging a sense of positivism.[33] The other monthly event is the *meitokusai* ritual, for the liberation of ancestors and spirits of the dead, held on the 16th of every month. The former ritual is held at Agonshū's Tokyo centre and the latter at its main temple near Kyoto; both rituals developed in the late 1980s at the period of its greatest expansion. Like other Agonshū rituals they are broadcast to its centres throughout Japan via satellite broadcasting on Agonshū's own media network, in a way that constructs a sense of community and of mutual participation even among those unable to be physically present (74). The two form a dyad in focusing respectively on this-worldly themes and the spirits of the dead. The *meitokusai* ritual is based, according to Agonshū, in esoteric Buddhist rites from the Tibetan Nyingmapa tradition transmitted to and mastered by Kiriyama, and it deals with ancestral spirits who cannot be liberated simply by personally conducted rituals at home. It has in recent years focused particularly on the spirits of the Japanese war dead and on memorializing them and paying homage to their legacy (this aspect will be discussed further in Chapter 4).[34] Members who undergo training in the *meitokusai* ritual techniques and practices and attend the ceremony in person can subsequently carry out the ritual at home as well.[35] Other calendar events include various festivals for deities venerated in Agonshū as well as divinatory activities aimed at interpreting one's fate and discerning whatever spiritual forces might be impeding one from fulfilling one's potential.

The most public event in Agonshū's calendar – indeed its main focus – is the annual Hoshi Matsuri. Since various descriptions of the event have been given elsewhere (e.g. Reader 1988, 1991, 1994; Baffelli 2016: 77–80) and a detailed photo-visual account of the festival is readily available online,[36] we will not go into great detail about the festival, but will restrict ourselves to a brief overview along with some observations about the key themes it involves.

Hoshi Matsuri translates as 'Star Festival' and as such refers to the importance attributed by Agonshū to astrology and horoscopes and, more in general, the idea of controlling one's own destiny.

This is explicitly stated in the presentation of the Hoshi Matsuri on Agonshū's website, in both the English and Japanese versions:

Hoshi means 'star' in Japanese, but the 'star' in the Hoshi Matsuri does not mean a star shining in the night sky.

When described in this context, it represents 'the star of destiny'.

It is this star that governs the joys and woes we encounter.

In 'esoteric Buddhism', one of the Buddhist schools, an excellent way to determine the cycle of people's luck was discovered by analyzing the star of destiny. This is called 'Mikkyo Senseijyutsu' (fortune-telling by Agon Buddhist astrology).

In addition to determining personal destiny, it is also one of the methods of improving a person's luck, by turning around his/her misfortune and further boosting the streak of good fortune. This is believed to be one of the ultimate secret methods of esoteric Buddhist prayer called 'Jokashofuku' – the miracle-working secret method of eliminating evil and changing luck for the better. This is the 'Hoshi Matsuri Goma-kuyo' or Fire Rites ceremony in which the 'stars' are dedicated by burning goma on the day of setsubun, which is a New Year Day in the lunar calendar.[37]

In an English pamphlet distributed during the 2017 festival the explanation of '*hoshi*' is less clear and only states that Agonshū 'refers to the Fire Rites Festival as Agon Hoshi Matsuri because the fire rites are conducted in the special manner of esoteric Buddhism, as a means of transforming destiny', while the Japanese version of the same pamphlet more explicitly refers to the 'stars of destiny' (*unmei no hoshi*) (Agon Shu 2017). Consultations about charting one's destiny by identifying one's 'stars of destiny' is one of the services offered at Agonshū centres and it figures prominently at the Hoshi Matsuri.

It is also important to note that 'Star Festivals' (*hoshi matsuri*) are not unique to Agonshū but are common in the esoteric Buddhist and Shugendō traditions as annual events performed usually at the New Year, Winter Solstice or *Setsubun* (the traditional Japanese beginning of spring) (Sekimori 2006: 218).[38] The emphasis of these rituals and festivals is on avoiding misfortune and ensuring long life (Sekimori 2006). This is another example, in other words, of Agonshū drawing on and incorporating elements from existing traditions into its own framework. It also draws on a long Japanese tradition of divination and fortune telling, in which people have sought to discern their potential futures through a variety of consultation practices, including astrology and palmistry.[39] Agonshū is just one of many new movements that have used divinatory techniques to offer followers various ways of trying to ascertain and find ways of improving their destinies.

While divination plays a role in Agonshū and the festival, the movement has in more recent times amended its English translation of the name of its main festival, both to emphasize the importance of its fire rituals and to emphasize how Shinto themes have become part of it. Since the mid-1990s Agonshū, while using the title Hoshi Matsuri, also refers to it in English as 'The Combined Shinto-Buddhist Fire Rites Festival' (Japanese: *Shinbutsu ryōkai daisaitō gomaku*).[40] It takes place on 11 February each year at Agonshū's main temple complex at Yamashina just outside Kyoto. February 11 is a public holiday, *Kenkoku kinenbi* (National Foundation Day), and one reason for choosing to hold the event on a public holiday is simply that this makes it easier for people to attend and boosts the potential crowd. There are clear underlying symbolic meanings to the choice as well, for the holiday has nationalist dimensions, referring back to the mythical foundation of the country by Emperor Jimmu (the descendant of the Amaterasu the Sun Goddess according to Shinto myths). The prevalence of nationalist images, from Japanese flags to references during the rituals to the spirits of past emperors and the like, has from the 1980s onwards given the occasion a nationalistic dimension that has attracted attention from outside observers (Reader 1988: 240).

Inaugurated in 1970 as a small event it grew in size until, by the late 1980s, it attracted over half a million visitors each year, with millions of *gomagi* being burnt on two huge pyres in a sustained event lasting much of the day. The size of the event owes much to Agonshū's publicity activities; it promotes the event widely via pamphlets, many of them delivered door-to-door,[41] television advertisements and the activities of its members. Agonshū is also aided, it appears, by tourist agencies and offices in the Kyoto area, which have put the event in their calendar of interesting things to see for visitors.[42] Many who attend are ordinary members of the public who may not necessarily be interested in joining the movement but who come along out of curiosity or interest aroused by the spectacular nature of the event. Its dramatic style – involving processions of Agonshū members in *yamabushi* clothing accompanied by martial-style music broadcast over loudspeakers, chanting, ritual dialogues, the lighting and the roaring flames of two massive pyres and numerous side events (including dancing by figures dressed in Shinto-style costumes and representing various deities) – is designed to attract attention and crowds, and it has succeeded in doing so for some decades. As such the Hoshi Matsuri offers a public gateway to Agonshū, and also a means through which anyone can engage with the movement's activities and offer prayers for their ancestors and personal benefits.

Central to the event are two large pyres on which *gomagi* are burnt in the ritual *goma* process (Figure 3.2). Initially there was only one pyre but as the event grew two pyres became necessary to accommodate the growing number of *goma* sticks. Located in the *kekkai* (the ritual arena, marked off by four bamboo gateways and with a huge altar on which are numerous offerings and a copy of the *shinsei busshari* casket) the two pyres represent respectively the realization of one's wishes (*hōshō*) and the liberation

Figure 3.2 Hoshi Matsuri pyres before the ritual begins. Photo by Ian Reader.

of the spirits of the dead (*gedatsu*). As such they replicate the orientations of the two rituals (the *tsuitachi goma* and *meitokusai*) mentioned above and combine two main themes (personal development and amelioration, and dealing with the spirits of the dead) we have identified as key to Agonshū's overall teaching and orientations. The burning of the pyres symbolically liberates the intentions written on the *goma* sticks being incinerated and extinguishes negative forces (Figure 3.3). As the flames consume the *gomagi*, they, according to esoteric Buddhism, release the wishes and bring them to the attention of the Buddhas. Fire also has a purifying dimension, as an agency removing the negative karmic forces of the dead. In this act of ritual incineration the *goma* sticks serve also as an offering to the gods and Buddhas.[43] Agonshū also – in order to allay any worries that might arise from the incineration of such large amounts of wood – includes a note in its publicity materials to say that the wood comes either from controlled afforestation projects in Indonesia or from waste timber in Japan, and that in both cases the movement follows closely laws on the protection of resources and the environment (Agon Shu 2017: 12).

In the 1980s the two pyres were referred to by Buddhist terms: the *taizōkai* (womb world) and *kongōkai* (diamond world). These two realms – the womb and diamond – represent the two mandalas prominent in esoteric Buddhism that signify the potential for enlightenment in this phenomenal realm (the womb), and the practices leading to enlightenment (the diamond). These symbolic designations and meanings are indicative of Agonshū's roots in Shingon Buddhism and Shugendō, and are, according to Agonshū officials, still present even though the Hoshi Matsuri has been depicted since 1993 as a combined Shinto-Buddhist ritual.[44] The two pyres have subsequently

Figure 3.3 Hoshi Matsuri performance. Photo by Ian Reader. From the Photo Archives of the Nanzan Institute for Religion and Culture, Nagoya, Japan.

been referred to as the *shinkai* (realm of the *kami* [Shinto gods]) and the *bukkai* (realm of the Buddhas), with the former representing the realization of wishes (*hōshō*) and the latter the liberation of the spirits of the dead (*gedatsu*).

As such the two pyres represent two major pillars of Japanese religiosity (this-worldly themes and caring for the spirits of the dead) while the ritual process of the Hoshi Matsuri combines Agonshū's main themes of caring for and liberating the spirits of the dead and of realizing human wishes, into one coherent framework. The pyres together also reflect the widely acknowledged orientations in Japan of its two older traditions, with Shinto being commonly viewed as concerned with issues in this life and Buddhism with matters of death and memorialization.[45] Together, they can be seen as sending out an implicit message that Agonshū is at core very much a Japanese religion that draws on and brings together the themes of its main traditions in a new form. The re-designation of the pyres and the emphasis nowadays on the festival as a combined Shinto-Buddhist rite also illustrate recent developments in the movement, in which themes more closely aligned to Shinto and to nationalist themes have become more prevalent as the movement has got older. These are themes we address more closely in the next chapter.

World Peace, internationalism and Japanese identity

While the Hoshi Matsuri exudes themes related to Japanese religious world views and Japan itself (the date itself with its nationalistic associations and the twin themes of this-worldly realization and the liberation of unhappy spirits of the dead), there is another dimension to the Hoshi Matsuri that is widely promoted by Agonshū and that (at least in theory) sits above these Japan-centric themes. This is the theme of world peace (*sekai heiwa*). In Agonshū teaching, threats to harmony and peace occur because of the karmic problems caused by unhappy spirits along with the unhappiness of those whose wishes and hopes of salvation are frustrated. To bring about world peace requires dealing with such issues, and this is what the pyres and rituals of the Hoshi Matsuri do according to Agonshū. This focus on world peace was from early on linked to Agonshū's messages about the potential calamities facing the world at the end of the last millennium and to the prophecies of Nostradamus, but it has remained an overarching theme in the movement and in its publicity even after the potential disasters of the late twentieth century have receded into history. The fact that the festival is held at Agonshū's holy site, designated as the 'new Sahet Mahet' from which Agonshū aims to spread 'complete Buddhism' to the world, reaffirms this sense of mission. The theme of world peace features strongly in the messages broadcast over the Hoshi Matsuri loudspeakers and in its *kanjin* campaigns. It is also emphasized in symbolic terms through the presence of various dignitaries from different faiths who have been invited to attend the festival; at different times we have noted the presence of Egyptian Muslim leaders (1988), Mayan Grand Elders (in 2010) and Sri Lankan and Bhutanese monks at the festival (as well as at Kiriyama's funeral in 2016). Loudspeaker announcements, too, have made sure that attendees at the festival are aware of the presence of such foreign religious figures, while members of the public, according to

Agonshū, have also voiced their appreciation of being able to make a contribution to world peace through their own attendance.[46]

Rituals remain the framework through which world peace may be achieved, according to Agonshū, and to this end it has carried out numerous public events with a message of world peace not just in Japan but overseas and/or with overseas religious leaders. These began in the Kannon Jikeikai period and continued through Agonshū's early years with fire rituals in sites associated with Japan's wartime engagements in the Pacific region (Reader 1994: 52) and in Japan with figures such as the Dalai Lama, with whom Kiriyama conducted a fire ceremony for world peace in Tokyo in 1984.[47] Subsequently they have been held in places as diverse as Ulan Bator in Mongolia (1996), New York (2000, 2001), Paris (2003), Auschwitz (2006), Siberia (2007), Israel[48] (2008), Jerusalem (2013) and – as in earlier years – at numerous sites around the Pacific. The first of these was at Palau in 1977 and subsequent rituals have been conducted in places such as Guadalcanal (2009). Many of these places (notably Siberia and the Pacific region sites) were places where there were many Japanese war dead, and these have become the prime focus of such rituals more recently.

Agonshū's ritual services have thus focused especially on pacifying the spirits of the dead while framing such actions within the wider rubric of world peace. The choice of sites such as Auschwitz and Jerusalem, too, has clear resonances with issues of war and remembrance; the 2013 Jerusalem fire ritual was to pray both for peace in the Middle East and for world peace, and at this time Agonshū also erected a Buddhist stupa in that city. They have also – as the various rituals in places such as Paris and New York, and rituals with figures such as the Dalai Lama, indicate – served to project Agonshū as a world religion active on the international stage. Often such rituals also display a seemingly ecumenical dimension in which religious actors from different traditions play roles – something on display in the One Peace Live Aura event Agonshū held at its Yamashina temple site on 7 November 2010. This involved a fire ritual conducted by Kiriyama and Agonshū devotees along with Mayan religious leaders from Guatemala, while messages of support were read out from religious and other leaders in Bhutan and Israel, and performers from Sri Lanka and Bhutan provided dance and musical accompaniment.[49] As with events in Japan such as the Hoshi Matsuri, these events are broadcast live and transmitted to Agonshū centres in Japan so that members can feel a sense of participation while seeing their leaders operating on an international stage. Agonshū's international orientations are also demonstrated by various overseas symbols that have been incorporated into its main ritual complex at Yamashina. There is, for example, a Bhutanese Buddhist Hall that contains Buddhist paintings from Bhutan, and the Jerusalem Peace and Friendship Square, in which stands the statue of a lion to symbolize friendship and peace (Figure 3.4).

Although there are clearly elements of international engagement and universal aspiration in all of this – and we have no doubt that Agonshū is sincere in its hopes for world peace – we consider that underlying these public events and demonstrations of international engagement is a pervasive sense of Japanese identity. As such these international dimensions are in many respects secondary to Agonshū's orientations as a movement born, developed and located in Japan. The emphasis on Japan as the spiritual centre from which world peace will come and from which Buddhism (the

Figure 3.4 Jerusalem Lion symbolizing overseas activities and world peace. Photo by Ian Reader.

only true and complete form thereof) will spread to the world reinforces this point. So does the presence and involvement in what are essentially Japanese rituals, of foreign dignitaries whose appearance serves to reaffirm (at least in the eyes of members) the universal stature of their movement. Likewise the sight of Agonshū leaders going to Auschwitz and Jerusalem to conduct rituals to pacify spirits and bring peace to the troubled regions of other nations through Japanese-style rituals sends out a message to members. The incorporation of motifs such as the Bhutanese Hall at Yamashina and the placing of an Agonshū stupa in Jerusalem also show how Agonshū's engagement with the world is one replete with symbolic meanings, in which Agonshū (and through it, Japan) can go out and save the world via its Japanese-centred interpretation of the causes and solutions of problems, while assimilating the wider world into Japan and domesticating it.

Perhaps the most striking example of this was at the 2012 Hoshi Matsuri. Although world peace remained an overarching theme, the real focus was very much, and understandably, on the terrible events of 11 March 2011, when the earthquake and tsunami disaster killed thousands, wrecked swathes of northern Japan, damaged the Fukushima nuclear reactor site, caused the area around it to become uninhabitable and aroused serious worries about nuclear contamination. The 2012 Hoshi Matsuri – the first one after the March 2011 tragedy – focused on praying for those who died in the disasters, rebuilding Japan and developing a new civilization (*bunmei*) out of the ruins of that tragedy.[50] Agonshū also ran several other events focusing on the tragedy in which it talked of reviving the Japanese spirit (*kokoro*) and offering 'prayers for Japan' (*Nihon no inori*) – the latter being the title of an Agonshū event involving Japanese traditional arts and drama along with lectures in Kyoto a week after the 2012 Hoshi Matsuri. At this event various participants spoke about ways to revive the Japanese spirit and focused on Japanese ancient myths that marked the country out as special.[51] While it is understandable that Japanese issues would be central to Agonshū's activities in the aftermath of the March 2011 disasters, at the same time such events also clearly shed light on the underlying focus in the movement as world peace took a back seat to the more immediate concerns of Japan. It was a further indicator of how Agonshū's universalist messages about world peace are underpinned by and ultimately best understood in the light of its nature as a Japanese movement, one whose nationalist orientations have become increasingly prominent as it has aged.

The importance of teachings, the meanings of practice

Teachings are important in new religions such as Agonshū. Developed via the experiences and insights of founders such as Kiriyama, they provide meaningful messages to ordinary people helping them understand their position in the world. They articulate moral codes and ways of living, explain why misfortunes happen and how they should be dealt with and provide cosmological explanations relating to deities and other figures of worship and their role in the universe. They reorient the world in the context of the founder's experiences; Kiriyama's pained earlier life and misfortunes such as his imprisonment serve as indicators of the problems that can hit anyone – even a future religious saviour – in this life and as a teaching of hope that even a convicted felon can achieve salvation and happiness. Such teachings and the practices they embrace create new frameworks of meaning for followers. They may also change in line with circumstances. For Agonshū the donation of the *shinsei busshari* was recognition of Kiriyama's status as a saviour and of his mission to spread Buddhism to the world. It was, in those terms, a logical and reasonable thing to amend Agonshū practice away from austerities and towards veneration of the relic – something that made it more accessible for greater numbers of people and thereby, in Agonshū's vision, increased the numbers who could perform rituals to pacify the dead and save the world. Whereas an outside viewer might consider that such changes might smack of a degree of opportunism (especially given the lack of clarity about how the relic was acquired) in order to increase membership levels and make practice easier for followers, within Agonshū the message was clear. In a sense, it replicated the transformation in Kiriyama's own life path when, in 1970, Juntei Kannon told him he had cut his karma and no longer needed to focus on a personal path of asceticism but should instead go out and spread his message to the world.

Agonshū offers followers a set of teachings that draw on Japanese folk and Buddhist ideas about the relationship of the spirit and human worlds, in which the spirits of the dead have influence in this world, both positively and negatively. To ensure the positive nature of such influences one has to pacify those spirits and enable them to attain buddhahood while cutting one's own karma and removing one's spiritual impediments. This is essential in order to achieve one's wishes and to attain peace for one's ancestors. Agonshū's practices are closely allied to, and are a means of enacting, its teachings; it is via rituals that practitioners pacify and liberate the spirits of the dead, cut their own karma and open the way to happiness, success and spiritual empowerment. Members thereby reinforce their sense of being and take part, along with their founder and other members, in a mission to transform the world. They also, as we have outlined above, express a sense of Japanese identity that underlies and implicitly subsumes the theme of world salvation and grounds the movement in its Japanese environment.

We have mentioned at several points how new religions have often been dismissed as lacking in serious meaning or as somehow deviant and contrary to Japanese norms. The academic Watanabe Masako (2011: 87) sums up an attitude found widely in Japan, especially among the mass media, that 'converting to a new religion also means cutting oneself off from the world of "common sense"'. However, as this chapter has shown, and as Watanabe herself implies (2011: 88), such views misunderstand and misrepresent what movements such as Agonshū are doing and saying. They fail also to recognize a central element in Japanese religious structure – that teachings and doctrines do not exist in a vacuum but correlate with and are articulated in and through practices. Far from cutting themselves off from normative values or 'common sense' in Japanese religious terms, what Agonshū members are doing, and are being encouraged by their movement to do, is express values that are grounded in commonly shared Japanese religious perspectives. The linking of karma – seen as governing all human activity and as a barrier to spiritual progress – to the idea of the spirits of the dead is not a departure from traditional customs or traditional concepts. Nor is the idea of ritual practice as an efficacious and innately moral code of conduct through which negative karma can be eradicated, moral codes expressed and society made better. These notions provide Agonshū members with a coherent framework through which to counter personal problems and to express their aspirations for a better world. Agonshū members know the importance of practice, without which teachings and moral codes are empty of meaning. As such they take part in rituals, at home and at Agonshū centres, and through them find a sense of belonging with the movement. The enthusiasm we have seen and heard about when conversing with devotees taking part at mass events such as the Hoshi Matsuri indicates how readily members can engage with the practices that support their teachings. Such mass events afford members an opportunity to step outside normative day-to-day routines to be a mountain ascetic practitioner and a ritual performer acting (in their eyes) to cut their own karma, strengthen their country and save the world.

There is a close symbiosis in Agonshū between the idea of a leader with special spiritual power, insight and knowledge, teachings that can be readily projected via the leader's insights, and practices and rituals that can be performed at home and communally. Together they form a whole that characterizes Agonshū and, we suggest, this is also reflective of a wider pattern among new religions in Japan. This nexus of founder/teacher/inspiration, with messages and understandable teachings about the world and the individual, and the rituals and practices that enact and give meaning to those teachings, was significant in Agonshū's rise and its acclamation, in the 1980s, as a 'new' new religion. They are themes that resonate across the historical spectrum as well, indicating that Agonshū, while being very new in Japanese terms, was at the same time doing things and expressing concepts that are deep-rooted historically.

This does not mean that a movement such as Agonshū will necessarily be successful in what it does, or that it will always be able to continue growing in the way it did when it first attracted mass attention. By the latter years of the past century and into the beginning of this one, a variety of problems began to surface that affected Agonshū's development, and that of other movements as well. As this happened, and as Agonshū moved from being a very new religion infused with an aura of dynamism into one that was (along with its leader) becoming older, some of the issues we have drawn attention to in this chapter – notably the underlying current of nationalism – have become more evident. It is to such matters that we turn in the next chapter.

4

From the World to Japan: The Nationalism of an Ageing Movement

Introduction: from 'number one' to the 'lost decade' and the 'danger' of religion

Movements such as Agonshū clearly tapped into a wider cultural mood of 1980s and early 1990s Japan, and it was in this period – especially the 1980s – that it grew rapidly, as did the numbers of *gomagi* burnt at the Hoshi Matsuri (Reader 1988). If there were concerns in the 1980s about a coming crisis and a sense of unease about where Japan fitted in the world, these concerns were balanced by an optimism and sense of confidence borne out of Japan's economic prowess. The notion of 'Japan as Number One' – as Ezra Vogel's (1979) famed book was titled – was manifested in a variety of contexts in Japanese popular and localized culture, from the *nihonjinron* discourses purporting to identify the Japanese as unique, special and different, and hence occupying a special enhanced status in the world (Befu 2009; Morris-Suzuki 1998), to the idea of Japan being the epicentre of a new spiritual culture that would solve the world's problems. Agonshū's rhetoric about the saviour from the East who had discovered what all other Buddhists had failed to discern – namely, the true essence of Buddhism – and about its mission to propagate 'original Buddhism', save the world from chaos and bring about a new spiritual age, clearly fed off this sense of Japan-centric confidence.

Yet within a short time much had changed. The 'Bubble economy' that sustained so much of Japan's 1980s development, burst in the early 1990s, with banks facing massive losses, major companies posting huge deficits, jobs being lost and the economy sliding into stagnation and recession, from which it has barely recovered in the decades since. The loss of public and international confidence that resulted, along with rising unemployment and a general sense that the Japanese political system that had helped deliver the economic good times was corrupt, broken and unable to deal with Japan's newly emerging economic and structural problems, made the notion of Japan as world leader look increasingly remote. Instead of being 'number one' the public rhetoric shifted to talk of a 'lost decade' (and, later, of lost decades).

Disasters in 1995 added to this sense of unease and impacted heavily on the religious world. The Hanshin earthquake that devastated the city of Kobe not only led to criticism and a loss of confidence in the government (seen as slow to react and provide relief) but also in religious movements in general for (according to critics) failing to provide succour to the suffering (Yamaori 1995; Umehara and Yamaori 1995). Just two months after the Kobe earthquake, on 20 March 1995, Aum Shinrikyō's sarin gas attack on the Tokyo subway happened. Since the Aum Affair has been widely discussed elsewhere, including its impact on the wider religious environment (Shimazono 1995; Lo Breglio 1997; Reader 2000a; Reader 2000b; Reader 2004a; Kisala and Mullins 2001; Dorman 2012; McLaughlin 2012; Baffelli and Reader 2012), it would be sufficient here just to highlight the impact that it had on the image of religion. As we have written elsewhere, the Aum Affair triggered a 'paradigm shift in public and political attitudes towards religious organisations' (Baffelli and Reader 2012: 8).

In the wake of the subway attack surveys showed public support for heightened state monitoring of religious movements and a widely held view that 'religion' was potentially dangerous (Baffelli and Reader 2012: 8). Furthermore the notion that being a member of or joining a religious movement (and especially a new religious movement) was tantamount to being 'brainwashed' or 'mind controlled' became a dominant element in public discourse. This naturally impacted on movements needing to gain new recruits through conversions and new affiliations in order to remain vibrant and replace older members who died.

While religious organizations in general faced problems after Aum, the problem was compounded for Agonshū for three reasons. One was that Aum had given millennialism and prophecy a bad name, and this impacted on movements such as Agonshū and Kōfuku no Kagaku that had emphasized millennial themes and Nostradamus's prophecies. While they had to find ways to distance themselves from earlier millennial proclamations and promises, their orientation as millennial movements made them particularly suspect in the eyes of many Japanese after Aum's attack. The second problem was that Asahara Shōkō had for a time, prior to establishing Aum, been a member of Agonshū and had participated in its practices, as well as adopting some aspects of Agonshū's teaching and orientations into his own movement. The third was that when the connection between Agonshū and Aum was first mooted in the media, Agonshū mishandled it by initially saying that Asahara had not been a member – an error it had to then backtrack on, initially by claiming that records of his membership had been filed in the wrong place (hence the denial), and then by saying he had only been a member in name rather than real engagement. Kiriyama (1995b) reinforced this latter point and sought to distance his movement from Asahara in a book published after the attack, in which he argued that if Asahara had been a real member and had really understood his teachings, he and Aum would never have gone down the path of violence.[1]

There is no mistaking some similarities between Aum's teaching and orientations and those of Agonshū. Aum also was interested in supernatural powers (*chōnōryoku*) and esoteric Buddhism, talked of different realms of existence, claimed to have restated 'original Buddhism' and emphasized the importance of eradicating karma. It also, like Agonshū, focused on themes of millennialism, Nostradamus and the idea of a saviour from the East. However, there were also significant differences. Aum's millennial focus was 'catastrophic' in nature in that it believed that a final apocalyptic war was not something to fear and avoid on the path to a new spiritual world, but a necessary happening in order to destroy the evils of the material world and bring about a new age.[2] Where Agonshū saw ritual services to pacify the dead as the means through which to transform the world and avoid catastrophe, Aum embraced violence and catastrophe as the way to realize it millennial visions. Aum was also structured differently, with a communal focus and an emphasis on renouncing the world to perform harsh austerities, a path very different from Agonshū.

Despite those differences, the Aum Affair was a serious crisis for Agonshū, and in some ways the stigma of Aum has continued to haunt it. To provide an example of this, in June 2006 Kiriyama performed a fire ritual in Auschwitz, Poland. The event attracted some controversy in the Polish media, which produced articles associating Agonshū with Aum and appearing to suggest that Asahara was a member of the group when the sarin gas happened:

> A guru of a mysterious Japanese cult called Agon Shu will appear as a guest of honour at the ceremony commemorating the day when the first prisoners were transported to Auschwitz. Asahara Shoko, who conducted the sarin gas attack in Tokyo metro, also comes from this sect. (Interia Fakty 2006: online)[3]

Such articles, over a decade after the sarin attack, indicate that Agonshū, although not directly involved in any of Aum's crimes, continues to face problems of 'guilt by association' with Asahara's group, at least in media portrayals that in turn impact on the group's status both in Japan and abroad.

Another critical change was that the year 1999 came and went without any apparent major upheavals, while Nostradamus – so prominent in the teachings of many new movements in the 1980s and early 1990s – unsurprisingly went out of fashion.[4] This caused a dilemma for groups that had been making prophetic comments about the threats of 1999 while offering hopes of world transformation and identifying themselves with Nostradamus's prophecies. The passing of the apparent crisis of 1999 removed a valuable recruiting tool for them. A common strategy in response was to claim that they had been responsible for or played a part in avoiding the cataclysms apparently foretold by Nostradamus and others. Agonshū, for instance, portrayed itself and Kiriyama as crucial factors in the avoidance of calamity at the end of the millennium, as did Kōfuku no Kagaku (Baffelli and Reader 2011).

However, even when proclaiming they had helped in this apparent 'escape' from the dangers of 1999, movements whose sense of dynamism and urgency had been so powerfully driven by the temporal proximity of the end of the millennium and by promises of world transformation faced new challenges. Given that Japan was in a period of economic malaise and facing social problems as a result, it was hard for movements such as Agonshū to claim that their activities had led to a brave new world of spiritual transformation and happiness. Rather, the new millennium appeared – especially when the shadow of global terror followed by wars in the Middle East erupted after 11 September 2001 – to bring new problems and worries, rather than some form of spiritually oriented amelioration. While Agonshū could rhetorically claim to have helped overcome the dangers of 1999, the brave new world that ensued could hardly be viewed as better than before, while the advent of the new millennium removed one area of Agonshū's appeal and weakened the sense of dynamic urgency that had previously impelled it.

These problems were exacerbated by a declining interest, especially among the young, in being part of or joining religious organizations, or in participating in memorial rituals for the ancestors and spirits of the dead. Although scholars have pointed out that some people continue to participate in some individualist 'spiritual' practices such as visiting power spots, or consulting spiritual experts (Horie 2011; 2017; Gaitanidis 2012), surveys have shown a decrease in many areas of religious engagement and in participation in traditional rituals (Ishii 2007; Reader 2012).

To attract new members, especially younger ones, in order to guarantee their continuing welfare and even survival, religious movements often need to reorient themselves and focus on new activities. This can be a particular problem for movements that, like Agonshū, present themselves as being in tune with or at the cutting edge of their times. They can quickly look out of touch – and hence lose their appeal – if they are unable to maintain such a dynamic and they can face serious dilemmas when broader social currents change. While they may need to innovate in order to look in tune with the times and attractive to potential new recruits, they also need to retain the support of their existing members, who may be getting older and less keen on change. Often current members resist changes and want their movement to remain the same, familiar and just as they know it – and they are usually the people who have provided the economic and human resources that helped the movement develop and that have kept it going. We have heard such comments from officials in a number of movements who have been caught in this dilemma, in which the changes they felt would be necessary to prevent stagnation and decline risked alienating long-term and older members who provided the movement's key financial support. As a consequence, they often ended up by adhering to themes and practices that attracted an earlier generation (such as superhuman powers and ancestor spirits in the case of Agonshū) but that appeared less appealing and even old-fashioned or bizarre by younger generations, who might be more concerned about the apparent 'dangers' of religion symbolized by Aum.

Ageing members, numerical problems and image restyling

These changing circumstances have had consequences for Agonshū. It is widely accepted that its main period of growth was during the 1980s, during which it probably increased its following more than tenfold. The figures it reported to the Bunkachō (Agency for Cultural Affairs) to be included in the annual *Shūkyō Nenkan* (Religions Year Book) showed 23,570 members in 1980 and 203,000 in 1985 – a figure that remained steady for many years thereafter. In recent reports to the Bunkachō, however, the figure has gone up to over 300,000 with a figure of 364,986 in the 2016 *Shūkyō Nenkan* (Bunkachō 2017: 97), which would appear to indicate a movement on the rise. However, there appears to be a discrepancy between this figures and the actual state of the movement. First, as has been mentioned before, scholars have repeatedly shown that assessing correct membership figures for religious groups in Japan is extremely difficult and that the data reported by religious groups is by no means a literal expression of the truth (Astley 2006: 96–8; Reader 1991: 195–6). In part this is because movements can be optimistic and inventive when reporting figures to the Bunkachō that will then be published. There are obvious promotional advantages to reporting high and growing membership figures, which serve as an attractive advertising tool, suggesting vibrancy and dynamism and refuting any notions of ageing and stagnation. This inventiveness can include (as some new religions have done) asking members to purchase multiple copies of a movement's magazine so as to distribute it as a means of proselytizing, and then counting each magazine sent out as indicating a membership, or operating on the assumption that if one person from a household has joined, their whole family would also be members. Some groups appear to add new members but do not remove those who leave (or die) from their lists. At times, too, this may be because movements – especially when they enter periods of decline – do not have adequate staff to keep membership lists up to date.[5] Examples of discrepancies abound. Kōfuku no Kagaku is one movement whose membership claims have been challenged by scholars. In the 1980s and 1990s it repeatedly claimed to be expanding rapidly, talking of a membership of several millions and even asserting that it was the largest movement in Japan, outstripping Sōka Gakkai, which is commonly acknowledged to be the largest single religious organization in the country (Ōkawa 1995a).[6] Such claims were met with widespread scepticism; Shimada Hiromi (1995: 90–2) drew attention to the movement's inability to fill arenas in which its leader held mass rallies, while Numata Ken'ya (1995: 193–6) commented on a gap between reported numbers and actuality. The general perception has been that the movement may pay more attention to the numbers of publications it sells than to the actual numbers who participate in its activities. Similar questions have been raised about whether Agonshū had as many followers as it reported in the 1980s (Reader 1991: 217, 258 fn. 45).[7]

As such, one should not place too much weight on the numerical claims of religious organizations in Japan. Our observations of Agonshū, along with discussions with members and officials, suggest that its apparent numerical increase is more of a chimera than an indication of actual strength. Agonshū members and representatives have in discussions with us at different times between 2010 and 2017 referred to an ageing and declining membership and, as one official put it, of elderly members no longer able to get to centres to attend rituals but to whom Agonshū continues to send seasonal greetings.[8] Such people appear to be members on paper although not in person. The Question and Answer session that we reported on in Chapter 2 – in which the issue of membership fees and practices was raised in the context of people leaving the movement – is pertinent here too. The member who raised the question was worried about people leaving Agonshū and Kiriyama's response – emphasizing the values of continuing to pay membership fees and persevere with the practices – recognized this underlying issue. As Baffelli (2016: 84) has commented, the numbers attending the monthly *tsuitachi goma* rituals in Tokyo when she did fieldwork in 2006–2007 were significantly lower than those reported by Reader (1991: 225) for similar events in the late 1980s.

There have been some events towards the end of Kiriyama's life, including his funeral ceremony, when Agonshū's Tokyo centre has been filled, and this may have been, as one participant informed one of the authors, because members thought it might be the last time they could see Kiriyama in person. Regular visits to other centres in more peripheral locations, for example, in Miyazaki city in Kyushu, however, showed very small numbers (around ten to fifteen as a rule) attending the monthly rituals. Also we have noted a difference in the recent Hoshi Matsuri crowds compared to such events in the late 1980s. The latter had started early in the morning, usually at 7 a.m., and went on all day, for around ten hours, with the viewing platforms around the fire area full until the late afternoon. In 2017, however, the event started later, at 9.30 a.m., at which time the viewing areas were not crowded and it was easy to move around to get better views (Figure 4.1) – a contrast to the experiences of the late 1980s. The event went on for only six or so hours, and by early afternoon the crowds had thinned out considerably and the event was winding down; by 3.30 p.m. there were very few people left watching.[9]

In conversations with adherents in recent years we have often heard comments about the problems of attracting new, younger members. Members stated that in the 1980s many joined because of Agonshū's distinctive characteristics, such as techniques to acquire superhuman powers, but that these now do not attract younger people, and that it is difficult to replace members who leave the organization (or who have died) with new, younger people who can add dynamism. For example, a female member, who has been a very active member of the organization for twenty-seven years,

Figure 4.1 Sparsely filled stands at the start of the Hoshi Matsuri in 2017. Photo by Ian Reader.

expressed her concerns about members leaving the organization after having only been members for a few years and the difficulties the group is facing in rebranding its distinctive features (Baffelli 2016: 86). Benod (2013: 33–4, 327, 351) has commented that the membership is predominantly made up of middle-aged people, many of whom had joined when in their twenties or thirties and who were now in their fifties or above. Our observations during events and rituals over the past fifteen years along with interviews with officials and members confirm this view of a movement that is ageing, in which young members are a minority and new recruits are rare.

As such, Agonshū had, in the first two decades of the current century, lost the impetus of its earlier period, seen its age profile increase and active participation decrease. Its founder had aged, and so had the movement. As a result it clearly was facing longer-term problems. This is not, we stress, a singular problem for Agonshū but one facing numerous movements in Japan. As Levi McLaughlin (2012, 2018) has shown, for example, Sōka Gakkai, long considered the largest and most successful of all new religions, has been facing problems of stagnation and potential decline in recent times. Tenrikyō is another example; it lost, according to its own studies, around 200,000 members each decade between 1986 and 2006, largely because of members dying and not being replaced by new converts and declining numbers of initiates able to carry out propagation activities (Katō 2017). These are not outliers so much as examples of a wider pattern, in which new religions, often viewed as the most dynamic institutional element in Japanese religious structures, have, along with the older religious establishment, experienced retrenchment and falling support levels in twenty-first-century Japan.[10]

The internet and other problems

Even in the area of media communications, where Agonshū had previously made a name for itself as an innovator, it had begun to look out of touch. Its satellite broadcasts might have been ahead of the field in the 1980s but, three decades later, they had not changed and stagnation rather than development appeared to be the norm (Baffelli 2016). It appeared slow to make use of newer technologies, as Benod (2013: 196) observed when he visited Agonshū's Tokyo centre in 2009 and saw that its audiovisual equipment had not been upgraded in some time and that it was using old cathode televisions that were no longer available on the market to display its videos. Although he found, on a subsequent visit in 2012, that the equipment had been upgraded to LCD screens and Agonshū was 'little by little' ('peu à peu'; Benod 2013: 196) replacing videos with DVDs, he was left with the impression of a movement no longer keeping up with new media and technological developments.

This has also been the case with the internet. As we have discussed in previous publications (Baffelli, Reader and Staemmler 2011; Baffelli 2011, 2016), Agonshū was, like many new religions, a latecomer to the internet and its website for several years only provided sparse information about its activities.[11] The website was rarely updated and even if, in the present day, it appears to be graphically appealing, it only provides limited information about the movement. For some time after Kiriyama died, for example, the website did not even mention the loss of Agonshū's founder (see next chapter) and its online English profile of Kiriyama had not (as of January 2018, over a year after his death) indicated that he had died.

Some attempts have been made to update things and provide a newer look; for example, a 2012 Agonshū advertising campaign to promote the Hoshi Matsuri featured young male and female *yamabushi* so as to convey an image of youthful vibrancy, and the movement signed up for social media accounts. However, these have barely made an impact. The Agonshū Twitter account, for instance, consists only of quotations from Kiriyama's writings. Bluntly, Agonshū appears out of touch in social media contexts and 'to have lost, over the years, its status as a user-friendly religion' (Baffelli 2016: 87).

As a consequence, Agonshū went from looking very modern to looking behind the times. Even attempts to tap into popular trends – something that marked Agonshū out in the 1980s – appeared to be more a case of not creating or being in at the start of a bandwagon, but of jumping on an existing one just as it was beginning to slow down. This was perhaps nowhere more evident than in its adoption of the idea of 'power spots' (*pāwā supotto*), places that supposedly exuded spiritual power that could be readily tapped into by visitors. The 'power spot' phenomenon was one of the trends that became widely commented on in the earlier years of the current century and, according to Tsukada and Ōmi (2011) it hit its peak in around 2010, after which it began to run out of steam. It was in 2010 that Agonshū inaugurated a number of 'power spots' around its main temple at Yamashina and at the Hoshi Matsuri. Alighting on a potentially attractive new trend just as it appeared to be passing its peak seemed symptomatic of the movement's struggles to adjust to the times.

Reorientations and strategies for renewal

The adoption of 'power spots' and the updating (even if slowly) of its facilities indicate that Agonshū, like other movements facing problems in contemporary Japan, is not simply being passive in the face of weakening support. The strategies that are being adopted vary widely and we can only draw attention to a few examples here. Sōka Gakkai, for example, has moved away from its earlier focus on aggressive and active recruitment, realizing that this is out of step with contemporary attitudes, and has instead become more inwardly focused on developing mechanisms and strategies to retain the support of existing members and keep them in the movement, rather than looking at ways to expand in the ways it had done in earlier decades (McLaughlin 2012). In so doing it appears to consider that devoting resources (which may be in decline because of the erosion of its membership) to recruitment activities in an environment that is largely hostile to religious movements is less viable than trying to ensure that it does not bleed more internal support. Trying to retain the loyalty of those who have been born into the movement and who will, of necessity, henceforth be the main support structure of the Gakkai appears to be its main strategy. This strategy of retaining loyalties is one that has also been pursued by older Buddhist sects, albeit not always with resounding success.[12] Tenrikyō has made attempts to use new media forms popular with younger people to try to give the movement a more modern image and engage with new generations.[13] It has also developed fresh training programmes designed to attract new members and to enable followers to develop and heighten their missionary skills so as to attract new people into the movement (Katō 2017).

Seichō no Ie has undergone one of the more radical reorientations among new movements in recent times. Known for its arch nationalism and for its links to right-wing political and Shinto associations[14] it has shifted course in more recent times to develop an environmentally oriented view of the world. This began around the year 2000 and has been advanced particularly by Taniguchi Masanobu, the grandson of the movement's founder Taniguchi Masaharu, who acceded to the leadership in 2009 and felt that his movement needed a change of direction if it were to remain relevant in the modern day. He has introduced some radical changes that have moved it away from its earlier Shinto-oriented nationalism to an environmentally focused stance that appeals to a younger clientele (Staemmler 2013), while engaging actively with social media. Whether these changes will bring in a new generation of members to revitalize an ageing movement is at present unclear, but it is an example of how leaders in some new movements can recognize the need for change and for creating an up-to-date image. It is an example that senior figures in other movements have drawn our attention to, while expressing the wish that their own movement could do something similarly innovative, and also noting that their older members, who provide their main financial support, were less keen on any such radical change.[15]

Some new movements have looked overseas as a potential source of new converts and a way of addressing problems in Japan. Isaac Gagné (2017: 154), in his study of the small movement Kagamikyō, a movement that splintered off from Sekai Kyūseikyō in the 1970s,[16] notes that it, like many new movements, has been facing problems of an ageing membership, declining financial support and few new recruits. To counter this it has adopted a strategy of reaching out overseas to try and attract new recruits – something that, Gagné notes, other new religions have also done (154). Overseas support is seen as enhancing the movement's prestige, which could then be used to draw in new followers in Japan as well.[17] At the same time, there are concerns within the movement that in so doing (and in amending its orientations to make it attractive to such new audiences) it may be alienating its older members who have been the bedrock of the movement – a dilemma that, as we noted above, is one that many movements currently face.

How far Kagamikyō's strategy will work is unclear. Thus far Japanese new movements have not generally been very successful in building a following beyond their Japanese bases.[18] Agonshū has sought to increase its profile outside of Japan and the examples we have given in previous chapters – from its numerous overseas rituals to its sponsorship of international bodies such as universities – are indicative of an overseas strategy that serves to demonstrate to a Japanese audience its status as a player on the international stage. Yet there is little evidence that it has developed any significant following outside of Japan (or, indeed, anything other a very few non-Japanese devotees). While it projects itself as a universalizing movement intent on world peace and with a mission to spread 'complete Buddhism' to the world at large, it remains deeply grounded within Japanese religious culture with its emphasis on Japanese beliefs about the spirits of the dead. Its membership remains predominantly if not almost wholly Japanese, and it has continued, even while talking about world peace and original Buddhism, to operate in ways that emphasized Japanese religious concepts and issues of Japanese identity and concern, as we discussed in the previous chapter. While such orientations contributed to its appeal in its country of origin, they have not made it especially accessible to people beyond Japan.

Looking back, 'coming home' and turning to the gods?

While it has tried to adopt what appear to be some of the newer trends in the Japanese religious world, Agonshū's main response to the problems it faces has involved what we see as a form of retrenchment, bringing its focus increasingly closer to its Japanese homeland, developing links with Shinto, incorporating Japanese deities and, increasingly, focusing on the spirits of the Japanese war dead. In so doing its nationalist orientations, which have been present along from its early days, have become intensified in recent years, and particularly since around 2010. In such terms it has, we consider, taken a path that is likely to appeal especially to an existing membership that may itself be getting more conservative as it ages. It is a strategic path more akin to that of Sōka Gakkai (a movement that, as we note in the next chapter, was formulating this strategy in a similar context to Agonshū, of a dominant, long-serving but ageing charismatic leader) than, for example, the more radical and modernizing steps taken by Seichō no Ie under the direction of its new leader.

While Agonshū continues to proclaim that it is a Buddhist movement striving for world peace, it has increasingly incorporated and focused on themes associated with the Shinto tradition and Japanese nationalism, including associating itself with controversial practices such as venerating the spirits of the war dead at Yasukuni Shrine in Tokyo. Yasukuni Shrine is highly controversial, not least because executed war criminals are among those enshrined there and because it has been seen both in Japan and across East Asia as a symbolic centre of Japanese militarism. It is both a focus of Japanese right-wing nationalist sentiments and a flash point in debates and controversies over the constitutional separation of state and religion. Over the years various mainly right-wing revisionist actors have tried to have it reinstated as a state-supported institution and to allow visits to the shrine by political figures such as the Prime Minister in their official capacity. Such issues have been seen by many opponents as potentially threatening the constitutional separation of religion and state that pertains in Japan and have led to numerous protests and lawsuits.[19]

Some commentators such as Mark Mullins (2012a, b) have perceived a growth in religiously oriented rightist nationalism in Japan in recent years, a growth symbolized and manifested by the rise in support for right-wing nationalist politicians and the activities of organizational groupings such as the influential Nippon Kaigi (Japan Conference).[20] This organization includes prominent political figures, including Japan's current (as of March 2018) Prime Minister Abe Shinzō, Ishihara Shintarō, the right-wing activist, former governor of Tokyo and friend of Kiriyama's (see below) and many other influential figures especially in the political world. It has close links with the Shintō Seiji Renmei (*Shinseiren*, Shinto Association of Spiritual Leadership), a Shinto political group with agendas to support the Imperial household, revise the Constitution, reform education in ways that cultivate patriotism and that are widely seen as replicating the nature of prewar Japanese education, and re-establish care and veneration of the spirits of the war dead enshrined at Yasukuni Shrine as a national ritual (Mullins 2012a: 73). Nippon Kaigi has supported these agendas and, given that it has Abe, the current Prime Minister, and various other powerful political figures among its number, it is widely viewed as a powerful pressure group and agency in contemporary Japan (McNeill 2015; Sasagase and Sato 2015). While it is not a religious organization but a political one, its agendas incorporate religious themes and indicate the extent to which support for the political right in Japan can be associated with nationalist-style religious themes. Agonshū increasingly seems to identify with such themes, as is manifest in the prominence of Shinto deities and Japanese spirits in its recent activities.

In the previous chapter we mentioned that in the 1990s the Hoshi Matsuri began to be referred to in Agonshū as a combined Shinto-Buddhist ritual, and that the pyres became the *shinkai* (realm of the Shinto gods) and *bukkai* (realm of the Buddhas). 'Complete Buddhism' thus was reinforced through this association with the Shinto gods. On one level one could see this as another example of a common pattern in terms of Japanese religious practice and engagement, of Buddhism absorbing themes from Shinto (and vice versa) and of Buddhist authorities claiming the Shinto deities as subsidiary elements or localized manifestations of universal Buddhist powers.[21] The two traditions have been closely interwoven historically, institutionally and in the lives of ordinary people in Japan, and in such respects it is not really surprising that Agonshū saw fit to incorporate Shinto deities into its framework of worship. Indeed, this could be seen as a way to enhance its appeal to a Japanese audience. Yet Agonshū's adoption of Shinto should not be seen simply as a process of accommodation or, indeed, of absorption of a local tradition into a universal one. Rather, it has been seen as a way of strengthening and enhancing Agonshū because of the prominence and power of the Shinto *kami*, who are clearly not portrayed in such terms as localized entities waiting to be absorbed by a greater tradition, but as significant reinforcements to that tradition. As we discuss in the next chapter, Agonshū has claimed that adding the *kami* to the world of 'complete Buddhism' has enhanced that tradition and made it more powerful than ever before.

Moreover, Agonshū's focus on and adoption of Shinto themes has become increasingly pronounced as Agonshū has got older. The Hoshi Matsuri initially was a Buddhist ritual with two pyres symbolizing complementary Buddhist esoteric realms and meanings. As it has become a combined Shinto-Buddhist rite (and not, we note, a combined Buddhist-Shinto one) the realm of the *kami* – the *shinkai* – has not simply overlaid the earlier symbolic Buddhist meanings of the pyre for the realization of wishes but has become the equal of the realm of the buddhas. This change came about after Agonshū conducted a combined Shinto-Buddhist fire ritual in Ise (the location of which are widely regarded as Shinto's most prominent shrines) on 24 October 1993 to commemorate the sixty-first rebuilding of the Ise shrines, an event that is often framed with nationalist and patriotic rhetoric and images.[22]

The origins of Agonshū's incorporation of Shinto deities, rituals and themes stems back, according to Kiriyama, to an encounter in the early 1970s with Koizumi

Futoshinomikoto, who ran a martial arts spiritual training centre and shrine at Ise, and who was revered by his entourage of disciples as *Ise no ikigamisama* ('the living deity of Ise').[23] According to Kiriyama (2005: 33–59), Koizumi, having read Kiriyama's 1971 book *Henshin no genri*, invited him to his centre at Ise. Kiriyama stayed overnight and had a dream in which he encountered numerous *kami*, but when he related this to Koizumi the next day, Koizumi said that this was not a dream but a real encounter, one that showed Koizumi that Kiriyama was in fact a reincarnation of the Japanese deity of the winds Susanoo – a powerful deity associated with the origins of Japan. For Koizumi this was a sign that Kiriyama had a special mission to revitalize Japan through the spiritual power of the *kami*. Kiriyama appears not to have dwelt on the claim by Koizumi associating him with Susanoo, although he states that he did at times narrate this encounter to followers in his sermons (33). Until the 1990s Shinto themes remained relatively in the background although Kiriyama has stated that Koizumi's comments revealed to him the importance of paying attention to the Shinto gods as intrinsic elements in Japan's traditional religious and moral system (1–8, 33–59). A further spirit encounter with *kami* in 1990, according to Kiriyama, intensified this feeling and increased his sense of mission, adding to the message he had received from the Buddha at Sahet Mahet and convincing him that salvation required the combined powers of the *kami* and buddhas (48–50).

As a result he began to emphasize that Japan had traditionally been grounded in a union of Shinto and Buddhism and of its figures of worship – the notion known in Japan as *shinbutsu shūgō*, the amalgamation or syncretic combination of the *kami* and buddhas as a unified religious system. For Kiriyama this combinatory system had been Japan's moral, spiritual and religious guideline until the Meiji era, in which Shinto and Buddhism had been separated and its religious tradition rent asunder. As a result of this, Japan had lost its moral compass and its people had failed to continue the traditions of their ancestors, leading to turmoil, social fracture and religious decline (Kiriyama 2005: 1–8). In order to revitalize Japan's religious spirit and re-establish social harmony, it had to reunite Shinto and Buddhism; hence an important element in Agonshū's mission was to bring the *kami* and Japan's Shinto heritage back into union with Buddhism. The renaming of the Hoshi Matsuri and its pyres, and the incorporation of various Shinto rites into the festival were elements in this process from the 1990s onwards and they have become increasingly prominent since. At the 2017 Hoshi Matsuri, for example, Shinto priests played a prominent role in the rituals enshrining Kiriyama, carrying his relics on a portable Shinto shrine (*mikoshi*) into the sacred arena, as well as performing acts of ritual purification before the main altar while shrine maidens performed traditional ritual dances.

Agonshū has also enshrined a number of Shinto deities into its pantheon over the years; it has instituted Susanoo shrines at several of its centres, while at Yamashina, it has shrines to Ebisu and Daikokuten, two of the *shichifukujin* (seven gods of good fortune) popular in Japan as providers of benefits and wealth (Reader and Tanabe 1998: 156–63). It is by no means uncommon (indeed it is much the norm) for Buddhist temples to incorporate shrines to Shinto *kami*, and so the presence of these figures at what Agonshū portrays as a Buddhist temple site is quite standard in Japanese contexts. However, two points are worthy of note here. One is that Daikokuten has generally been viewed as a Buddhist figure, initially associated with a Hindu deity later adopted into the Buddhist pantheon, although he has also been identified with a Shinto *kami*, Ōkuninushi no mikoto.[24] Agonshū portrays Daikokuten specifically as a Shinto deity, with a Shinto-style shrine. The second is that Agonshū claims that since being enshrined by the movement these two deities 'have obtained profound new power in addition to their original power to provide the [*sic*] money and fortune' (Agon Shu 2017: 7). Buddhist figures can thus be incorporated into Agonshū as Shinto *kami* and can have their powers enhanced as a result, while their incorporation strengthens Agonshū's identity as a Japanese movement in which both buddhas and *kami* are venerated.

Agonshū has not just brought Shinto *kami* into its pantheon and accorded them an equal status in the pyres of the Hoshi Matsuri. It has also developed links with a number of Shinto shrines around Japan. It has close connections to Nakayama Shrine in Shimonoseki in Yamaguchi prefecture, and it was from there that the aforementioned Shinto priests and shrine maidens who performed ritual roles at the 2017 Hoshi Matsuri came. Other shrines that Agonshū has developed connections with include Suwa Taisha (shrine) and Yasukuni Shrine, both of which sent messages of condolence to Agonshū on the occasion of Kiriyama's death and funeral. Agonshū has also been involved in rituals and acts of worship at Shinto shrines. In the last few years before his death, Kiriyama made annual organized visits with an Agonshū delegation to Yasukuni Shrine to venerate the spirits of the war dead. These visits, usually on 15 July (the date of the annual *urabon* festival of the dead), have continued after his death, and are now part of the movement's annual ritual calendar. They also involve visiting the nearby Chidorigafuchi National Cemetery and performing formal memorial rituals for the war dead there.

Yasukuni, the war, regrets and revisions

The acts of veneration at Yasukuni are especially significant in the light of the ways in which Agonshū and Kiriyama have spoken about the Pacific War (as it is usually referred to in Agonshū) in recent times. In Chapter 2 we mentioned that in 1983 Kiriyama had written that it was good he had been unable to go to war because of ill health because if he had gone to war he might have committed bad deeds – a comment that could be read as an implicit admission that the wartime behaviour of Japan's troops might not always have been of the highest standards. Yet as he entered his final years he began to talk more regretfully about his inability to fight. In a discussion with the playwright and director Kuramoto Sō published as an Agonshū advertising feature in the *Sankei Shinbun* on 15 August 2012 (this being the anniversary of Japan's surrender and the end of the Pacific War, and a date on which the war dead are remembered) Kiriyama regretted having been unable to participate in the war. He spoke of his sense of powerlessness and frustration over this; it was, he said, 'regrettable, because I was not even able to die for my country'.[25] In fact, he claimed during this discussion, it was for such reasons that he decided to become a religious figure with a mission to perform memorial rituals for those who had given their lives protecting the country (*kuni o mamoru*).[26]

Kiriyama reiterated these thoughts in various other media around this time. In May 2012 the *Meitokusai Nyūsu*, an Agonshū newsletter related to its *meitoku* memorial rituals, announced a memorial service for the spirits of the Japanese war dead (Agonshū 2012). In the newsletter Kiriyama states that it was thanks to those who died in the war that contemporary Japan has been able to experience its subsequent economic development, and that he thinks that all Japanese today are the bereaved family (*izoku*) of the Pacific War.[27] These comments indicate not simply an increased stress on remembering and commemorating Japan's war dead – and we should emphasize that the war dead, as associated with Yasukuni, are those who died while in the service of Japan, that is, they are the military war dead and government officials – but an apparent reappraisal of the past through which the war dead are elevated into guardians and benefactors of the present nation.

A subsequent Agonshū public relations feature in the *Sankei Shinbun* on 15 August 2012, the seventieth anniversary of the ending of the war, reported on a visit to Yasukuni on 15 July by Kiriyama and a delegation of disciples. It also outlined Kiriyama's thoughts on the war. These indicated a militant revisionist posture that would have resonated well with the right-wing nationalist supporters of the Nippon Kaigi and the Shintō Seiji Renmei. Kiriyama emphasized the continuing need to perform memorials for those who died, and worried that since a large part of the Japanese population (over 80 per cent) had been born since the war, memories of what really happened might be lost. For Kiriyama, Western colonialism was a factor in the conflict; Japan, he said, had sought to become equal with the colonial nations but had been unable to do so because of discriminatory economic policies against it by the United States, Britain and others. As such, even though it did not wish to go to war it was pushed to such extremes because of discriminatory acts against it and for the sake of its self-existence and self-defence (*jison jiei*) – something that, he felt, contemporary Japanese do not understand. He stated that he wanted to fight but was unable to do so because of illness, while friends of his did go and died. As such, Kiriyama mused, his wish to worship at Yasukuni may be in part on behalf and because of those friends who died and as an apology to them because he had survived. He further stated his belief that the living have a duty to make sure those who died (in war) did not die in vain (*muda*) and that they must not forget those who said, 'Let's meet again at Yasukuni' – a clear reference to the military slogans of the war period and to the kamikaze pilots who set off on their suicide missions saying to each other that they would meet again (in spirit) at Yasukuni Shrine. Kiriyama said he could not comprehend Japanese people that question *Yasukuni sanpai* (veneration at Yasukuni), which is something he thinks is *atarimae* – obvious or natural.[28] It was for such reasons that he had felt, ever since Agonshū's first overseas rituals in Palau in 1977, it was an important mission for him to perform memorial services and repatriate the bones of the war dead. He also mentioned the atomic bombs at Hiroshima and Nagasaki, calling them war crimes and commenting that it is the views of the victors that get legitimated afterwards.

The *Sankei Shinbun* feature also mentioned Kiriyama's visit to Jerusalem in 2013 to perform rituals for the war dead and pray for world peace; for Kiriyama there was no contradiction between such acts for peace and his prayer visits to Yasukuni. Both, he said, are manifestations of his country's history and awareness of its obligations to its past. The *Sankei Shinbun* publicity article also outlined the activities of the former Tokyo governor Ishihara Shintarō, who performs an act of veneration at Yasukuni Shrine each year on 15 August. Ishihara had also accompanied the 93-year-old Kiriyama on his 15 July 2015 visit to Yasukuni and had written a prayer for Japan's rebuilding (*Nippon saiken*) on an Agonshū *gomagi* – a prayer reiterating the messages of Agonshū's 2012 Hoshi Matsuri about reviving the Japanese spirit and building a new civilization. Ishihara is a well-known writer, politician and right-wing nationalist, and he is a member of and an advisor to Nippon Kaigi (Sasagase and Sato 2015). He has written provocatively and critically about Japan's relationship with foreign powers, and has been accused of xenophobia, for example, in suggesting that foreigners in Japan were the cause of violent crime, in referring to China in insulting terms and in saying that he would like to wage war and defeat the Chinese. Controversially, too, he initially, before backing down and apologizing, described the tsunami disaster of 11 March 2011 as a 'divine punishment' (*tenbatsu*) for Japan's moral decline.[29]

He developed a friendship with Kiriyama and, besides going to Yasukuni Shrine with him, delivered the eulogy at Kiriyama's funeral, acclaiming him as a patriot and calling him *sensei* (teacher).[30] Kiriyama and Ishihara engaged in a dialogue (*taidan*) together in the journal *Seiron* in June 2012.[31] *Seiron* is a monthly magazine published by the *Sankei Shinbun* company – the news organization in whose newspaper Agonshū publishes publicity articles such as those cited above. The *Sankei Shinbun* is a conservative newspaper and its publishing arm (which includes *Seiron*) has a reputation for publishing right-wing nationalist and revisionist materials that resonate with the views of groups such as Nippon Kaigi.[32] To that extent Agonshū's use of the *Sankei Shinbun* and its affiliates for its advertisements seems to indicate the potential type of audience it is looking for.[33]

In this *Seiron* discussion Kiriyama, in referring to Ishihara's reference to the March 2011 tsunami as a *tenbatsu* (divine punishment), states that in his view the criticisms directed at him for this were unfair (*hikyō*), and that similar comments were made in the past about previous disasters such as the 1923 Kantō earthquake that killed thousands in the Tokyo region. In Kiriyama's view one had to be aware of the historical meanings and reasons behind natural disasters – a comment that implies that some form of retribution might have been involved, in his view, in the calamity. Those who did not pay full attention to caring for their ancestor spirits would not be able to improve their lives – a point that reiterated Agonshū's beliefs about the relationship between the spirits of the dead and the situation of people in this world. It also dovetails with Ishihara's (pre-apology) interpretation of the tsunami disaster as having a moral foundation; Ishihara had said that the 'divine punishment' occurred because Japanese people were becoming selfish and greedy. Kiriyama's statement that those who did not pay full attention to the ancestors would not be able to live full lives appears to reiterate, in a slightly different mode, this view by implying that ignoring or not paying proper attention to the ancestors is a sign of greed and selfishness that incurs retribution.

Since Kiriyama's death, senior figures in the movement have reiterated the movement's connections to Shinto, and reinforced the nationalist views that Kiriyama had articulated. In an interview in Sankei Square (an online publication of the *Sankei*

Shinbun company) after Kiriyama's death and in connection with an Agonshū memorial service for the spirits of the Japanese war dead, Wada Naoko, the administrative head of the movement, said that Kiriyama had informed her that if he had not been invalided out of the war, he might have ended up being enshrined at Yasukuni along with his school friends. Although he did not have a familial blood relationship (*ketsuen*) with the souls of war dead, he was part of their bereaved family (*izoku*) because they were the spirits of Japanese people. In other words Kiriyama viewed the war dead as familial ancestors of the Japanese populace as a whole, a point evident also in his comments cited above, about the economic benefits of contemporary Japan emanating from the sacrifices of those who died for their country. According to Wada, Kiriyama emphasized that it was natural for Japanese people to perform memorials for the war dead at Yasukuni Shrine and that he had said that 'Japan would have no future if they forgot to give thanks to those who had died saying "let's meet again at Yasukuni"'.[34] Not long after Kiriyama's death, too, as we discuss in more detail in the next chapter, lectures were being given at Agonshū's centre in Tokyo that reiterated and intensified Kiriyama's comments by appearing to exonerate Japan from blame for the war by portraying it as a noble endeavour against the evils of colonialism while idealizing those who fought as benefactors of the modern nation and affirming the value of visiting Yasukuni Shrine. Japan itself was referred to in strikingly nationalistic terms as a 'divine country/country of the (Shinto) gods' (*shinkoku*) in Agonshū publications such as the Agonshū Magazine members' magazine of March–April 2017 (Agonshū 2017, 3–4: 37). These declarations, as well as the dialogue with Ishihara, showed the extent to which nationalist sentiments of the type Ishihara represented had become part of Kiriyama's own thinking, and how, in recent years, Agonshū appeared to share common ground with the agendas of rightist nationalist political organizations.

Pacifying the spirits and bringing them home

Agonshū's focus on Japan was clearly emphasized, as we described in Chapter 3, in the 2012 Hoshi Matsuri and related events in which the movement prayed for Japan's revival after the tsunami tragedy. While praying for Japan's revival was understandable in the context of the disasters and something that religious movements across the country had engaged in, the ways in which such messages were developed – with invocations of Japanese myths, and talk of reviving the Japanese spirit and developing a new civilization (*bunmei*) – were indicative of Agonshū's nationalistic direction of travel in the last years of the founder's life. This can be seen also in its overseas rituals for the spirits of the dead, both in Kiriyama's life and subsequently. As we indicated earlier, these began with rituals for those who died in the Pacific region during the Second World War and expanded to include rituals in various locations around the world, including those with potent symbolic dimensions such as Auschwitz and Jerusalem. The geographical spread along with a broad emphasis on the spirits of the dead appeared to indicate the universalism of Agonshū's message; even if operating within Japanese frameworks of thought its pacification rituals were for all those unhappy spirits whose lives were ruptured in war.

However, the primary focus of its rituals and the area in which most of them have been held are where Japanese military lost their lives. Moreover, several of its more recent overseas rituals appear to have focused specifically on the Japanese war dead. In 2007, for example, Agonshū conducted rites at Khabarovsk in Siberia for the captured Japanese military personnel who died in Russian camps in the war. Japanese military personnel were not the only people who died in such camps in Siberia, but it appears that Agonshū's ritual focused on them and on repatriating their spirits to be enshrined in Japan. According to the English-language section of Agonshū's website the ritual was for 'victims in the concentration camps of Siberia and for world peace'[35] but earlier reports that outlined the movement's plans indicated that its focus was on the Japanese dead[36] while the movement's Japanese-language web pages clearly show that it was for the spirits of approximately 60,000 members of the former Japanese military who were 'interned and sacrificed' in Siberia.[37] It does not mention others who died, just the Japanese.[38]

Nishimura Akira (2013) has drawn attention to the visits (which he views through the lens of pilgrimage) to Pacific War battlefields and areas where Japanese military personnel lost their lives, carried out by bereaved family members and descendants and former soldiers in recent times. Often this involves collecting traces of the dead (e.g. bones and other remains) to bring them back to their Japanese homeland, and in many respects what Agonshū is doing is much the same. It appears to us, based on Kiriyama's comments above about his sense of loss because of friends who died in the war and his motives in memorializing them, that he was, in later years, on a form of personal pilgrimage to perform memorial rituals for the spirits of dead soldiers at various Pacific sites.

The focus on the Japanese fallen – and on conducting rituals in the area around Japan – was emphasized, too, in the rituals Agonshū began to perform at sea in 2012. The first of these was titled the 'Buddhist memorial service on the seas' (*yōjō hōyō*), and involved Kiriyama, then aged 91, boarding a boat in Yokohama harbour along with 570 followers and going on a 7,800-kilometre voyage taking in former war sites in places such as Iwo Jima, the Philippines, Taiwan, Okinawa and Kagoshima, and ending in Kobe. During the voyage rituals for the spirits of the dead were performed at various points. While the English-language web page stated that the rituals were for world peace and the spirits of the war dead who lost their lives in such places, the Japanese-language pages were more specific in indicating that these were the Japanese war dead. Noting that not just soldiers but those in other branches of the military such as sailors and those on merchant ships lost their lives in the conflict Agonshū declared that in this mission it had 'after 67 years brought back to their home country the spirits of the dead'.[39] It also stated that after returning to Japan (*kikokugo*) the spirits were enshrined at Agonshū's temple at Yamashina.[40] The Japanese-language account of the boat ritual thus shows clearly that the focus was on the Japanese dead and on bringing them back to their home country and enshrining them there.

Since the ritual was also said to be for world peace, the implication was that a first step for the realization of world peace was for the Japanese war dead to be appropriately memorialized and pacified. At the time of Kiriyama's death, a plan was afoot to conduct another such sea ritual voyage, this time to the seas north of Japan and to islands once held by Japan but taken over by Russia at the end of the war. This voyage was, according to Agonshū, a reflection of Kiriyama's desire to continue the mission of memorializing the Japanese dead and repatriating them. We will discuss this further (and the voyage itself, which was carried out in July 2017) in the next chapter. Here we note that not only did that subsequent voyage include repatriating the spirits of the Japanese dead but also the *kami* (Shinto deities) who had been left 'homeless' after their shrines had been destroyed after the northern islands mentioned above were absorbed by Russia in 1945. A subsequent fire ritual – its thirtieth in all for 'world peace' according to Agonshū's website – held in Okinawa on 30 November 2015, also indicated the emphasis on Japan, since the themes of the ritual were listed on the website as 'pacifying the nation in face of national difficulties, the power of divine revelation/miracles, and the rebirth of Japan' (*kokunan chingo. shin'i jigen. Nihon shinsei*).[41]

Paradoxical orientations: the nationalism of a universal movement

While Agonshū had a nationalist dimension from early on, this has become increasingly prominent as Kiriyama came to the end of his life and began to talk about the war in revisionist terms, blaming the war on perfidious colonialist foreigners and talking of the war dead as benefactors whose sacrifice aided the nation. While it is difficult to ascertain all the factors behind such increasingly nationalistic orientations, we consider a number of elements played a part. It could in part be a simple progression that was intensified by the sentiments of an ageing leader reflecting on his lost friends in his final years. The interviews, events and comments we have cited in this chapter relate to the very last years of Kiriyama's life, largely from around the time when he reached 90, and the apparent change in his views about the war – from relief at not having to fight to regrets at not so doing – might well be part of a wider reinterpretation of his life as he approached death. It is possible, too, that he was influenced by those around him who assumed greater responsibility for the movement as he became weaker; as we discuss in the next chapter, in his final years Kiriyama was largely a symbolic figure in Agonshū ritual terms, and those around him took more active public roles in the movement. They also, as we show, have intensified the nationalist themes we have outlined in this chapter, suggesting that these themes were as important to those in the upper echelons of the movement around Kiriyama as they were to him.

If this is the case, it would not be unique, for other Japanese religious movements have become more nationalistic in the wake of losing their founders. Nagaoka Takashi (2015) has discussed how, after Nakayama Miki died in 1887, Tenrikyō (influenced by the prevailing sociopolitical winds of the age and the ways in which religious organizations were expected to support state endeavours) became more nationalistic in orientation. Tenrikyō's practice of *hinokishin*, voluntary service for others, was portrayed as patriotic service for the country, while the movement became supportive of the state. Nagaoka contends that these changes were not brought about by state pressures on new movements but because of internal changes in the movement after the death of its charismatic founder, in which its teachings were systematized to be in line with government regulations that required religious doctrines to accord with State Shinto (75–7). We are not suggesting that all new movements in Japan have displayed a turn towards heightened nationalism in response to the demise of their founder, and we do not suggest that this is necessarily a common pattern. However, Nagaoka's study does suggest that such a turn can occur, and our examination of Agonshū appears to reiterate this point.

This nationalistic turn could also be a strategic development to address the problems of a movement that was beginning to age and was finding it hard to get new recruits. By appealing to a tide of nationalism epitomized by the apparent popularity of right-wing nationalists in Japan, and by placing its advertising features in news media associated with the political right, Agonshū appears to be both trying to capitalize on that trend and to cater to the sentiments of a membership that is itself getting older. The earlier Agonshū, as it sought to attract young Japanese in the 1980s, expressed a sense of Japanese importance and mission that was implicitly nationalist but without dealing with the forms of explicit expressions (such as, e.g. visiting Yasukuni Shrine) that might have worried a younger audience. The ageing of the movement and its membership may well have removed any such concerns.

Agonshū's direction of nationalist travel raises a number of issues about nationalism in religious contexts in Japan and about its relationship with themes that Agonshū – like other new religions – has affirmed to be central to its nature, namely, that it offers hope, messages and meaning for all humanity and speaks in universal terms. The views that Kiriyama has expressed in his last years, along with his associations with nationalists such as Ishihara, seem to sit rather awkwardly with the proclaimed stance of a religious leader whose key mission is one of world peace. His comments about Western colonialism that exude a sense of moral indignation over the war and implicitly exonerate Japan from war guilt, his statements that a major factor in his becoming a religious leader was to perform memorials for his friends who died in the war and his regrets at not having been able to fight and die for his country appear contrary to the notions of world peace and salvation that Agonshū proclaims as its universal mission.

To understand this apparent disjunction, one first has to recognize that at root Agonshū is a product of the Japanese environment, that its prime original audience is Japanese, and at present it is struggling to retain followers. As such the importance of its Japanese base becomes ever more acute. Religious movements and traditions in Japan have generally espoused or articulated themes related to issues of identity and meaning within a Japanese framework. Nationalism in various forms and associations between religion, the state and national identity have been a recurrent element in Japanese religious structures historically as well as in the present. Shinto's role in supporting the state and its associations with notions of a special Japanese identity and of myths that portray Japan as a divine and chosen land have been widely discussed, and nationalistic themes remain integral to that tradition.[42] Buddhism, too, has a long history of supporting the state and its structures, and its activities in fomenting an aggressive militaristic nationalism in the period leading up to and during the Second World War have been widely documented.[43]

In such contexts Japanese new religions are not doing anything new. Indeed, by emphasizing nationalist sentiments they are in a real sense identifying themselves as normative in the Japanese religious spectrum. As we noted in Chapter 1, even as Japanese new religions have talked in universal terms with claims of world salvation, their main message and focus has been about Japan and has spoken particularly to a Japanese audience. By offering followers the apparent potential to be part of a world salvation mission through the avenue of Japanese concepts and rituals (as Agonshū has done) followers are offered a sense of meaning in which their Japanese identity is reinforced and given added value by dint of being able to provide meaning and spiritual salvation for the world. Given that they have arisen in a time frame in which Japan has been increasingly engaged with the wider world – and hence has needed to deal with questions about its relationship with and identity in the context of the wider world – it is unsurprising that these issues have been of concern to the new movements that have emerged in the period in which Japan has developed as a modern nation state. Agonshū has dealt with such issues by positing a universal message, portraying its leader as a prophesied saviour at a time of world crisis and offering a message of peace, while asserting that it is because of its position as a Japanese movement that such grand visions can be achieved.

It is a message that was potent in the era when Agonshū first really grew – a period when the image of 'Japan as Number One' reinforced the sense that Japan had a special message for the wider world. Numerous studies have drawn attention to the nationalist themes expressed by movements across the new religions spectrum that were fused with images of universalism in placing Japan at the centre of the world (Pye 1986; Reader 1988, 2002; Shimazono 1997, 2001; Cornille 1999; Berthon and Kashio 2000, Tsukada 2012). Some of these studies have seen this dynamic as a reaction to Japan's earlier war defeat, and the humiliation of occupation that followed. Catherine Cornille (1999), for example, has argued that the nationalism evident in the new religions that sprang to prominence from the 1980s was more pronounced than in earlier new religions, and she links this to the effects of Japan's defeat in 1945. While the centrality of Japan in the worldviews of earlier new religions could be attributed in part to the point that their founders were largely of rural stock and with limited knowledge of the wider world, for movements that developed in the post–Second World War era, according to Cornille, nationalism 'may be regarded as a reactionary attempt to return to the past glory of Japan in the face of the humiliation of defeat in war. The resurgent nationalistic voices in new Japanese religions toward the end of the twentieth century sound distinctly triumphalistic, linking the religious importance of Japan to the country's economic success' (239). Cornille is one of a number of scholars who have drawn attention to how the universalism projected by many new religions centres around notions of Japanese uniqueness and of it being a chosen land: 'While new religions seem to be consciously universalistic in their teaching and scope, many of them gave also developed explicitly nationalistic and ethnocentric teachings regarding Japan as the origin of creation and the cradle of salvation, the Japanese as the chosen people, and Japanese language and culture as a unique vehicle of salvation' (229). Shimazono

(1997, 2001) and Tsukada (2012) have also argued along similar lines, and viewed the new religions of the 1980s as having a particularly strong nationalistic orientation. Tsukada (2012) has emphasized the tendency of many such movements to portray Japan as a chosen land and a fount of spiritual supremacy, something he identifies as evident in Mahikari (in which Japan is a chosen land and the place of origin of the human race) and Kōfuku no Kagaku (145–50). Tsukada argues that Mahikari and Kōfuku no Kagaku base their claims to Japanese spiritual supremacy on different foundations. Mahikari's perspective, in which it draws on myths that place Japan at the spiritual centre of the world, is 'ultratraditional' in that it attaches a distinctive meaning to traditionalism, while Kōfuku no Kagaku is, he contends, 'supratraditional' in that it exhibits a form of Japanese spiritual nationalism (*Nihon seishin nashonarizumu*) (135) in which the spiritual nature of the Japanese provides the foundation for nationalist sentiments and in which Japan's economic prowess (at least up to the Bubble) provided the basis for its emergence as a 'spiritually advanced country' in the global age (149–50). Kōfuku no Kagaku's leader Ōkawa Ryūhō (1995a: 105) has emphasized this point by linking Japan's economic growth to its emergence as what he terms 'the source for the new spiritual movement' (Baffelli 2005). Such themes of spiritual supremacy also can invoke (either explicitly or implicitly) the idea of overturning the dominance of Western civilization (Berthon and Kashio 2000).

Agonshū reflects many of the points made by Cornille and Tsukada. One can see, in its developing narrative about the war, a reactionary revisionist impulse that seeks to counter the humiliation of war defeat and the opprobrium that went with it, by externalizing blame for the war, emphasizing the sacrifice of those who died fighting and making their spiritual well-being central to the mission of peace in the present day. Agonshū also combines aspects of both what Tsukada calls the ultratraditional and the supratraditional. Its incorporation of Shinto images and emphasis on Japanese ritual practices and ideas about the spirits of the dead draw heavily on an ultratraditional reading of the world, and by portraying its main temple as the new epicentre of Buddhism for the world, it is closely allying itself to the idea of a chosen land. It also demonstrates elements of supratraditionalism in that it clearly associates its mission of world salvation with Japan's development as a major power and the economic prowess that enables Agonshū to finance and conduct rituals for peace and make donations to various international institutions that bring it recognition on a wider stage.

Acquisitional nationalism and retrenchment

There is also a further aspect that we think aptly describes Agonshū's universalistic and Japan-centric views. In its dealings with the wider world we consider that Agonshū has been engaged in a process of what we term 'acquisitional nationalism' – a process of acquiring recognition in both symbolic and material forms from overseas that is used to enhance its image and self-representation as a Japanese movement speaking to a Japanese audience. Over the years it and its founder have acquired a variety of objects and honours from overseas. From honorary titles given by international academic institutions to special ordinations and titles from various Buddhist organizations outside Japan, Agonshū has developed a dynamic in which the international and global world is acquired and brought to Japan for the purpose of enhancing the movement's Japanese base. In the period in which Kiriyama has acquired honorary titles and recognition – widely emphasized in Agonshū's publications and its website – from international academic bodies, he increasingly articulated nationalist revisionist messages about the war and focused on Japanese spirits of the dead as the key to Agonshū's practice.

The acquisition of Buddhist titles and objects from outside Japan has also helped in this process. The *shinsei busshari* relic from Sri Lanka is portrayed in Agonshū as being given in recognition of its position as the purveyor of original Buddhism. In the 1990s Kiriyama also received honorary titles from Sri Lankan Buddhist temples and a sapling grafted from the Bodhi tree (itself said to be an offshoot of the original tree at Bodh Gaya, under which the Buddha gained enlightenment) at Tantirimale Raja Maha Temple in Sri Lanka that was replanted at Agonshū's temple in Japan.[44] He received an *abhisheka* initiation from monks from Sri Lanka at an Agonshū event celebrating the New Year festival and Kiriyama's birthday that one of us attended in 2014. Agonshū has cultivated links with Bhutanese Buddhists in recent years and through such links Kiriyama was, in 2010 and 2011, awarded a number of titles and ranks in the Bhutanese Buddhist tradition. Agonshū has brought Bhutanese Buddhist monks and performers to Japan to participate in rituals and public performances, and in 2015 it opened a Bhutan Hall within its main temple complex; the Bhutanese monks in attendance at the opening ceremony along with representatives of the Bhutanese government also present were invited guests of the movement.[45] Bhutanese monks were also present and performed rituals at the 2017 Hoshi Matsuri, when a mandala from Bhutan was displayed on the main altar.

Kiriyama commented, on the opening of the Bhutan Hall, that Agonshū's aim in developing links with Bhutanese Buddhists was to draw on the main branches of Buddhism in order to develop a more holistic and complete form of the tradition.[46] Yet Agonshū's focus is clearly not simply on incorporating or bringing to Japan elements of other Buddhist cultures, as the ritual events involving Mayan figures (see Chapter 3) and the building of a Jerusalem Peace and Friendship Square at its main temple indicate. It has sought to build an image of international recognition by going beyond Buddhist institutions and bringing people from outside the Buddhist world to perform at its rituals. While it has developed links with other Buddhist cultures as part of a drive to build a complete Buddhism, these have occurred during the period when Agonshū has manifested increasingly nationalistic orientations, developed links to Shinto and to Japanese nationalists and focused on praying for the spirits of the Japanese military war dead and repatriating their spirits to Japan. In the next chapter, too, we note that these dynamics – not simply towards an increasingly Japan-centric focus but to one that at times appears almost exclusively concerned with Japanese interests – have continued and may have intensified since Kiriyama's death.

Agonshū in the 1980s appeared to be projecting itself as an international, universal movement with a Japanese core, based in Japanese ideas and rituals and with a confidence in the special nature and mission of its leader and of Japan in spreading Buddhism to the world, thereby solving world problems, averting millennial upheavals and bringing about world peace. It appeared to reach out and engage in a variety of overseas activities, building on Japan's economic power and using its own wealth to facilitate such engagements, while its messages of a universal mission world salvation appeared to resonate with the popular mood in Japan. As its support has receded and Japan's sense of confidence has been affected by decades of stagnation and other problems, Agonshū has turned inward, moving from the idea of spreading outwards via a mission of world salvation from Japan to the world at large, to bringing back to Japan the spirits of the Japanese dead and paying increased attention to symbols of Japanese nationalism and identity. The theme of world peace may still be articulated in Agonshū rituals (especially, we note, in its English language publicity) but this apparent goal now appears – as the boat voyage rituals outlined above indicate – to be less prominent in its Japanese publications, and to revolve increasingly around the idea that universal aims can only be achieved by focusing on specifically Japanese concerns, worshipping at Yasukuni Shrine and articulating nationalist messages. In such contexts universalism appears to be on some levels a veneer that helped Agonshū develop an international profile through which it could enhance its standing in Japan, and through which it could acquire items of international recognition and domesticate them to reinforce the messages of implicit superiority that lie behind the nationalist rhetoric with which it has associated itself.

We do not see Agonshū's acquisitional nationalism and overseas activities primarily as an example of the globalizing dimensions of the movement as it takes its message and practices overseas, to a global audience and market. While Agonshū has tried, via its engagements overseas, to export its message, this has hardly borne fruit in terms of overseas recruitment, and it has been subservient to the more dominant theme of enhancing Agonshū's standing and support in Japan. This is evident in an increasing focus on repatriating Japanese spirits and performing rituals for dead Japanese soldiers and sailors, along with Agonshū's increased links to Shinto and expressions of Japanese nationalism. This in turn indicates a repatriating of Agonshū's core identity as a Japanese movement in which nationalist messages have overtaken the idea of spreading Agonshū to the world. What has been happening in recent years in Agonshū appears not so much a process of globalization in terms of developing new forms through global encounters – something that has occurred in some Japanese religious contexts[47] – as of retrenchment and nationalistic introversion, in which Agonshū's encounters with the global have become focused on a process of acquisition that reinforces the local and intensifies its sense of Japanese identity. Agonshū initially went abroad with its rituals and messages in its early days of expansion in Japan, but it has turned inwards as it has aged and as its founder came to revisit his memories of the past and realign them with those of revisionist nationalists such as Ishihara. This in turn has helped develop a backward-looking atmosphere in the movement, one that has been enhanced further by the death of its founder and the repercussions of that event. It is to such matters that we turn next.

5

Transcending Death: The Birth and Spiritual Messages of the Second Buddha

Introduction: dealing with the death of a founder

The death of Kiriyama in August 2016 represented a major rite of passage for Agonshū. It was already facing a dilemma that confronts movements when their charismatic founder ages and appears less able to perform the roles or show the dynamism they previously did. Even if they can still make use of the founder's presence, as Agonshū did in Kiriyama's later years when, although visibly weak, he continued to appear at ritual events, the loss of visible vitality may cause problems. Death presents an even greater dilemma. What happens when the figure whose insights and communications with spiritual realms provide the foundations of the movement's truth claims is no longer physically present to provide a direct link with the spiritual realm?

Once the founder dies, the movement has to deal both with the loss of physical presence and the problem of how to regard the deceased figure. It also may face problems of succession and secession – something that has occurred frequently among Japanese religious movements in modern times. Once the leader departs, the question of how to continue the movement and who, if any, might be able to manifest the attributes needed to do so becomes a moot question. As Christal Whelan has stated, after the death of the funder, 'acute tension gives way to an actual crisis as contention arises over the true spiritual heir of the religion' (2015 online).

Whelan was writing particularly about GLA after the death of its founder Takahashi Shinji. Prior to his death Takahashi had conferred the mantle of leadership on his 19-year-old daughter, Keiko, but her succession was opposed by many in the movement, who claimed that when he did this Takahashi had been extremely ill and was unable to act rationally, as a result of which his choice was invalid. A number of secessions and defections occurred led by senior devotees who felt they had more right to succession than Keiko; GLA's Kansai branch, one of the movement's greatest strongholds during Takahashi Shinji's lifetime, split off as a result. So, too, did Chino Shōhō who, believing she should inherit Takahashi's mantle, seceded to found Panawave Laboratory. Although GLA has subsequently stabilized under Keiko's leadership – which has succeeded in strengthening it overall – the Kansai branch of GLA remains separate (Whelan 2015).

Another example is Mahikari, where Okada Kōtama's death led to a conflict between his adopted daughter Okada Sachiko and a senior disciple, Sekiguchi Sakae, each claiming to have been designated by Okada as the new leader. As a result the movement split initially into two and later, with another secession, into three separate parts (Davis 1980: 2–5; Reader 1991: 20). Tenrikyō, Oomoto, Sekai Kyūseikyō and Reiyūkai, just to name religious movements commonly included in the category of the 'new', have all faced secessions and seen new movements emerge out of their organizations.[1] Secessions are not uncommon, in other words, and, as the examples of Mahikari and GLA indicate, while the charisma of a founder may be highly valued while s/he is alive, it can be challenged when the founder becomes subject to the normative human conditions of infirmity and mortality. Those with aspirations to leadership – perhaps because they viewed themselves as chosen or the most senior disciples – may in such cases seek to restrict the founder's charismatic authority by, for example, depicting him or her as not being capable of conferring leadership on a successor.

How a movement deals with the loss of its foundational inspiration, the extent to which it remains focused on that founder after death or feels it needs to move on and establish new parameters are all crucial issues at this stage. The path those who are leading Agonshū in the aftermath of Kiriyama's death have chosen has been to focus on Kiriyama as if he were continuing to lead the movement from the spiritual realms and to use that spiritual leadership as a way of maintaining the solidarity of the movement and, simultaneously, of affirming their own legitimacy. Their strategy has been to preserve and enhance Kiriyama's charisma by transforming him from being a human founder into an enlightened Buddha who remains a continuing presence and guiding light in the movement, and who continues to transmit spiritual messages to them. This appears, at least initially, to have avoided any significant secessions or overt conflicts thus far, although provoking some unease online by people claiming to be unhappy Agonshū members.[2]

Not only has the movement used Kiriyama after death as a stabilizing element and, in effect, its continuing leader, but it has also elevated him into its de facto main focus of veneration. We identify this process as 'losing the leader, and preserving, elevating and transforming the founder', and suggest that it represents a response often found in charismatic movements, of spiritually transforming a leader and placing him/her on a level beyond the human. This tends to happen when the movement is still young, and often within the first generation of leadership, when a founder, having initially been portrayed primarily as a teacher and prophet, then acquires the status of a saviour or something more exalted. As we discussed in Chapter 2, such figures might also be perceived, in their lifetimes, a living deity or a manifestation of a Buddha. In other cases it is after death that elevation to a higher spiritual level occurs; Agonshū is an example here, for while Kiriyama was regarded in high esteem, as the successor to Shakyamuni and a world saviour, and accorded respect that was tantamount to veneration in life, it has been after he died that he has become an actual figure and object of worship. His charisma has been memorialized and, through the enshrinement of his relics, preserved as a material presence, while he continues to be portrayed as a living spiritual entity and key source of authority guiding the movement.

In examining these issues through the lens of Agonshū, we also ask further questions. One is whether transforming the founder into a focus of veneration alters the dynamic and nature of movements, making them potentially backward looking, nostalgic and more focused on the past than the present and future. Another is the extent to which this makes movements more introverted, conservative and focused on the cultures from which they emerge, suggesting a turn away from universal messages towards an enhanced focus on reaffirmations of cultural particularism. This, we suggest, is especially pertinent in the context of Japanese new religions, which often have a strong emphasis on issues of Japanese identity and nationalism. As the previous chapter indicated, as it has aged, Agonshū has become more oriented towards nationalist themes, and in this chapter we look at how the loss of the founder may be exacerbating this tendency. Another issue we discuss is why Agonshū's post-Kiriyama leadership has chosen to portray him in the ways it has, as a realized Buddha seemingly more exalted than the original Buddha.

At the service of his followers: the leader in his final years

Even as Kiriyama became increasingly frail he continued to play a public role in Agonshū's rituals. Although Agonshū officials we have spoken to insist that Kiriyama remained fully active in the movement right up to the time of his death, our observations suggest something different. Agonshū produces videos of its ritual events that can be watched at Agonshū centres and these often show him in his later years not speaking or doing much apart from a few hand gestures or being lifted by officials to bestow a cursory benediction. We have also observed this at rituals we have attended. For example, at the *meitokusai* ritual event at Tokyo centre on 16 May 2012, instead of the usual live ritual, a video was shown of Kiriyama performing a memorial service (*kuyō*) for dead soldiers from a boat (one of the events discussed in Chapter 4). Kiriyama looked very weak and fragile, an image that could not be more different from the images of a younger and physically strong leader that occupied most of Agonshū's magazines in the 1980s. Similarly, at the *hatsugoma* ritual at Agonshū's Tokyo centre in January 2014 Kiriyama (93 years old at the time) was unable to deliver a sermon coherently, reading the same lines again a number of times. We witnessed a similar scene during the *kuyō* rituals in July of the same year. In his later years he appeared to be more of a presiding spirit than an active performer, remaining seated and passive as other officials carried out the *goma* rituals, before he was physically carried forward to perform brief ritual blessings at the end.[3]

Agonshū tailored and amended its rituals accordingly because of his increasingly weakened state. The Hoshi Matsuri had become shorter for such reasons; in the previous chapter we mentioned that the event in recent years has started later and ended earlier than in the 1980s. While one factor in making it shorter was that the crowds had become smaller than in Agonshū's heyday of the late 1980s, a prime reason was that, as Agonshū officials have confirmed to us, in his later years Kiriyama was unable to last the whole day.

The ageing of the founder also had an emotional effect on followers, who were clearly aware of his physical frailty and potential demise. Attendees at Agonshū rituals in Kiriyama's latter years said that they had made special efforts to attend because it might be the last time they ever saw him.[4] At Kiriyama's funeral in October 2016, Agonshū broadcast films of ritual performances in earlier eras, notably the 1980s, and many members were crying at the images of their founder in his younger, more dynamic days. Showing such films in itself suggested a sense of nostalgia for those days, while the emotions devotees demonstrated might well also have been tinged with their own feelings not just for the younger, more dynamic Kiriyama but for a similar period in their own lives.

Agonshū thus reformulated its ritual performances towards the end of Kiriyama's life in ways that relieved him of his previous levels of involvement, but which also maintained his presence for followers and gave the rituals his charismatic imprimatur. As such, in his later years, rather than directing the movement, he was at the service of his followers and of those who ran the movement's everyday operations. To that extent we would suggest he had moved from being the prime ritual performer to being the major ritual presence in Agonshū ceremonies. After death, the ritualization of his presence has continued, with Kiriyama transformed into an ever-present spiritual and (via his relics) physical entity at the service of the movement.

From exalted human to living spiritual presence

Although Kiriyama's sermons and teachings portrayed him as a role model whose path anyone could follow and stated that followers could be like him and overcome their problems, cut their karma and achieve great things, in reality there was a gulf of difference between him and his followers. There was a constant emphasis in Agonshū on his special nature as the founder, teacher and discoverer of the inner truths of original Buddhism. It was *he* who received the transmission from Shakyamuni, *he* who was the saviour prophesied by Nostradamus and *he* who was the person who could carry out important rituals to eradicate members' karmic hindrances. It was he who presided over the Hoshi Matsuri, formulated Agonshū's teachings and dominated its publications. This clearly created a cult of personality around Kiriyama (Benod 2013: 156–8) that was reinforced by the ways in which, as we noted in Chapter 2, Agonshū portrayed him as someone with a multiplicity of skills and talents beyond those of ordinary followers. The titles and honours he acquired from universities and Buddhist lineages from other countries similarly marked him out.

Yet even if Kiriyama had attained an advanced spiritual level, could perceive the spiritual presence of numerous deities and was on familiar spiritual terms with the Buddha, he was still a human being. Unlike the founders of many Japanese new religions, he was not portrayed while alive as a living god (*ikigami*) or a living Buddha (*ikibotoke*). In one of our first interviews with Agonshū officials, in July 1987, on asking about Kiriyama's status the response was unequivocal: he was a human being, not an *ikibotoke* (living Buddha), a response we have heard from ordinary members as well. Unlike figures such as Ōkawa Ryūhō of Kōfuku no Kagaku, who claimed to be the founding deity of this world, El Cantāre, and the eternal Buddha, Kiriyama did not proclaim himself to be a Buddha, deity or similarly transcendent spiritual being.[5]

Nor did Kiriyama or Agonshū seek to enhance his status by claiming, during his lifetime, that he had had exalted past lives and incarnations. Kiriyama (1993, 2000a) claimed to have developed clairvoyant powers and the ability to perceive the past lives of people, abilities he used to discern the karmic forces from previous lives that might afflict people suffering in this realm. Yet he did not make public claims about his own past lives, even though (from his assertions about his powers of clairvoyance) he claimed the ability to perceive such things. While he did at times refer to Koizumi Futoshinomikoto's claim that he was Susanoo reincarnated (Kiriyama 2005; see also Chapter 4) and we have heard that Kiriyama had claimed a connection to Susanoo on occasion,[6] he does not appear to have made direct and specific public claims on this matter. There is nothing in his writings on reincarnation to this effect, or, indeed, towards claiming any special past status for himself.[7] This contrasts with other leaders from the 1980s such as Ōkawa Ryūhō or Asahara Shōkō, who not only claimed the power to discern previous lives but used that power to elevate their own past status. Ōkawa, for instance, claimed numerous grand previous incarnations, such as being the Greek god Hermes (Numata 1995: 191–205; Winter 2013), while Aum Shinrikyō's Asahara had, in previous lives, been Imtophep, the creator of the Pyramids, and the Buddha Maitreya (Asahara and Yamaori 1992: 95).[8] It has only been in death that Kiriyama appears to have transcended his previous human condition.

Preparations, death and response

It is clear that the movement had paid some attention to the issue of succession while Kiriyama was alive. We first learnt of this in July 1987, during lengthy interviews with Agonshū figures in Tokyo at a time when Kiriyama was very active and seemingly at the height of his powers. When asked about future succession, officials did not shy away from the question and replied that he would be succeeded from within the organization, but that Kiriyama's charisma was his alone and would not transfer to others. However, officials stated, the movement would continue to be blessed with great spiritual force, since it had the *shinsei busshari* – Shakyamuni's relic, the living presence of the Buddha – and this would serve thereafter as the movement's focus, source of authority and spiritual power. Shakyamuni, in other words, would be Agonshū's main image of worship and its living charismatic presence. Subsequently, in 2014, a follow-up interview with Agonshū representatives also indicated that there was no designated successor and that the movement would be run by a board of senior members when Kiriyama departed. The position, therefore, appeared not to have changed between 1987 and 2014. Nor does there appear to have been any official announcement from Kiriyama while alive about succession. It would appear that from early on it was understood that there would be no direct successor and that the focus of charismatic and spiritual power in Agonshū would be placed in its main object of worship. At the same time it is not beyond the bounds of speculation that the lack of a clearly designated successor may also have been a source of tension in the group and made those running it uneasy.

We certainly sense that his death caused problems, given that Agonshū took some time to publicly react to or announce the death. He died on 29 August 2016, but the death was not made public until two weeks later, on 12 September, when a number of newspapers reported the news.[9] Members we have talked to appeared as unaware as the general public that their founder had died, only finding out just before the public announcement was made.[10] Agonshū's official website was not updated and even some time after his death continued to mention future events, such as the 2017 Hoshi Matsuri, at which Kiriyama would preside and referring to him in ways that implied he was still alive.[11] *Agon Magazine*, the movement's Japanese-language bimonthly members' magazine of September–October 2016, made no mention of his demise[12] and even after the death had become public knowledge the movement appeared to say little about the matter. When one of us visited an Agonshū centre in Kyushu on 1 October 2016, during the usual first of the month fire ritual (*Tsuitachi engi hōshō goma*) there was no evident sign at the centre that the leader had passed away and the members participated in the ritual transmitted on screen as they had done on previous occasions. The priest celebrating the rituals only very briefly mentioned the leader's departure in his speech, and the funeral ceremony on 16 October was announced among other event announcements at the end, but without specific details about its schedule. Even several months after his death Agonshū's official website appeared not to register the death and funeral. In its profile of Kiriyama even as late as July 2017 the last event recorded was the award of a peace prize to Kiriyama in 2016; the website's list of 'news' (*oshirase*) at this time included events such as an annual Go contest sponsored by Agonshū in which the prize is the Kiriyama Cup, reports on the annual Agonshū ceremony at the National Cemetery in June 2016 and an announcement about the June 2017 National Cemetery ceremony. It contained no mention of his death or funeral.

This does not mean that Agonshū was in denial over the death. To some extent, the absence of information on its website might simply be a manifestation of something we referred to in Chapter 4, about the movement not being particularly in touch with the most modern technological developments. Agonshū acknowledged his death with the aforementioned announcement at the 1 October ritual, and in reports released to the media, and it held a funeral on 16 October 2017, while at subsequent events such as the Hoshi Matsuri of 2017 not only was his death acknowledged but his relics were memorialized and enshrined. As we indicate below, the way that his death has been interpreted and a posthumous role developed for him suggests that the delay in public announcements might have been in order to organize a strategy and develop an understanding in the movement about the founder's posthumous role.

A narrative has emerged to counter any suggestion that in his last years he had ceased to be active in any sense other than as a visibly weakened presence carried in by helpers to add lustre to Agonshū rituals. In interviews with different Agonshū officials in February 2017, they insisted that he remained alert until the end. One stated that Kiriyama's handshake remained firm, that he continued to be lucid and to give sermons right up to the time of his death and that he had died on his way back to Agonshū's headquarters after having given a sermon in Hokkaidō. According to this official, Kiriyama knew when he was going to die and had said it would be by the end of August. He had, it would appear from this narrative, chosen the time to go.[13] An article in Sankei Square reported that Kiriyama continued to carry out various engagements, including his annual act of veneration at Yasukuni Shrine and at the National Cemetery as well as visiting various parts of the country before, on 29 August 2016, giving a peaceful smile in front of his followers and dying.[14]

Whether this is a hagiographic narrative developed subsequent to the event to create the impression of someone who, despite the visible signs of ageing evident to observers, never lost his vitality and who could foresee and choose the time of his own death[15] is unclear. However, it is clear that an underlying message within the narrative that has developed around his death is of a leader who remained in touch to the very end even as he was aware of his imminent death.

The narrative does, however, appear to be at odds with the apparent time it took to make any sort of public announcement about the death. When we have asked why it took so long to make the death publicly known, we have been told that this was in order for Agonshū to make appropriate preparations for dealing with the situation. However, we have not been able to ascertain why it would take two weeks to do this, not simply because of Kiriyama's age and frailty but because the above narrative implies that Kiriyama (and presumably those around him, if as the Agonshū narrative insists he remained capable of communications) knew when his time was coming to an end. What the delay between his death and its public announcement suggests to us is that Agonshū's active leadership was struggling to work out how to deal with the most significant event in its recent history, while also seeking to retain its authority in this transition period. At a critical point in its trajectory Agonshū's leaders had to choose how to legitimate their own succession. Even if the plan had been for senior figures already highly placed in the movement to continue in charge, they needed to show that their assumption of authority was legitimate and reassure the membership at this time of unease.

From the evidence available thus far, they have chosen to do this by using Kiriyama's own voice – from beyond the grave – and by co-opting his charismatic authority in this process. The comments we heard from senior officials that Kiriyama was in good spirits and lucid until the very end, and the Sankei Square report that he smiled at those around him at the last moment of his life, provides a narrative that guards against the sort of arguments and accusations that emerged in GLA in 1976, when senior disciples, aggrieved at the accession of his young daughter, argued that Takahashi Shinji could not have been in the appropriate state of mind to properly ordain a successor. It also helps protect the image of Kiriyama as a spiritually advanced being, preserving an aura around him that not only counters any suggestion that he might have become weak and lost his personal powers but actually enhances his power by showing he chose when to leave his body. Ensuring that a charismatic figure is not seen to be weak and reduced to the all-too-human state of age and infirmity is a viable strategy for both preserving charismatic status and ensuring that a founder or leader can be transformed into something even more potent at death. This strategy appears, at present, to be used by Sōka Gakkai regarding its leader Ikeda Daisaku, who is now in his nineties, and who has not been seen in public since 2010. This lack of visibility has in turn raised questions of whether he is simply incapable through infirmity to appear in the public gaze, or whether senior figures around him have taken the decision to not expose him because of his frailty and instead to preserve his aura by emphasizing his writings.[16]

In the case of Agonshū, the group did not withdraw the leader from view but instead exposed his frail and aged body to members until the very end. This, we think, was because Agonshū has constantly placed so much emphasis on the performance of rituals that withdrawing their chief ritual performer would have created a greater image of infirmity, fallibility and weakness than would keeping him, in his enfeebled state, in public view. Kiriyama was central not just to Agonshū's teaching but the public performances around which much of the interest in the movement had been built. He was, in effect, the embodiment of his teaching. As we discussed in Chapter 3, Agonshū's doctrine focuses on the idea of 'cutting karma' in order to liberate negative influences by spirits causing illness and misfortunes. As we showed in Chapter 2, Kiriyama's life history has become a representation of this teaching, showing how he was able to overcome several misfortunes to cut his karma. Similarly, the narrative of his body being strong and his mind being fully alert until the very end provides a final (and decisive) proof about the validity of his teachings. In order to do this, he needed to be publicly visible, even if weak, with his weakness simultaneously denied. In this process it appears that in order to support the charismatic relationship between the leader and his followers, the leader's body needed, both in its physical sense and in its 'glorified' aspect (by which we mean how it is perceived and interpreted by members), to be put on display, controlled (and finally owned) by the organization. By exposing the leader's body and by its glorification, 'tension can be maintained in the followers' emotional connection with their leader' (Huang 2009: 39).

Funeral and aftermath

Kiriyama's funeral service was held at Agonshū's temple at Yamashina on 16 October 2016. The ceremony (called *Agonshūsō*, Agonshū funeral rite) was scheduled to start at 1 p.m. and an impressive crowd from all over Japan and also from overseas came to say goodbye to their leader. They started arriving at the site several hours in advance and were asked to register and then told where to sit. Along with the seats inside the temple, attendees started filling a tent outside the temple and other areas that were set up nearby with television screens to broadcast the ritual from inside the temple. All participants wore black, as is customary for funeral services in Japan. However, the event was organized more as a celebration than a mourning ceremony; the emphasis on celebration was to become clearer in later months (see below) when the event came to be portrayed in Agonshū not as a death but as a transformation and as the beginning of a new era of empowerment. The ceremony (unusually for a Japanese funeral) started with music and dance performances, including *gagaku* (imperial court music often used in Shinto rituals) and *taiko* drums. A video of Kiriyama's life in Agonshū was played to remind attendees the reason for the ceremony, and many started crying. The chanting during the rituals were performed by monks from different Buddhist denominations and from China, Sri Lanka and Bhutan, while the memorial fire ritual, called *Agonshū kaiso Kiriyama Seiyū Daisōjō Agonshūsō Gomahōsō* (Agonshū Memorial Fire Buddhist Memorial Service for the Great Priest Kiriyama Seiyū Founder of Agonshū) was performed by Fukada Seia, who has been designated the official leader (*kanchō*) of the movement and is its chief ritual officer. Following this a member of Agonshū's board of governors, representing all members, expressed their gratitude (*hōon kansha*) and good intentions (*kokorozashi*) towards Kiriyama.

The ceremony continued with Ishihara Shintarō, the well-known right-wing former governor of Tokyo who, as we mentioned in Chapter 4, had close links with Kiriyama, delivering a eulogy describing Kiriyama as a great patriot. The celebration continued with a long list of condolences affirming the greatness of the leader, including messages from the former President of Taiwan and political and religious representatives from Bhutan, Israel, China and Sri Lanka, as well as from Japanese Shinto shrine priests and institutions, including Yasukuni Shrine. Other organizations (such as the Japanese national broadcaster NHK) and academic institutions (including the University of San Francisco and SOAS University of London) also sent messages of condolence. This long list served to affirm to the audience that their deceased leader was a recognized authority in both the secular and religious domains nationally and internationally. After the main ceremony, attendees were invited to enter the temple building where Kiriyama's embalmed body, dressed in ritual clothes, was displayed in a glass coffin. Attendees were given the opportunity to 'worship the founder' (*kaiso reihai*) and they queued until late at night in order to say a final goodbye. Members who attended the service later posted comments online about the emotions that were stirred and the tears they shed at seeing their deceased leader for the last time.[17] On this occasion too, just as it had in the various rituals at which the frail Kiriyama had been present in his final years of life, the exposure of the physical body of the leader played a central role in creating a community of emotions with and between members. It also demonstrated that his body was still intact – something that helped Kiriyama's subsequent transformation. Afterwards he was cremated (as is normal in Japan) and his relics collected and placed in a reliquary that has now become an object of veneration in the movement.

The death meant that a new leader (*kanchō*) had to be named, and the person who assumed this role, as was mentioned earlier, was Fukada Seia, an ordained Agonshū priest in his eighties who had been performing major ritual roles in the movement for some time. Wada Naoko, who had been the movement's administrative head (*rijichō*) while Kiriyama was alive, continued in that role. According to various members we have talked to, she runs the organization and is the chief driving force behind the movement now; she also performed the first ringing of the bell used to usher out the old and welcome in the New Year of 2017 and led Agonshū's New Year's celebrations (*Agon Magazine* 2017, 1/2: 1). Other figures in Agonshū have also been visually prominent in the period since Kiriyama's death, including ordained Agonshū priests such as Kiyokawa Hakuhō, who have conducted various rituals and delivered talks (see below) outlining the movement's teachings and presenting its interpretations of Kiriyama's post-death status.[18]

While Fukada has been designated as the official leader, he does not have (at the time of writing) the same levels of authority or ranks and titles that Kiriyama had in life; while Fukada is simply *kanchō* (leader) and is referred to as Fukada Seia Shōsōjō (literally, 'junior priest') Kiriyama was *kanchō geika* (the latter word meaning 'his holiness') and Kiriyama Daisōjō (great priest). Kiriyama's continuing superior status was evident at the 2017 Hoshi Matsuri; Fukada had a seat before the pyres and altar from where he physically conducted the rituals, but this was overshadowed by another chair on a dais above where he sat (Figure 5.1). The empty chair conveyed a clear message; this was Kiriyama's seat, the place from whence he had presided over past festivals and rituals and where, even in death, he continued to preside. As such, Kiriyama remained present in spirit not just on the altar where his relics were enshrined, but in the ritual arena, where Agonshū paid homage to him through the symbolism of the empty chair above that of the physically present new leader Fukada. Not only that but the empty chair faced the altar where his relics were being enshrined; the proceedings were also broadcast on a large screen overlooking the ritual arena and at one point an image from behind Kiriyama's empty seat was displayed on the screen as his relics were being placed on the altar. The image was striking; Kiriyama was not just presiding in spirit over the entire ritual but was watching himself be enshrined. In death, Kiriyama was as present and in charge of the festival as he had been in life. We will return to the 2017 Hoshi Matsuri shortly.

Kiriyama's presence has also been evident in other Agonshū's ceremonies and rituals in the months after his death. Agonshū's first fire ritual ceremony of the year (the *hatsugoma*) was, according to Agonshū's website, overseen by Kiriyama's protective spirit (*reiryoku shugo*)[19] while, at the 1 October 2016 *hatsugoma* the monk who oversaw the ritual ended by briefly mentioning that Kiriyama had passed away,

Figure 5.1 Fukada at the Hoshi Matsuri in 2017 and Kiriyama's empty chair. Photo by Ian Reader.

concluded by asking everyone to recite the five chants (*sa zaruzō* and so on) that Kiriyama used to conclude his sermons and *hatsugoma* rituals. Kiriyama's legacy was thus being continued with ritual officials and worshippers alike repeating what he did.

Communicating from beyond the grave: the founder's spirit speaks

The transformation of Kiriyama and of his charismatic authority has accelerated since his death. Stories circulated among members about miraculous happenings surrounding the funeral, with one person posting online comments about seeing a golden dragon spirit hovering above the founder's body as if to protect it, and other posters referring to miraculous events performed by Kiriyama at his funeral.[20]

His relics became a focus of veneration with the power to bestow blessings on worshippers, and around four months after his death, after an initial period of apparent silence, his spirit began to deliver messages to senior figures in the movement that have been recorded and relayed to members via Agonshū publications. Since his death Kiriyama has been referred to in Agonshū as the *kaiso* (with, as we noted above, followers being asked to 'worship the founder' [*kaiso reihai*] at the end of his funeral).[21] The spirit messages he delivers are known as the *kaiso reiyu* (The founder's spiritual instructions) and collectively they emphasize his continuing presence in the movement, affirm his position as its spiritual leader and are delivered using his posthumous name and title Kongō Seiyū (see also below).

According to Agonshū officials we have questioned, Kiriyama's spirit expresses these messages to senior figures in the movement, with the implication that he speaks not to one single person but at least to two senior figures.[22] The notion that a deceased founder can remain spiritually present as a guiding spirit and that s/he can continue to transmit messages to followers is a phenomenon found in other religious movements besides Agonshū. The founder of Byakkō Shinkōkai, Goi Masahisa, for example, continued to transmit messages to the movement via a senior female disciple, Saionji Masami, who thus occupied the titular leadership of the movement, while Goi remained as its guiding spirit (Pye 1986). Agonshū's current leaders, in communicating with Kiriyama and invoking his spirit to transmit messages and encourage followers, are thus doing something that is by no means new in the Japanese religious environment, where claims of receiving spirit messages from past figures are not uncommon.[23] Indeed they are following the path set out by Kiriyama himself, in his claim to have received a spiritual communication from the historical Buddha at Sahet Mahet entrusting him with the mission of spreading Buddhism to the rest of the world. As such the Sahet Mahet message was not just the transmission of the mantle of Buddhism from Shakyamuni to Kiriyama and evidence that sacred figures who have achieved nirvana can continue to communicate with the living, but also the foundation of the subsequent transmission of authority to the next generation of leaders in Agonshū. It also plays a significant role in the ways that Agonshū seeks to represent Kiriyama in his post-death manifestation.

What appears to be the first *kaiso reiyu* message appeared towards the end of 2016. This was printed on plain paper, in an eighteen-page document dated December

2016 and circulated to members by Agonshū.[24] It does not indicate why Kiriyama is communicating from beyond the grave or through whom he is speaking. The message begins by stating that there are two types of nirvana (full enlightenment): nirvana in this body (*uyoe*) and after death (*muyoe*). Kiriyama[25] informed followers in this message that he had achieved the former (nirvana in this body); on 29 August 2016 (i.e. the day he died) he left his physical body, entered complete nirvana and ascended to the highest spiritual realm, namely, the Buddha realm (*bukkai*).[26] He outlined his life in ways that drew parallels with the story of the Buddha, emphasized that in 1980 he had received a 'vibration' from the Buddha when he was in India and spoke of his feeling that he would became a complete or realized Buddha before his death – and that he would be able to die when he had achieved total Buddhahood.[27] After this (i.e. after his death) he would be able to help and guide his followers from the Buddha realm. He states that followers might have been upset when they heard he had died but he counsels them not to feel like this. As he had explained in various sermons, Shakyamuni's relics were the true body of the living Buddha; when he returned to the Buddha realm at physical death his relics became the living body of Buddha in this world, placed in a stupa and venerated by his disciples. The same is true for Kiriyama; while he has left his physical body and returned to the Buddha realm, he continues to be a living presence in this world. By enshrining and venerating his relics Agonshū is following the same path as the Buddha's disciples, while he (Kiriyama) remains the 'living founder' (*ikite iru kaiso*) who, just as in life, continues to bestow spiritual power on his followers while also helping them from the Buddha realm. Emphasizing that it is very difficult to attain enlightenment, and that it can only be achieved via the path he has set out, he decided to return to the *bukkai* (Buddha realm) to assist his followers. Whenever they are in need they can call out to '*kaiso Kiriyama Seiyū*' and he will step in to help them.[28] Of course, he assures them, all the Buddhas and gods (*kami*) will also aid them.

He continues that his true relics will be enshrined using the *Tōzanryū gomahō* (literally, 'the Kiriyama[29] style of performing the *goma*') – the ritual method he devised – at the first *goma* ritual of the year and then at the Hoshi Matsuri.[30] He emphasizes that his spiritual powers have increased because of his ascent to the Buddha realm and that his spiritual presence will be there in each *goma* stick at Agonshū rituals. He then speaks of Agonshū as the only true religion (*makoto no shūkyō*); it has brought together Shakyamuni's path of becoming Buddha, with the power of Bhutanese Buddhism, and the ancient law of the gods (*shinpō*) of Japan. As a result only Agonshū has the power to eradicate the world's bad karma and save all humanity; only Agonshū is lighting *goma* fires around the world to pacify the spirits of the dead and save people. Only Agonshū conducts a great ritual event – the Hoshi Matsuri – to this end.

Thus he implores followers to strive to collect as many *gomagi* as possible for the Hoshi Matsuri so as to create the good karma needed to save the world. He finishes with a reminder of a planned future event, in which Agonshū will perform rituals in the sea areas north of Japan to pacify the spirits of the Japanese war dead, something that will help bring happiness to the Japanese people, safety to the Far East region and world peace. He then makes a brief reference to a special pendant (about which we will say more later) offered to devotees who collect a substantial number of *gomagi* for the Hoshi Matsuri, exhorts his followers to venerate his true bodily relics and ends by affirming his desire to bestow his spiritual power on them from the highest realms. As the living *kaiso*, he will be with them and wants them all to strive their utmost alongside him to support Agonshū's ideals and activities.

A further *kaiso reiyu* appeared before Agonshū's first *goma* ritual of 2017, and this was printed in the first issue of the members' magazine of 2017 (*Agon Magazine* 2017, 1/2). Much of it replicates the themes of the earlier message. This *kaiso reiyu* begins with Kiriyama's spirit offering a New Year's greeting, and affirming his continued presence in the movement via his relics, with the phrase 'my true bodily relics that are in and of themselves the living founder'[31] (*Agon Magazine* 2017, 1/2: 5). These relics, enshrined in the head temple through Kiriyama's special *goma* ritual (the *Tōzanryū gomahō*), were protecting all Agonshū members and empowering the *gomagi* they used in their rituals (7). He warns that the world was entering a phase of great change because the karma (*innen*) of many countries was about to erupt – and people are losing spiritual power because they are hidebound by their karma. Japan, too, faces upheavals but there is a difference, for it is the country where Agonshū's teaching is present[32] and as such is the only place which has the teaching to liberate karma (*innen o gedatsu*) (8). Japan is destined to be transformed and become the world leader (*sekai no rīdā*), but to accomplish this it is necessary for 'all of you' (*shokun*, i.e. all Agonshū members) to proselytize and bring about the spiritual manifestation (*reisei kengen*) of human salvation through the sacred fires of the *goma*. To this end he exhorts members to make the forthcoming Hoshi Matsuri a huge success and further the mission to save humankind by bringing many *gomagi* to the festival (8). He emphasizes that his relics will be present at the *kekkai* (the sacred arena containing the altar and the two pyres) when the sacred fire (*seika*) for human salvation is lit, and that he will be there in spirit with all those taking part (8). He then speaks again of the planned ritual services and commemorations in the seas north of Japan for the Japanese war dead and for world peace in July 2017, and reiterates that Agonshū is the only religion that has the power to eliminate bad karma, uplift people's spiritual powers and save humanity (9). As such he exhorts them to continue striving to build a spiritual society, says that he will be at their side and tells them to realize their spiritual abilities, and 'this year too strive to do your best together with me'[33] (10).

Kiriyama issued two *kaiso reiyu* messages prior to the 2017 Hoshi Matsuri, both of which were later published in *Agon Magazine* (2017, 3/4). In the first, on 10 February 2017, he said that tomorrow's festival is when 'my true body relics' would be enshrined, and repeated previous messages that he would enter the *kekkai* with the practitioners and do the ritual practices alongside them. He would also go to places outside the *kekkai* where others are doing *shugyō* and help there. He reiterated his wish for everyone to do even more practice, affirmed that his spirit was striving for them to reach highest spiritual levels, talked of how they were a 'a group of holy people' (*seisha no shūdan*) seeking salvation for humanity and ended by exhorting them to strive tomorrow with him. He restated this message in another, shorter, *kaiso reiyu* at 5.20 a.m. on the morning of the Hoshi Matsuri, emphasizing again that his true body relics would be enshrined and that he would be spiritually present, while encouraging his followers to enhance their practice.

Another striking spiritual message delivered via the new leadership appeared in a leaflet circulated in Agonshū prior to the Hoshi Matsuri in February 2017. The leaflet offered devotees the chance to acquire a special spiritually charged pendant that would bring the wearer special benefits and spiritual protection. This was the 'Saishō Kongō Seiyū daikakuson reirikishugo pendanto' (a literal translation would be 'most victorious Diamond Seiyū most enlightened venerated spiritually powerful protector pendant'), and it contains various terms illustrative of Agonshū's post-death depiction of Kiriyama. Seiyū is of course Kiriyama's given name, and the terms related to it (such as 'most victorious' and 'most enlightened') are elements in Kiriyama's posthumous name[34]; kongō (diamond) is a term found notably in esoteric Buddhism, and signifies unchanging wisdom. In Shingon Buddhism it is part of the term of reverence that that sect uses (*Namu daishi henjō kongō*) for its founder figure, Kūkai, in his posthumous miracle-working and transcendent guise of Kōbō Daishi.[35] Kiriyama's posthumous title thus portrays him as a spiritually powerful protective and enlightened figure of veneration. The leaflet indicates that Kiriyama's spirit is immanently present in the pendant, which is a *bunshin* of the founder; *bunshin* is a term signifying a manifestation or spiritual presence of a deity or similar sacred entity. Shinto *kami* and Buddhist figures of worship can appear spiritually in the form of *bunshin* manifest in statues and amulets, while a standard explanation for the efficacy and significance of items such as amulets is that they are *bunshin* of the gods and Buddha figures venerated at the shrines and temples that vend them (Reader and Tanabe 1998). In other words, Kiriyama is being portrayed in a similar mode to Shinto deities and Buddhist figures of worship, with his *bunshin* or spiritual presence, according to the leaflet, enabling the pendant wearer to further penetrate into the teachings and practices of Agonshū, and to be together with Kiriyama's spirit. The leaflet further exalts Kiriyama as an enlightened being whose spirit remains present in this world with the power to grant benefits to the living.

The pendant is given to those who have solicited (*kanjin*) 2,000 *gomagi* for ritual incineration at the 2017 Hoshi Matsuri. Since one *gomagi* stick costs 100 yen, collecting 2,000 such sticks (whether by encouraging others to purchase them or, perhaps, paying for some oneself as well) means that a member has collected a minimum of 200,000 yen (in UK terms as of January 2018, over £1,300) for the movement. Agonshū had previously offered other rewards for those who had solicited large numbers of *gomagi* for the Hoshi Matsuri, and in harnessing Kiriyama's spirit to encourage donations and sales in the aftermath of his death the new leadership is clearly continuing this practice and showing that it retains the commercial and entrepreneurial spirit of the Kiriyama era.

The leaflet also contained an extract from the above December 2016 *kaiso reiyu* in which Kiriyama exhorted followers to make the Hoshi Matsuri a success by soliciting as many *goma* sticks as possible. He also validated the spiritual nature of the pendant as a living embodiment of his spirit, expressed his delight that the pendant, his *bunshin*, was available and affirmed that, having entered the realms of enlightenment, he could transmit spiritual power to the wearer.[36]

The 2017 Hoshi Matsuri: enshrining the founder in his presence

Kiriyama's relics were initially enshrined on 1 January 2017 during Agonshū's first *goma* ritual of the year, at which the new leaders spoke of how his spirit continued to protect the movement (*Agon Magazine* 2017, 1/2: 2) while the founder's spirit message exhorted followers to make the Hoshi Matsuri a success and to continue Agonshū's mission of world salvation. The relics were also central to the 2017 Hoshi Matsuri, where they were enshrined on the main altar. The Hoshi Matsuri marked a further point in his post-death elevation, in which he not only joined the Buddha as a figure of worship and as a continuing material presence but also surpassed him to become Agonshū's de facto central focus of veneration.

Much at the 2017 festival replicated earlier Hoshi Matsuri. These included a background of dramatic martial-style music, processions by members dressed as *yamabushi*, invocations to gods and Buddhas, the lighting of the two pyres and the burning of millions of *gomagi* for worldly benefits and the liberation of unhappy spirits. It also involved, as in previous years, shrines and stalls where visitors could purchase amulets, have divinations done and acquire various Agonshū goods, and groups of Agonshū members dressed as various deities, chanting, soliciting alms and offering various amulets and other Agonshū goods for sale. Yet the occasion was different from previous years in three ways that signified the changes and the continuities produced by Kiriyama's death. The three crucial differences were the physical absence of Kiriyama as a living physical figure in the ritual arena, the overarching presence of Kiriyama as a spiritual and (via his relics) physical presence and authority, and the commemoration and enshrinement of his spirit and relics. Together they sent out a potent message reinforced by the narrative broadcast over loudspeakers, by Agonshū's subsequent report of the event, and by the explanation – by an Agonshū priest – of the meanings of Kiriyama's demise that was published in the Agon members' magazine after the Hoshi Matsuri.

On its website and in pre-festival publicity, Agonshū offered people the opportunity to offer 'prayers to the great spiritual power of a Buddha!'[37] Accompanying this invocation was a photograph of Kiriyama and a message about the 'manifestation of the spiritual power' (*reiriki kengen*) of the founder.[38] Kiriyama was hailed as a Buddha whose spirit would be present at the festival – a promise that Kiriyama had already made in a *kaiso reiyu* prior to the event – and the 2017 Hoshi Matsuri was proclaimed as the 'festival of the great rebirth of the second Buddha' (*dai ni no budda oofukkatsu sai*). At the festival loudspeaker announcements informed the gathered throng that Kiriyama was now the 'second Buddha' (*dai ni no budda*) who had joined the 'first Buddha' (*dai ichi no budda*) Shakyamuni, the *shinsei busshari* who was Agonshū's main image of worship.[39]

The festival started, according to Agonshū's subsequent report, with a ritual in the main temple at which the bodily relics of the living (*ikeru*) Agonshū founder Kiriyama Seiyū Daishōjō Geika (his title when alive) were 'reverently accepted' (*hōtaisare*) on a Shinto-style *mikoshi* and carried by Shinto priests in procession (Figure 5.2),

Figure 5.2 Shrine maidens (*miko*) and Shinto priests at the Hoshi Matsuri. Photo by Ian Reader.

accompanied by music, chants and Agonshū practitioners in *yamabushi* garb, to the main ritual arena (*kekkai*). The Agonshū report thus conveyed the message that Kiriyama, although dead, was still alive and it reinforced this by using the title he had when alive. The casket containing the relics was draped in a gold cloth and before it were placed Kiriyama's personal ritual implements. The arena was covered with a layer of snow but, according to the magazine report, as the relics were brought down to it, the snow stopped, the clouds cleared and the sun burst through.[40] The relics were then ritually enshrined on the altar in an extended process in which Shinto priests offered prayers and invocations, Shinto shrine maidens performed traditional Shinto *kagura* ritual dances and various *yamabushi* practitioners made offerings. A *yamabushi mondō* (dialogue) was broadcast outlining Kiriyama's achievements in life and attributing all manner of innovations, spectacular spiritual deeds and accomplishments to him. Fukada Seia, as Agonshū's chief ritualist and *kanchō*, oversaw the process although, as we noted above, Kiriyama's empty chair indicated who the presiding spirit was – a point affirmed in the subsequent *Agon Magazine* report that stated that Kiriyama's spirit had presided over the whole affair and that everyone present had felt the spiritual power of the 'second Buddha's vibration' (*Agon Magazine* 2017, 3/4: 20, 34).

The relic casket, draped with gold cloth, was then carried by a *yamabushi* to the altar and placed there, strikingly (to our eye), in front of the *shinsei busshari* casket of Shakyamuni in a way that partially obscured the latter. As this enshrinement was taking place, the riveting image mentioned earlier, of the view from Kiriyama's empty chair facing the altar, appeared on the large screen, to transmit the message that Kiriyama was not simply overseeing the ritual but was 'watching' and presiding over his own enshrinement. Throughout this process the loudspeaker commentary highlighted his life and achievements, from his mastery of various ascetic and esoteric practices, to his founding of Agonshū, his mission of world salvation, the establishment of 'original Buddhism' and of 'complete Buddhism', and his activities in discovering the path to spiritual liberation (*gedatsu*) and the pacification of unhappy spirits. Not only had he unified Buddhism but he had also united the (Shinto) *kami* and the Buddhas, and striven for world peace and the salvation of humanity (*jinrui kyūsai*) via numerous rituals around the world.

His international profile was emphasized with a recitation of how he had been recognized through honours and titles bestowed by Buddhists in other countries. The entire narrative emphasized what had been manifest via the various *kaiso reiyu* and leaflets cited above: that Kiriyama was no longer a human founder but a spiritual presence and figure of worship, on a level with the Buddha. *Agon Magazine*, the Japanese-language members' magazine, elaborated further on this by reminding followers of how in 1980 Kiriyama had received the vibration at Sahet Mahet in India, followed by the true Buddha relics (*shinsei busshari*) and how, through these, Shakyamuni was enshrined at temple as the '*dai ichi no budda*'. With the addition of Kiriyama's relics as the 'second Buddha' the sacred site had now become the incomparable sacred centre of complete Buddhism.[41] Agonshū was proclaimed as the 'group of holy people' (*seisha no shūdan*) dedicated to transmitting the true law (*shōbō*)[42] in order to save all humanity. If the first stage in the ritual transformation of Kiriyama had occurred at his funeral in October 2016 when followers were encouraged to 'worship the founder' as he remained bodily intact prior to cremation, the Hoshi Matsuri represented the completion of this process of turning him into a figure of worship materially enshrined through his relics so that he could be ever-present hereafter. It was also, according to Agonshū, a turning point for the movement; with 'the festival of the rebirth of the second Buddha' Agonshū's mission of spiritual awakening aimed at cutting the world's karma was starting in earnest (*Agon Magazine* 2017, 3/4: 46). As such Kiriyama's death and enshrinement were not end or crisis points in the movement's history or in the life trajectory of its founder, but points of departure and of a new beginning in the mission to save humanity and realize a new era filled with sacred spiritual light.

In the same Agon members' magazine devotees who participated in the festival reiterated such themes, and indicated that the promise made by their founder in his spiritual messages, to be present with them and oversee their practices at the Hoshi Matsuri, had been fulfilled. They spoke of how they had been together with their 'sacred teacher' (*seishi*, one of the terms of endearment and veneration used for Kiriyama) at the holy fires, that they had felt that Kiriyama's power was with them and of how it had spread through the *goma* sticks and amulets onto the attendees (*Agon Magazine* 2017, 3/4: 64–72). This magazine account thus affirms the view promoted by the movement that Kiriyama remains spiritually present and that, despite his physical demise, his power permeates every activity it undertakes.

Elevating the founder, surpassing the Buddha

The 2017 Hoshi Matsuri was all about Kiriyama in ways that appeared to eclipse Agonshū's main image of worship, the *shinsei busshari* of the Buddha Shakyamuni. Although Agonshū had previously described the *shinsei busshari* relic as the manifestation of the living Shakyamuni and the highest figure of worship in Buddhism,[43] by proclaiming Kiriyama as the second Buddha it appeared to raise him to a similar category. Yet it went further than that. The symbolic imagery of the Hoshi Matsuri enshrinement, in which Kiriyama's reliquary was placed on the altar in front of the *shinsei busshari* casket, suggested that his relics were taking precedence over the *shinsei busshari* and that the deceased founder's spirit was surpassing that of Shakyamuni.

These themes were developed further by the Agonshū priest Kiyokawa Hakuhō in an article in *Agon Magazine* that followed on from its report on the 2017 Hoshi Matsuri (Kiyokawa 2017). In it Kiyokawa expanded on the symbolic themes of the festival and explained how Agonshū regarded its departed founder. The following is a summary of Kiyokawa's article, which was underpinned by extensive references to Kiriyama's own writings.

According to Kiyokawa, while Shakyamuni is the 'first Buddha', the focus of his discussion is the 'second Buddha' (*dai ni no budda*, i.e. Kiriyama). He repeats the story of how Kiriyama turned to Buddhism, saw the truth in the Āgamas and established the correct way of becoming a Buddha (*jōbutsuhō*). Shakyamuni had died over 2,000 years ago, Kiyokawa reminded readers, and now there was a need for a new Buddha (*nyorai*) to promulgate true Buddhism for this current age. This Buddha is the *kaiso* (i.e. Kiriyama) (Kiyokawa 2017: 48) who has come to bring salvation to all. Kiyokawa emphasized the importance of the Sahet Mahet vibration, through which Shakyamuni transmitted his spiritual fiat to Kiriyama, and through which the world's sacred centre moved to Japan (48), a transmission subsequently affirmed by the 1986 donation of the Buddha relic from Sri Lanka. According to Kiyokawa, Kiriyama also received vibrations from the Buddha relic and became the mediator of the *shinsei busshari*'s sacred power. This gives Agonshū a special link to Shakyamuni because Kiriyama was the direct disciple (*deshi*) of the first Buddha (48–9).

In August 2016, during an Agonshū ritual, Kiriyama attained complete buddhahood[44] (*kanzen na budda to nararemashita*) and this and his direct link to the *dai ichi no budda* meant that henceforth Agonshū followers, as disciples of the *kaiso*, could receive the spiritual power of Buddha and themselves attain buddhahood. Kiyokawa then explained the difference between the two Buddhas (Shakyamuni and Kiriyama); the former's power can only be accessed indirectly (*masetsu*) and mediated via Kiriyama, whereas the powers of the 'second Buddha' Kiriyama can be directly accessed by devotees (Kiyokawa 2017: 49).

Not only is the *dai ni no budda* directly accessible but he appears to be more powerful than the original Buddha. According to Kiyokawa, Shakyamuni developed a system for cutting karma and enhancing spiritual awareness that was pertinent for the times in which he lived. However, that was a simpler world than now. Because of rapid changes and increasing numbers of people today Shakyamuni's system was no longer sufficient to save everyone; the world needed a new way to develop the spiritual power of greater numbers of people. This, Kiyokawa stated, was what Kiriyama, the second Buddha, had done; he had made Shakyamuni's system more powerful by incorporating elements from Bhutanese Buddhism – the most powerful and dynamic strand within the Tibetan lineage of Buddhism – that were not known in Shakyamuni's time, thereby creating a 'complete Buddhism' (*kanzen bukkyō*). To this 'complete Buddhism' he had further added the power of the Shinto gods. To this extent Agonshū's association with Shinto that we reported on in Chapter 4 serves not just as evidence of how Agonshū has embraced nationalism and developed links to the wider frameworks of religion in Japan, but it provides a mechanism whereby the movement can claim it has both made Buddhism complete and gone beyond it.

As such Agonshū is more powerful than earlier Buddhism while the 'second Buddha' has manifested greater powers of salvation than the first Buddha (Kiyokawa 2017: 49).[45] It was Kiriyama (rather than Shakyamuni) who developed the teaching of the Āgamas, the core sutras of Buddhism. Kiriyama not only received Shakyamuni's imprimatur but had also been identified by Nostradamus's prophecies as the saviour destined to lead the world out of turmoil. His power was enhanced because it was combined with that of Shakyamuni. Moreover his spiritual standing had been recognized by various influential forces around the world, with Kiriyama's meeting with the Pope cited as an example of this.

Kiriyama's role as a world saviour came at a turning point in history according to Kiyokawa, for Christian power (i.e. the power of Western states) is coming to an end. Kiriyama had said, in his book *1999 nen karuma to reishō kara no dasshutsu karuma*, that Nostradamus's prophecies signified the end of the era in which Christian Western culture dominated the world. Kiyokawa now confirmed that this was the case; Western culture and Christianity are at a point of implosion due to their emphasis on materialism (Kiyokawa 2017: 54). We are now at a time when the world needs a Buddhist spiritual culture inspired by the power of the *dai ni no budda* to eradicate the destructive karma of Christian-inspired culture and materialism and to heighten spiritual awareness (54–5). Citing Agonshū's rituals for peace around the world in places such as Jerusalem as examples of this process in action, Kiyokawa further emphasized the ability of Agonshū to enable the spirits of the dead to attain buddhahood, because it possesses the power of Kiriyama the second Buddha (56).

Kiyokawa then thanked the founder (*kaiso*) for all of this. While cautioning followers that the founder had said that the world is in crisis Kiyokawa reminded them that he had also told followers that they were destined to build a new realm of light and peace. Kiriyama's return to this world as the *dai ni no budda* was in order to realize this. The *kaiso*, Kiyokawa (2017: 57) concluded, had explained everything and all we (i.e. his disciples) needed to do was to walk the path outlined by him and unfailingly realize the ideals and vows of the holy teacher (*seishi*).

The Northern Seas, the spirits of the dead, the *kami* and reflections on the war

We will discuss some of the implications of the spirit messages, enshrinement and posthumous treatment of Kiriyama shortly. First we wish to look at another significant event carried out by Agonshū after Kiriyama's death that was in the pipeline before he died. This was the *Hoppō Yōjō hōyō* or Northern Seas memorial service, of June 2017, another in the series of rituals for the spirits of the war dead carried out by Agonshū in regions where battles and losses of life had occurred during the Pacific War. The Northern Seas event involved memorial services at sea and *goma* rituals on the island of Sakhalin (now belonging to Russia but formerly Japanese) for the Japanese who lost their lives in the naval encounters between Japan and Russia at the end of the war. Kiriyama had, according to Agonshū, wanted to do this ritual and, as was indicated above, his spirit had reminded followers about this plan and about his wish that it would be fulfilled.

The preparations for the event were reported in the Agon members' magazine for May–June 2017 (*Agon Magazine* 2017, 5/6), while a series of newspaper reports that Agonshū displays on its website afterwards have provided accounts (from an Agonshū perspective) of the event.[46] On 9 April 2017, Agonshū held a special meeting to highlight the forthcoming event. Interestingly, on this occasion, there was no *kaiso reiyu*; instead, Wada Naoko, the administrative head, spoke on Kiriyama's behalf, reporting various things he had said to her and reiterating that it had been the *kaiso's* wish that this venture would take place and be a great success. As Kiriyama's disciples (*deshi*) she and the movement's members had a duty to continue his work.

She mentioned various previous rituals Kiriyama had done for the war dead and stated that he would be present (in the form of his relics, which Agonshū was taking on board the ship) for the coming event. Its aim was not just to perform pacification rituals for the Japanese war dead and for the protection of country. Before 1945 the northern islands such as Sakhalin had been Japanese territory and on them were Shinto shrines enshrining Japanese deities (*kami*). The shrines had disappeared at the end of war (when the islands were taken over by Russia) and hence the *kami* there had no home. So, besides pacifying and repatriating the spirits of the Japanese war dead, the aim was also to bring the *kami* who had lost their shrines, back to Japan and give them a home there. This again was the founder's wish.

Wada then turned to recent world events, including an American missile strike on war-torn Syria that had occurred just two days previously on 7 April 2017, to highlight the continuing dangers the world faced, and to reiterate Kiriyama's message about Japan's role as a peace-bringer; the founder had told her that there is no country as blessed and peaceful as Japan. Moreover, Wada said, they (in Japan) were fortunate to have the *kaiso* to teach and help them become a great religious movement working not only for their own sakes but also for the whole world. Repeating an early spirit message of Kiriyama she spoke of the world in turmoil and of the need to build a *seisha no shūdan*, a group of holy people, in order to save Japan and carry out Agonshū's mission of realizing world peace through prayer. Only Japan could do this; emphasizing that this had been a recurrent theme of Kiriyama's talks, she said it was their duty to achieve his wishes via events such as the *Hoppō Yōjō hōyō* to cut Japan's karma and make the country the world's leader. Repeating Kiriyama's standard exhortations, she ended by asking everyone to work together to achieve his wishes (*Agon Magazine* 2017, 5/6: 25–31).

The magazine followed this account by reporting an invited lecture (titled *Hoppō no eirei he no omoi* 'thoughts about the spirits of the northern seas') given to Agonshū members by Kamijima Yoshirō on the day before Wada's talk. Kamijima was a journalist who had interviewed Kiriyama on many occasions, and who has written for the *Sankei Shinbun*. He subsequently wrote a positive article about the Northern Seas ritual (in which he participated) for the *Sankei Shinbun* – an article now displayed also on Agonshū's website.[47] In his lecture Kamijima outlined nationalist revisionist views about the war that reiterated and intensified Kiriyama's comments, cited in the previous chapter and reported in the *Sankei Shinbun* in 2012, in which Kiriyama claimed that Japan was forced to go to war because of Western colonial policies and to defend itself. Kamijima emphasized Kiriyama's patriotism, citing his visits to Yasukuni Shrine and Kiriyama's frequent comments about how fortunate he was to have been born Japanese. Kiriyama, Kamijima noted, had also emphasized the importance of ancestors and had told him that the Japanese would have no future if they failed to pay attention to them. Kamijima then showed the audience a map of Asia before the Pacific War – a map showing that, apart from Japan and Thailand, the region had been colonized and dominated by white Western colonial powers. While Japan had expanded into Korea and elsewhere, this was not due to a desire to colonize such places but for defensive reasons; fearing the threat of Russia, Japan had had to create a protective barrier around itself. Indeed, Kamijima claimed, a factor in Japan's war was the wish to abolish discrimination, and he 'demonstrated' this with a map showing that by 1942 whole areas had been removed from colonial rule (and, he said, subsequently the countries of Asia had attained freedom). While not denying that Japan had caused some problems for Asian peoples he refuted the idea that it had waged war against Asians; the war was against white colonial forces. Indeed, he cited the 1943 establishment of the Greater East Asian Co-Prosperity Sphere, instituted by the Japanese government and representatives of the areas it controlled, to emphasize this point. This area, he noted, was where Kiriyama's *jōbutsuhō* rituals for the spirits of the dead have been primarily focused – rituals that were, Kamijima asserted, not just for the Japanese but for all the Asian dead. Kiriyama focused mainly on Japanese spirits because to attain world peace one first has to care for one's own spirits of dead; he was, Kamijima (2017: 33–49) said, a patriot (a point, Kamijima noted, that Ishihara Shintarō had made in his eulogy at Kiriyama's funeral) but a patriot with a universal message who had established a universal religion to bring about world peace.

The talks by Wada and Kamijima in different ways outline the continuing nationalist orientations of Agonshū and suggest that it is becoming stronger. Kamijima's speech appears to be little more than revisionist right-wing nationalist apologetics about Japan's actions in the war. Given that it was an invited speech to Agonshū, by a figure who was presented as someone who knew Kiriyama well and was in tune with his thinking, it indicates that the increasing focus on a Japanese nationalist agenda outlined in the previous chapter was a product of Kiriyama's thinking that remains strong in Agonshū after his death.

The *Hoppō Yōjō hōyō* occurred between 30 June and 6 July 2017, when a ship chartered by Agonshū travelled around the Northern Seas carrying Agonshū members, led by Wada and Fukada, who conducted various rituals there, while a Bhutanese Buddhist ritual was also held for world peace during the voyage. Kiriyama's relics were on board the ship and hence he symbolically oversaw the whole ritual. On return to

Japan the party visited Yasukuni Shrine to pay their respects there before going to the Chidorigafuchi National Cemetery to enshrine the souls of the war dead there.[48]

New titles, new rituals, new exhortations

In the months after the Northern Seas' rituals Agonshū has added further events focused on its founder to its ritual calendar, published further *kaiso reiyu* said to be from Kiriyama, expanded its set of five canonical chants by adding a reference to him and given him a further title of respect and reverence. Its magazine has continued to reproduce the texts of earlier sermons and new pamphlets and flyers advertising Agonshū events and new encouragement for those who solicit large numbers of *gomagi* for forthcoming rituals such as the Hoshi Matsuri have appeared.

The anniversary of his funeral was commemorated by a new ritual that was preceded by a new *kaiso reiyu* reiterating many of the themes of earlier messages while expressing Kiriyama's happiness that the event was taking place. The spiritual message also reminded followers that they needed to continue in their practice and exhorted them to continue spreading the word of Agonshū. Fukada performed the *goma* ritual and spoke about Agonshū's activities of the past year, such as the Northern Seas voyage along with the reception of Kiriyama's *kaiso reiyu*. He also referred to Kiriyama not just as the *dai ni no budda* but as the *dai ni no oogu no nyorai*. This term basically draws on a standard Buddhist lexicon and refers to a venerable (*oogu*) Buddha (*nyorai*) or enlightened being,[49] and reiterates the earlier term of reverence ('second Buddha'). The term *oogu no nyorai* appears to have entered Agonshū's terminology during 2017 and adds a further degree of reverence and authority, along with an additional title of respect, to Kiriyama. In 2017 Kiriyama's spiritual presence was further affirmed in an addition to the five chants; as well as chanting that they will succeed members also now add a sixth pledge: *watashi wa seishi to tomo ni ayumu* ('I will walk together with the sacred teacher', i.e. Kiriyama).[50]

Kiriyama's presence was highly evident also at the *hatsugoma* or first *goma* ritual of 2018. This was performed in Kyoto and transmitted live to other Agonshū centres including the Tokyo main centre, where one of us observed it. Fukada again oversaw the *goma* ritual, in which prayers were directed to three figures: Buddha, the Japanese deity Susanoo and Kiriyama the second Buddha. At one point the recorded voice of Kiriyama was broadcast, overlapping Fukada's voice in chanting the sutras, and at another a video of a younger Kiriyama performing an esoteric ritual also appeared on screen and was integrated into the ceremony. The camera at times also zoomed in on the altar (something of a recurrent trope in Agonshū broadcasts) to show the reliquaries there; as at the Hoshi Matsuri Kiriyama's relic casket was placed in front of the Buddha's *shinsei busshari* casket. Kiriyama was thus a living part of the ceremony, incorporated into it via his historical, physical personage as a ritual performer and highlighted as a sacred object of reverence placed in front of the Buddha.

Fukada then gave a talk in which he first announced the creation of a new event in Agonshū's calendar – the celebration of the founder's birth, to be held annually on 7 January. Following this he introduced a new *kaiso reiyu* that again reiterated the exhortations of earlier messages while emphasizing that it is Kiriyama's spirit who continues to guide the movement and that it is his instructions that are being followed. Perhaps unsurprisingly, the message also contained an exhortation to solicit and purchase many *gomagi*. Fukada ended the message by asking everyone to chant the canonical chants (now six). The ceremony continued with a short talk from Wada Naoko about her activities in which she visited China and went to various temples and universities Kiriyama had previously visited; the image produced was one that in effect reiterated the idea outlined in the sixth (and new) chant of following in the sacred teacher's footsteps.[51]

According to a flyer obtained on the occasion of the *hatsugoma*, the schedule for the forthcoming celebration of the founder's birthday (*kaiso seitansai*) was to follow a pattern not dissimilar to the first of the year ritual. It was to start with a *goma* ritual, followed by a speech of gratitude to Kiriyama and a video of one of his sermons. Then would come a preview of the forthcoming Hoshi Matsuri and preparations for collecting *gomagi*, and a sermon from Wada Naoko, after which a video of the founder performing an esoteric ritual blessing would end the celebration.[52]

Another flyer collected at the Tokyo centre on the occasion of the *hatsugoma* related to the 2018 Hoshi Matsuri. As with the flyer in 2017 offering a sacred pendant that contained Kiriyama's spirit for those who solicited 2,000 *gomagi*, this one offered a reward for those who collected 2,000 *gomagi* for the 2018 event. On this occasion the reward was a sacred mandala (the *reikō himitsu mandara* or secret spiritual light mandala) containing the second Buddha's secret inner spiritual light. The mandala, the flyer stated, was an aid to a secret meditation method. There was an accompanying excerpt from one of Kiriyama's spiritual messages in which he encouraged followers to get this mandala (by, of course, collecting 2,000 *gomagi*) and talked about it as a powerful meditation aide. In the spiritual message Kiriyama states that he had previously taught them traditional meditation techniques but henceforth he planned (from this spring, i.e. spring 2018) to teach a new secret meditation technique (*okugi no meisōhō*). The new mandala would be an aide in this meditation. The flyer did not indicate how he would do this teaching from beyond the grave but the implications within it – that a new meditation technique was going to be used and that a new mandala was needed for this – were clear.

Enshrinement, legitimation and not letting go

We have outlined the spirit messages of Kiriyama, the above account by an Agonshū priest, the more recent discussions around the Northern Seas ritual event and the most recent developments at the start of 2018, at length because they together express clearly how the movement and its leadership are currently framing their deceased founder and how they are seeking to direct the movement in the wake of his loss. Here, again, we stress the importance of understanding how a movement functions through examining how it presents itself and represents events associated with it. There is an internalized logic at work here – just as there was, as we discussed in Chapter 2, in the hagiographic constructions through which movements portray the early lives of their founders. Understanding such logic is vital for understanding how a religious movement such as Agonshū operates and what meanings it presents to and contains for followers.

Agonshū was heavily 'Kiriyama focused' while he was alive. It was a movement created by him and centred on his charisma and ideas. Agonshū rituals focused on him, as did its publications and public narratives, all of which served to reinforce his charismatic standing in the eyes of his followers. Kiriyama did not designate who would follow him as leader, and there was no scope, while he was alive, for another charismatic figure to emerge as an obvious successor. There were (at least in the last decade or more) no family members who appear to have been active in Agonshū and who might, as has happened in many Japanese new religions, have been able to inherit the leadership. The operative leadership of Kiriyama's later years, in which Wada held the main administrative role and Fukada the senior ritual one, has continued after Kiriyama's death. It is evident that they were central to Agonshū's functioning in the period before Kiriyama died; even if the Agonshū narrative portrays Kiriyama as having been lucid and healthy until the very moment of death, the need for him to be aided in carrying out blessings and his inability to deliver sermons in his final years suggests that he had become a figurehead more than an active hands-on leader.

Yet even if Wada, Fukada and other senior followers were actively running the movement and taking leading ritual roles prior to Kiriyama's death, they still faced dilemmas of legitimacy when he died. As the secessions and succession disputes in movements such as Mahikari and GLA have shown, the death of a founder is a precarious moment for new movements, one that not only raises questions of succession but of how to retain a sense of potency and spiritual dynamism when a primary source of such things, epitomized by the leader's charisma, is lost. This can, in its turn, also be a source of worry to first-generation devotees (especially in comparatively new movements such as Agonshū) who have joined the movement to be part of an imminently realizable mission led by, and alongside, their charismatic founder and leader, and who might feel that now that the leader has gone, the mission itself has become impossible. They are bound also to be concerned when the movement they have joined has placed such a profound focus on the performance of rituals, which their founder had repeatedly emphasized were essential in order to pacify the spirits of the dead and solve both world and individual problems, and when the lynchpin of such rituals dies.

The narratives of Kiriyama's state of being immediately prior to death and of his spiritual messages – the *kaiso reiyu* – afterwards, along with the enshrinement of his relics, affirmations of his special spiritual power and of the rebirth of the second Buddha show us how these dilemmas are being handled. They illustrate how Agonshū's current leaders are seeking to assuage members' concerns while legitimizing their own positions. Fukada and Wada both play public roles, Fukada particularly with *goma* rituals but both reporting on events in the movement and outlining the founder's spiritual messages. It is they who report the contents of Kiriyama's spiritual messages, and they thus serve as representatives and manifestations of his authority; they are, in effect, the voices of legitimacy who have not just assumed the mantle of current leadership by default but have had it bestowed on them by the founder. They speak for him by narrating his words and commenting on them. The first *kaiso reiyu* we cited provides a reason for his death and projects it not as the result of old age and infirmity but because of his achievement in life. Becoming a totally realized Buddha enabled him to dispense with his physical body and be liberated from this physical realm. Thus Kiriyama in life had transcended the normative human condition and the frailties of age and death; rather than being struck down by death, he was able to die and to dispense with his physical body because of achieving total enlightenment. The story so projected – that he left his body when he reached the highest levels of realization – thus affirms that he was in control at death and that those now running the movement had his benediction to do so. Indeed, it shows that he left his body so that he could continue his work in the higher realms and because he was happy with his successors to Agonshū's leadership in this realm.

Agonshū's current leaders have thus developed a strategy of dealing with Kiriyama that affirms their position of authority, while seeking to console and encourage followers who might feel less enthused about the movement after losing their founder. They have done this by enhancing his spiritual status in death and projecting him not simply a human founder who started the movement and who, as a result, deserves respect for pointing the way to higher truths, and not just as a spiritual entity in another realm. From being the figure that developed a connection to the main focus of worship in Agonshū, he has become that main focus, more powerful, indeed, than the official main image of worship. As his spiritual messages indicate, he exists in the highest Buddhist realms helping raise Agonshū followers to those realms but he is also immanent and active in this world, personified by his relics and by his spiritual presence, relaying messages, manifesting himself in pendants and leading his followers to world salvation. He is, as Kiyokawa's account sets out, a *more* powerful spiritual presence than before, more so than the Buddha – and he, of course, belongs to Agonshū alone. This not only reaffirms Agonshū's uniqueness as the only avenue for salvation and as the only true religion, but it further emphasizes the potency and special nature of Japan. As Kiyokawa noted, the addition of the powers of the *kami* have made Agonshū more potent and have made the second Buddha more powerful than Shakyamuni. Because of this Japan has become the epicentre of the world, the country with the true teaching of Agonshū and its mission of world salvation.

The talks prior to the *Hoppō Yōjō hōyō* events of June–July 2017 show that the nationalist orientations of Agonshū have become stronger as well. This is evident in Wada's speech evoking the memory of Kiriyama and urging followers to support the rituals in order to realize his wishes, and the intensely nationalist revisionism of Kamijima's talk – itself picking up on themes articulated by Kiriyama in his later years. Moreover, by using Bhutanese rituals Agonshū appears to be engaging in further acts of nationalist appropriation by using the priests and Buddhist practices of another Asian country to pacify, repatriate and enshrine the spirits of Japanese soldiers and sailors. In such terms, Bhutanese ritual practices have become subservient to Japanese motivations.

What is striking, too, is that the death of Kiriyama has been used not just to reinforce a nationalist message but also to intensify the immediacy of Agonshū's mission and to argue that the loss of the founder is actually a means through which it can be fulfilled.

Because Kiriyama has gone to another realm, the movement is stronger spiritually. It now has its sacred founder present both in this world, via his relics and spirit, and in the Buddha realm. Agonshū's mission, so its narrative states, is not weakened because of its leader's departure from this world, but stronger because of it.

Agonshū's leaders thus seek to counter any loss of hope among members at the demise of their leader by claiming that because of Kiriyama's enhanced post-death status, and because he has now shed his human body to enter the realms of ultimate enlightenment, they now have the power to realize their mission. The loss of the founder is the start of the new mission – something that, in this narrative, is heightened by reaffirmations of Japan's special position in the world. As such followers are encouraged not to lose heart but to intensify their practice and work on behalf of Agonshū. Striving harder for salvation in the wake of the founder's death and rebirth as a Buddha sits alongside striving harder to collect more *gomagi* for the ritual.

The memorialization, preservation and co-option of charisma

Clearly the ways in which Agonshū's leaders have dealt with their founder's death serve to strengthen their authority while seeking to maintain a movement that has faced problems because of an ageing and perhaps eroding membership. The recurrent invocations to 'strive with me' articulated in the *kaiso reiyu* and in Wada's subsequent talk evoke memories of the living, vital Kiriyama of earlier years, while the constant calls for members to do *kanjin* and gather *gomagi* for the Hoshi Matsuri serve as a sign of the need the leaders place on trying to draw in sufficient economic resources. While some might see the calls for increased alms and donations gathering to smack of a mercenary nature and exploitation of members grieving at the loss of their founder, these can also be seen as continuations of the ways Agonshū operated while Kiriyama was alive – as our comments on *kanjin* and on Kiriyama's replies to questions about the costs of membership (see Chapter 3) indicated.

What is occurring in Agonshū on one level is a memorialization of charisma. The founder's charismatic authority was key to the development of Agonshū – as it has in many other Japanese new religions. It remains critical for his successors and disciples to preserve that charismatic aura, and this is generally only feasible by elevating the founder to a new level and making him/her a focus of worship. Charismatic authority and potency have been retained in the spirit of Kiriyama along with his material presence in this world via his relics. The Agon members' magazine of May–June 2017, besides reporting Wada and Kamijima's talks about the Northern Seas' ritual, also inaugurated a new series that reprinted some of Kiriyama's sermons, under the title *Kaiso hōwa shiri-zu* ('The founder's sermon series'), as if to reiterate the centrality of Kiriyama in the movement's doctrinal structure; the first sermon chosen for the series dates from 1992 and discusses spiritual hindrances, karma and Agonshū's processes for transforming the spirits of the dead into realized buddhas (Kiriyama 2017 [1992]). It is, in essence, a reiteration of Agonshū core teachings, while its publication and the series it headlines transmit the message that, although the founder is no longer here, the essential teachings remain the same and that Agonshū and the new leadership thus represent continuity not disjuncture. The use of videos showing him performing esoteric rituals and his 'presence' via recordings of his chanting during contemporary rituals further emphasize this notion of continuity and of immanence. The founder may have died but the founder remains present and even, as the new leaflets indicate, ready to teach a new secret meditation technique.

Agonshū is an example of how a new movement deals with the loss of the immediacy charisma as manifested in the living physical body and presence of its founder. In Chapter 2 we talked of how charisma is relational, and how those around a leader help to create and reinforce his/her charismatic nature and status. The ways in which Agonshū leaders such as Wada, Fukada and Kiyokawa have enhanced Kiriyama's post-death status by publishing messages that they portray as coming from Kiriyama, taking part in rituals while placing themselves in a symbolically subservient position to the departed yet spiritually present founder and talking of him as a second yet more powerful Buddha show this relational dynamic need not only be operative during a leader's lifetime. In continuing their elevation and praise of Kiriyama after death and in using his voice as a continuing spiritual presence, the new leaders are further enhancing the idea of a charisma that does not die or evaporate at death but is maintained, continued and transformed thereafter.

Rather than Weber's argument that charisma is followed by routinization, what seems to be happening in Agonshū is both a memorialization of charisma, and, via his relics, a preservation of it in a material form that keeps the (dead) leader symbolically alive. It could also be seen as an attempt at enhancing that charismatic status by asserting that the posthumous founder has become ever more potent spiritually. While some degree of routinization has occurred in Agonshū, in that Fukada has become the official leader and has assumed the main ritual roles in the movement, and in that Wada runs the administration and plays a role in relaying messages and overseeing events, this appears at present to be a subservient routinization, one that remains in thrall to a higher form, as symbolized by Kiriyama's empty chair above Fukada at the Hoshi Matsuri, by the title – *Shōsōjō* – Fukada has compared to that of his predecessor and by the fact that when Wada delivers talks such as that before the Northern Seas event, she relies heavily on invocations of Kiriyama's spirit and his words. Their position of authority and their routinized stature as leaders are reliant on being representatives of the dead yet charismatically present founder.

By enshrining Kiriyama's relics and declaring him to be a main image of worship Agonshū is also demonstrating how movements may be reluctant to let go of the past and of sacred figures so important to their dynamic. Andrea Castiglioni (forthcoming) has recently directly addressed these questions in Japanese contexts through examining the relationship between the ascetics of Mount Yudono and their lay devotees and patrons during the Edo period (1600–1868). By mummifying the body of the ascetic to transform it into a 'flesh body icon', devotees were able to ensure that the performance of charismatic authority by these ascetics continued after death. Their devotees put on exhibitions of the ascetic's mummified body and conducted ceremonies in which that (deceased yet preserved as if alive) body was re-clothed. As such, Castiglioni raises the question about who it was that produced the ascetic's charisma, 'owned' his body in both life and after death and had the authority and power to define and shape its performance.[53] Agonshū showed similar orientations when, in later life, it continued to use Kiriyama in rituals, while, in death, his physical remains continue to play a role in the movement. By showing that his death was not some terminal event but instead a shedding of the human form because Kiriyama had attained total enlightenment, and by continuing to relay the messages he is said to emit to them, they are also continuing in this mode. They are not just showing an unwillingness to let him go but are subtly trying to strengthen their own position and status. As the representatives and transmitters of this sacred figure's messages and spirit, and controllers of his relics, they are in essence co-opting his charisma and, just as happened in his latter years, when his frail body was used as a symbol in Agonshū rituals, so too now are his relics and spirit used in similar ways.

Agonshū's operative leaders, we have suggested, already had control of Kiriyama as a physical presence when he was still alive but apparently no longer physically able to sustain the performance of demanding public rituals and sermons. In death they have retained that control not by proclaiming themselves as leaders in his place but by confirming him as the all-powerful founder-leader and continuing spiritual presence and, now, the main focus of worship. They have done this by interpreting the writings he did while alive (as Kiyokawa has done) and by relaying the spiritual messages – the *kaiso reiyu* – that are, according to the current leadership, transmitted by Kiriyama. By channelling his spirit they are affirming their right to leadership while seeking to strengthen their position and authority by seemingly demeaning it through their deference to Kiriyama the *kaiso* who continues to issue instructions and bestow spiritual teachings and benefits. They merely serve as mouthpieces of the founder; their authority is thus grounded in a posture of seeming subservience.

Of course, this relies on their claims to be spoken to by his spirit and we are aware that some members have raised concerns about this on some internet discussions boards. Claims that Wada in particular is seeking to control the movement, and concerns that the repeated encouragement for members to make Agonshū events a success and to gather *goma* sticks are little more than attempts to increase the movement's revenues (and perhaps shore up a movement that is losing members) have appeared in such locations. Such comments need to be treated with caution, not just because internet discussion forums allow for posters to hide their identities and make claims (e.g. some participants who express hostile attitudes to the current state of the movement claim to be long-term members – a claim that cannot be verified) but because many such boards and threads are explicitly oriented towards drumming up hostility to Agonshū and other new movements, and some display prejudices and unsubstantiated allegations.[54]

Nonetheless they indicate the possibility that some members may feel uneasy about the latest developments in the movement. The repeated calls (in *kaiso reiyu*, for example) for followers to solicit *gomagi* could raise concerns among members. Likewise the idea of new meditation techniques that require a mandala (as indicated by the flyer put out before the 2018 Hoshi Matsuri) indicates a potential further requirement and demand on members, some of who (as we indicated earlier) might already be struggling because of the movement's demands. The extent to which the movement might be facing problems and hence needing to get more support from existing members is unclear, but the various developments since Kiriyama's death, such as the development of new festivals and the call to learn new meditation techniques, appear to suggest a drive towards increasing the mechanisms for gaining financial support from members.

At the same time, however, there are clear barriers to much overt questioning of these developments. For a start, challenging the authority of the current leaders implicitly means challenging that of the founder himself and doubting his charisma and spiritual power; if he is as advanced as a spiritual leader as followers believe, it would seem evident that he could send messages to them from higher spiritual realms. After all, Shakyamuni – in the context of Agonshū belief – did just that to Kiriyama in 1980 and that spiritual communication was intrinsic to Agonshū's construction of its self-image as a movement with a mission, and accepted as such by members.

Continuity and the seeds of transformation

By making Kiriyama the continuing spiritual leader and immanent presence Agonshū is countering the loss of the charismatic physical presence of their founder by transforming, preserving, sanctifying and elevating that charisma, in the persona of Kiriyama the *kaiso*, the founder who has died but remains alive and spiritually present. To that degree they are clearly trying to assert a form of continuity and to reassure members that their founder's teachings and practices will carry on as before. They are also demonstrating that they are able to continue interpreting that charisma and transmitting his teaching. Kiyokawa's article shows that the leaders not only understand the inner nuances of the teaching but can also interpret it to show why Kiriyama is now the second Buddha and why Agonshū is so strong. Being able to systematize and interpret the teachings of a founder is a clear way to achieve or at least lay claims to authority. In Kiyokawa's words we can see this strategy in action.

This also opens the door to potential new teachings, modes of interpretation and transformations. In Chapter 3 we drew attention to Kiriyama's teaching that everyone could attain buddhahood. Although Kiriyama in life was repeatedly portrayed as existing at a more advanced spiritual level than his disciples, the notion that one could realize enlightenment was nonetheless a theme that remained prevalent in Agonshū. Since his death and elevation to the Buddha realms, however, there appear to be suggestions of a departure from this position. In the *kaiso reiyu* of December 2016 Kiriyama states that attaining buddhahood is very difficult and he appears to indicate a shift of focus by saying that people should call out to him for assistance. He, as such, will serve as an agency operating from the Buddha realms to help people achieve post-death transcendence. This in a sense looks potentially akin to the stance of Pure Land Buddhism, which adheres to the notion of the difficulty or impossibility of buddhahood and says that to achieve salvation (in the form of rebirth in the Pure Land) one needs to call out the name of Amida Buddha, who will thereby grant salvation. Kiriyama's spirit, as an enlightened Buddha in the Buddha realms, appears to be portrayed in a similar light in this *kaiso reiyu*. Whether Agonshū is developing in this way, as a movement that emphasizes the salvific powers of a Buddha figure (in the guise of its founder) is unclear. It is evident at least in Kiyokawa's talk, which draws on Kiriyama's writings while portraying him in a new light as more powerful than Shakyamuni, that Agonshū's teaching and worship are in the process of being reinterpreted and reoriented in the aftermath of his death. How far this process will go remains to be seen, but such examples, in the short period since his death, indicate that not only is the current leadership seeking to stabilize the movement and affirm its own authority by focusing on the posthumous Kiriyama but they may be developing the grounds through which to reinterpret his teachings, and thus Agonshū, in the longer run.

Looking back to the glorious past?

Agonshū is intent on preserving its founder's charisma and retaining a focus on charismatic leadership not through the ascent of a second charismatic leader figure (something that rarely occurs in the context of new religious movements, at least in the immediate aftermath of the loss of a founder)[55] but through the veneration of its initial founder. This raises the question of whether Agonshū (and other movements that appear to venerate their founders) may be looking back to an earlier period when its leader was younger and alive and when the movement appeared to be more in tune with the mood of the age, rather than looking forward. While the use of videos depicting the younger Kiriyama performing rituals and the use of his voice in the chanting of sutras during *goma* rituals can be seen as a way of maintaining the living dynamic presence of the founder, it clearly contains a backward looking nostalgic dimension, back to the time when he (and the movement) were younger and not impaired by the processes of physical ageing and (in the case of the movement) of a loss of dynamic. The emotional responses of members at his funeral, watching films of a younger Kiriyama, certainly also indicated emotive feelings for a past when the membership itself was younger and the movement appeared to be stronger.

On one level one could argue that Agonshū was always operating with a retrospective dynamic; its talk of a return to 'original Buddhism' implied a return to a 'time when' and to an image of purity and origins. Yet it was also infused with a sense of optimism and confidence that this 'return to origins' was also a new beginning, a regeneration of the idealized past in the present in order to construct an idealized future. Its travails in the past two or so decades, as the confidence of the 1980s evaporated, removed that optimism. This influenced the move away from messages of world salvation towards a more overt emphasis on nationalist themes. With Kiriyama's death and enshrinement the possibility of becoming ever-more entrenched in considerations of the past has become stronger.

By focusing on Kiriyama's spirit Agonshū also is continuing, we argue, with a process of internalization and a more overt Japan-centred orientation. In its emphasis on repatriating the Japanese spirits of the war dead, along with the *kami* of the islands formerly under Japanese rule, and in its visits to Yasukuni Shrine Agonshū has been turning inwards as it has aged. The enshrinement of Kiriyama is a continuation of this process. The 2017 Hoshi Matsuri narrative of Kiriyama's life certainly indicated a major focus on the past, even as it sought to portray the event as a rebirth and an occasion for regeneration and the onset of a newly galvanized mission.

The enshrinement of his relics and the ways in which followers asked to act as he did (e.g. by chanting the five positive phrases as Kiriyama used to, and now adding a sixth that innately ties them to his path) indicate a focus on doing what the founder did. While messages in the *kaiso reiyu* mention how Kiriyama's death and rebirth as a Buddha have opened up a new opportunity for world salvation, they also contain a nostalgic dimension. It was in its heyday in the 1980s that Agonshū was so intent on talking about a world mission of salvation and when Kiriyama, interpreting the prophecies of Nostradamus, saw himself as the saviour who had come to stop the world falling into chaos and catastrophe. While this vision of world salvation has always been present in Agonshū it had, in recent years, become somewhat marginalized as the movement faced difficulties, ceased to expand and became increasingly focused on nationalist themes. That tendency does not look like abating. Yet by also using rhetorical images redolent of Agonshū's earlier era, which tell members that the time for their mission has now come, and by drawing on the image of their departed yet present founder to do so, Agonshū appears to be trying to move forward by using nostalgic notions of past glory to promise future regeneration.

We cannot at present tell the extent to which Agonshū will continue to do this and become like other new movements that appear to all intents and purposes to have turned their founders into their main focuses of worship, somewhat displacing the initial deities that their founders venerated. At present, from the evidence in the short period since Kiriyama's death, the signs are that this process is under way in Agonshū and that it is becoming not so much a religion founded by Kiriyama Seiyū, as a religion centred on him and seeking to bring back the glories of the past when it had a mission of world salvation and believed it was about to spread its truth to the world, while drawing on his image in order to sustain its support structures in the present.

6

Concluding Comments: Founder Worship and the Problem of the 'New'

Introduction: the trajectory of a 'new' movement

In this book we have looked at the trajectory of a movement commonly described as a 'new religion' in Japan, from its early days to the time shortly after its founder's death. In this period Agonshū has experienced rapid growth, undergone changes, introduced new focuses of worship, faced retrenchment, lost its inspirational founder and transformed him after death into a transcendental figure of worship. In its brief history from its origins through to the heady days of the 1980s when it appeared to be in touch with the popular mood, to the problematic era from the 1990s onwards, and to the ageing and death of its founder, Agonshū provides a good example of how new movements centred around charismatic founders can experience rapid changes and turning points.

While Agonshū has retained stability in its teachings and doctrines on karma and the spirits of the dead it has also experienced various changes in short order during its development. Kiriyama's life story itself can be seen as a series of dramatic ruptures and developments, from the suicide and salvation story of 1954, to the 1970 revelation from Juntei Kannon that indicates his turn from asceticism to religious leadership with a mission, to his claimed discovery in 1978 of the importance of the Āgamas. The 1980 Sahet Mahet transmission story that has become a major focal point of Agonshū's narrative, and the acquisition of the relic from Sri Lanka proclaimed as the true living relic of the Buddha reinforced Agonshū's self-identity as a universal Buddhist movement with a mission of salvation from Japan to the wider world and signified further important points in its trajectory. While such stories and turning points have clearly been projected, constructed and interpreted in particular ways by Kiriyama and Agonshū, they form crucial elements in the movement's self-identity, narrative and appeal to followers.

As Kiriyama aged, changes were less rapid and the focus appeared to shift more to solidifying existing elements within the movement. There were less dramatic shifts of the type evident in the first decade or so of its existence; by that time Agonshū had built a sizeable membership and could be seen as no longer being a very new movement but one entering – in first-generational terms – a middle period, in which the leader and those who had been around him from the outset entered the later decades of their lives. It was a period in which key rituals and structures, from doctrines to ritual formats, and a main image of worship, had all been settled. Stability did not mean stagnation as such, for some changes occurred – notably that the nationalist themes present from its early days became more potent, evident in visits to Yasukuni Shrine, rituals to repatriate the spirits of the Japanese war dead and a growing nationalistic revisionist rhetoric about the war. In this later period the movement has had to adjust to the reality that its initial burst of growth and the time when it appeared to be ahead of the field was over. The movement had aged along with its leader; just as he appeared to have become more inward looking and reflecting on the past and the friends he lost in the war, so did the movement as a whole, focusing more on Japanese issues and appealing to nationalist sentiments.

Agonshū has now entered another phase in its life cycle, one it was bound to face at some stage, as Kiriyama's death has meant it has had to deal with the loss of its founder and the change of leadership that has followed it. This is always a critical phase in a movement's development; losing the founder may not only trigger succession disputes but can also unsettle members who, in a first-generation movement, are liable to have joined because they have been inspired by and felt a direct personal connection to the founder. By enshrining Kiriyama his successors are sending out a message of continuity and letting members know that the founder continues to be central to the movement. How this will work out in the longer run is unclear but, as we indicated, one evident change is the transformation of Agonshū into a movement in which its deceased founder is becoming a (or the) main focus of worship. If Agonshū previously shifted its main focus of worship from Juntei Kannon to the Buddha and the *shinsei busshari*, it now appears to be making a further shift, from Shakyamuni and the *shinsei busshari* to Kiriyama the second (and more powerful) Buddha.

The developments we have traced in the trajectory of a quite new Japanese religious movement within the immediate time span of its founder's life and in the immediate period after his death raise a number of questions not just about Agonshū but about what we have throughout referred to as 'new religions'. Whether Agonshū is becoming a founder veneration movement is one such question, and alongside it we ask whether this represents a normative pattern in Japan and perhaps for 'new religions' in general. Another is whether, rather than being somehow 'new' and different, Agonshū is simply replicating normative Japanese religious structures. A third is whether, in the light of the transition under way in Agonshū, in which it is no longer a first-generational movement in terms of leadership, the term 'new religion' remains viable for it and, indeed, for other movements that have thus far been examined under the label of 'new religions' (*shinshūkyō*) in Japan and beyond.

Agonshū as founder veneration

Kiriyama's death and the way it has been handled in Agonshū are illustrative not simply of how a movement deals with the crisis of the loss of a founder, but of how such events can presage changes in orientation and teaching. In Agonshū's case a number of points can be readily discerned. The most striking is how a human founder has at death been transformed into a Buddha with salvific powers and has moved from being a leader to a main focus of worship. Another is that, based on the themes being mapped out in the *kaiso reiyu*, the concept of worship and faith as a means to salvation – themes that became central to Agonshū after the acquisition of the *shinsei busshari* in 1986 – have been intensified by the death and transformation of Kiriyama.

In an interview with a senior Agonshū figure in February 2017, one of us remarked that, given the enshrinement of Kiriyama's relics as a main object of worship, the notion that his spirit remains present and accompanying members as they perform their religious practices, and the proclamations that he was now the second Buddha, we wondered if Agonshū was turning into what we described as '*Kiriyamakyō*' (literally, 'Kiriyama religion'). He agreed that this did appear to be the case. The evidence we presented in the previous chapter, in which we discussed how Agonshū has made Kiriyama into the '*dai ni no budda*' whose reliquary was placed on the Hoshi Matsuri altar in front of that of the Buddha, and whose power is, according to Agonshū interpretations, greater than Shakyamuni's, appears to confirm this. If Shakyamuni originated Buddhism, Kiriyama, according to Agonshū, made it 'complete' (*kanzen*) and added to it the power of the *kami* to present an enhanced teaching able to match the complexity and problems of the modern world. His spirit in the Buddha realms aiding devotees to attain better rebirths, his physical presence as a living entity in this world via his relics, as well as in pendants, and his messages via the *kaiso reiyu*, all indicate that for Agonshū he remains as central to Agonshū after death as in life.

Agonshū's founder veneration is unsurprising. It is in many ways a personalized religion, born out of Kiriyama's experiences. Kiriyama, in seeking to understand why his life was going wrong, developed a way of thinking and practice that solved his problems – and he externalized that understanding, and made it universal and applicable to all. In so doing he drew on Japanese concepts grounded in the folk and Buddhist realms, about karma, ancestors and the spirits of the dead, and on practices found in Japanese traditions such as mountain asceticism, esoteric Buddhism and ancestor veneration rituals. Through them he found personal liberation, something confirmed by personal messages he claimed to have received from Buddhist figures such as Juntei Kannon, who affirmed that he had cut his karma and authorized him to become a religious leader seeking to save the world, and Shakyamuni, who conferred a universalizing mission on him.

One can detect other highly personalized dimensions in Agonshū's development. We can see this, for example, in the emphasis on the spirits of the war dead, evident in Agonshū's international rituals that have centred on places where large losses of life occurred in the Second World War, from Auschwitz to the Pacific War zone, and later the specific emphasis on spirits of the Japanese war dead coupled with Agonshū's focus on rituals and memorial visits to the National Cemetery and Yasukuni Shrine. The war and the feelings about the war dead are clearly elements that affected Kiriyama personally; as we discussed earlier, he became more focused on such issues as he got older and closer to death, even regretting that he had not been able to fight and die for his country. As we noted in Chapter 2, movements do revise their leaders' biographies to accord with new developments and fit with their new messages, and we consider it highly likely that this has happened with Agonshū's portrayals of Kiriyama's regrets in the period when it has become more overtly nationalistic.

His personal experiences not only provided the basis around which Agonshū emerged and developed; they also form the framework around which followers should deal with their own lives, following his example, performing his rituals and, now, venerating his spirit and relics. They indicate that Agonshū is not simply a religion founded by Kiriyama but a religion of Kiriyama, in which he remains alive and present according to Agonshū's current teaching and in which his spiritual voice is used to guide the movement and validate its current direction, while his physical presence in the form of his relics serves as the focus of its worship.

A common pattern in the new religions

Agonshū is, in such respects, illustrating a pattern found widely among Japanese religious movements of modern times, in which human founders are transformed into figures of worship by the movements they founded or inspired. As we stated in Chapter 1, a normative pattern for the foundation of new movements in Japan is for charismatic figures to reveal (or claim to have revealed to them) new deities that entrust them with a sacred mission, or to discern new truths in ancient scriptures. A further common pattern – and Agonshū clearly exemplifies this – is for such movements to then memorialize their founder and inspirational leader as a figure of worship.

Byron Earhart has shown how this process operated in Gedatsukai, whose founder, Okano Eizō, was given the title Gedatsu Kongō (literally 'diamond of liberation') after he died in 1948. A memorial was built to Okano at Gedatsukai's sacred centre on the outskirts of Kyoto and he became, in the guise of Gedatsu Kongō, one of three 'divinities' (as Earhart terms them) worshipped in Gedatsu's sacred triad both at its holy centres and in members' homes (Earhart 1989: 39). Founder memorialization is evident in Shinnyoen, which has built at its main centre a replica of the original place where Itō Shinjō began his religious mission. It has marked it with signs and symbols of his and his family's earlier life, as if to keep it alive for devotees. It is clearly evident in Tenrikyō, where the spirit of the founder Nakayama Miki is considered to be present at its sacred centre in Tenri, watching over the movement and her disciples. Her house is preserved and each day a newspaper is set out for her and her bath is run. Nakayama is not portrayed as a deceased founder but as Oyasama (honourable parent), a term that closely relates her to the (theoretical) main focus of Tenrikyō worship, who is referred to as God the Parent (Tenri-o-no-mikoto).

The process of elevating a leader to a position of higher spiritual authority that transcends death is evident, too, in Sōka Gakkai which, according to Levi McLaughlin (2012, 2018), has, since the 1990s, focused almost exclusively on the charismatic leadership of its third (and longest-lasting) leader Ikeda Daisaku. Sōka Gakkai is in some respects an anomaly among Japanese new religions in that its origins are not in the revelatory experiences of a charismatic founder but in the ethical and educative views of its first leader Makiguchi Tsunesaburō, who established it initially as a moral and educational society promoting concepts grounded in Nichiren Buddhism. It was after the ascent of Ikeda (initially a leading disciple of Toda Jōsei, the Gakkai's second leader) to its leadership and as a result of his long tenure (he became leader aged 32 in 1960) that the movement became increasingly centred on Ikeda's personality, teachings and meetings with famed figures from around the world. Sōka Gakkai has publicized what it portrays as Ikeda's various talents (such as photography) and has reported his many honorary degrees and other awards to help enhance an image of him as a charismatic and multitalented figure. Such is the emphasis in Sōka Gakkai on Ikeda now that the movement has been portrayed by some external critics as little more than 'Ikeda-kyō', 'the religion of Ikeda' (McLaughlin 2012: 137). McLaughlin also indicates that charismatic leadership of the organization will end with Ikeda (who is, as we write, 90 years old). This likely future is reiterated by Clark Chilson (2014) in his examination of how Ikeda promoted the mentor-disciple relationship in Sōka Gakkai, and of how this relationship is oriented towards preserving Ikeda's charismatic status and influence in Sōka Gakkai beyond his death. Ikeda became the president of Sōka Gakkai (according to his later account) because he was closest disciple of Toda, the previous leader, and in his own writings Ikeda has emphasized the importance of the mentor-disciple relationship. By portraying himself as learning from – and hence continuing the teachings of – Toda, including accepting his harsh criticisms, which were for his own betterment, Ikeda thus has created a sense of intimacy with the previous leadership, which is continued through his own person. Chilson shows that Ikeda has nurtured a belief in his followers about his own extraordinary qualities through such means, and in so doing has promulgated a similar mentor-disciple link between him and his followers. Since Ikeda has emphasized the importance of obedience to the leader (in his case, Toda) this informs disciples that they should be similarly obedient to Ikeda. This process of creating intimacy and identification between Ikeda and Gakkai disciples is one that, the current President of Sōka Gakkai, Harada Minoru, informed Chilson, should continue after Ikeda's demise. It was the mission of Sōka Gakkai to preserve this mentor-disciple relationship with Ikeda after he had departed this realm, so as to transmit his spirit to future generations (76).

Similar processes (but more acutely) are under way in Kōfuku no Kagaku. In this case, Ōkawa has already 'achieved' various exalted levels of spiritual status; he is, the movement proclaims, the creator figure El Cantāre and the Eternal Buddha. Hence it would hardly be surprising if his movement did not become focused on venerating its founder when he passes on. It has already taken various steps in this direction. The place where Ōkawa was born (a small village in Shikoku) has been turned into a pilgrimage site for disciples, who are issued with a *seichi junrei* (sacred place pilgrimage) guidebook to aid their visits, and plans are afoot to build a new holy centre of worship there as well (Akiya 2015: 18–19). The site also includes a building in memory of Ōkawa's father, who helped found the movement, and among the items displayed there are the original cassette tapes on which were recorded the first spirit messages (*reigen*) that Ōkawa claimed to have received, and which played a significant role in the founding of the movement. Before Ōkawa started Kōfuku no Kagaku he initially worked for a business company in Nagoya, Japan, where he lived in a company dormitory. This place, too, has been acquired by the movement, and turned into a place of pilgrimage where disciples can gain insights into the life he lived as a company worker, enter a reconstruction of his bedroom and see where Ōkawa placed his shoes and had dinner. His movement is already, it would appear, constructing the frameworks of founder veneration in the lifetime of its founder, and building for its future by highlighting his past.

A common Japanese religious trait?

Elevating human figures to positions of worship and venerating founders is not limited, in Japanese contexts, to the new religions. The example of Shingon Buddhism, one of Japan's oldest established Buddhist sects, provides a striking example that resonates with the stories and veneration of the founders of Japanese new religions. When Kūkai, the founder of Shingon in Japan and the monk who established its main headquarters at Kōyasan, died, a series of legends grew around him. He was given the posthumous title Kōbō Daishi and in this guise a series of legends grew around him. He had not died but had entered eternal meditation at Kōyasan, where his spiritual presence could still be felt and imbibed by disciples and pilgrims as he sat awaiting the coming of the future Buddha Maitreya, while those buried in the graveyard around his mausoleum were to rise again at that time (Schopen 1987: 202–203; Astley 2016).

At the mausoleum offerings are made daily to Kūkai, who remains, according to Shingon legend, seated in eternal meditation and enlightenment in the mausoleum. His spiritual presence is not confined to Kōyasan for, in his posthumous guise as the wandering pilgrim and miracle-worker Kōbō Daishi, he also is, according to the plethora of legends (*Kōbō densetsu*) associated with him, forever walking around Japan dispensing miracles and graces. The expansion of Shingon was aided by the sect's focus on its revered founder in his posthumous guise as a wandering and as an ever-present miracle worker, a human who transcended normative bounds to become an enlightened sage and spiritual force able to aid and intercede on behalf of the living. He also became a role model for ascetics who helped spread the Shingon faith and encourage pilgrimages to Kōyasan, as well as for pilgrims in general.[1] A key element in Shingon's growth, in other words, was because of the popular tales and miracle stories centred on Kōbō Daishi and his position as a source of benefits and miracles, and as a focus of veneration. This was so much the case, as Shingon scholars such as Saitō (1984) have shown, that while technically the main focus of worship in Shingon is Dainichi Nyorai (the Cosmic Buddha) in reality, it is Kōbō Daishi who is viewed in this way. Saitō's survey of ordained Shingon priests showed that even the priests and official clerical hierarchy of the sect tends to view Kōbō Daishi as the central focus of worship. Tanabe (2002: 672) reiterates the point that in Shingon Kōbō Daishi is effectively viewed as a saviour and a deity to whom devotees dedicate their chants and prayers. Moreover, the living presence, in the Shingon imaginary, of Kūkai/Kōbō Daishi at Kōyasan is manifested in the daily rituals there in which Shingon monks provide ritual meals for the holy figure, seated in eternal meditation in his mausoleum (Nicoloff 2008: 236–7), in a not dissimilar way to how Tenrikyō devotees provide for Nakayama Miki at her sacred centre at Tenri. Kūkai and the veneration of Kōbō Daishi provide the most striking example in the older established Buddhist sectarian traditions of founder veneration, but one can discern similar nuances in other sects as well. In earlier eras in the Sōtō Zen sect, for example, its initial founder in Japan, Dōgen, was portrayed as an intercessionary figure who could bestow benefits and boons on petitioners (Faure 1987: 50–1), while both Dōgen and the sect's second founder, Keizan, are the focus of reverence as sect ancestors.[2] Even on a more localized level one can see this process in action, as in the example of a small pilgrimage confraternity in Shiga prefecture, the Shiga Shingyōkai, whose deceased founder, Naitō Kinpō, after death, became a focus of veneration for the confraternity in ways that made him appear more prominent at the group's hall of worship than the figures (Dainichi Nyorai and Kōbō Daishi) who had initially been the Shiga Shingyōkai main focuses of veneration (Reader 1996: 280–4).

These are examples of a recurrent pattern within the wider contours of the Japanese religious world in which human figures – and not just the founders of religious institutions and sectarian traditions – can attain divine or transcendent status. The notion that Japan is a culture in which humans can become deities is seen in the folk and Shinto traditions, where many of the *kami* (deities) have human origins, whether in reality or legend. Satō Hiroo (2016) has discussed this matter also by drawing attention to examples of deifying human figures in Japanese religious contexts.

Among the most famous examples is the ninth-century educator and scholar Sugawara no Michizane who, after his death, was ritually enshrined and revered as the deity of education Tenjin, with major shrines built for him across the country. Imperial, aristocratic, military and political leaders are among the many who have attained the status of *kami* after death. Tokugawa Ieyasu, the seventeenth-century military and political ruler, for example, is enshrined as the deity Tōshō Daigongen at the Tōshō Shrine at Nikkō. Other examples (in perhaps more prosaic forms) include the merchant who suffered from haemorrhoids and, after death, was apotheosized into a deity offering relief to those suffering from that complaint (Reader and Tanabe 1998: 236–7). There is, in other words, an extensive culture of making humans into spiritual entities whether in life (as is the case with those who are proclaimed living gods, *ikigami* or buddhas, *ikibotoke*) or, even more extensively, in death. It is a tendency that permeates the wider terrain of religion in Japan.

Charismatic movements and founder worship

Nor is the pattern of movements founded by charismatic figures becoming movements that venerate their founders, especially after death, as deities or something similar, limited to Japan. In their discussion of charisma and of 'making saints' in modern Chinese religious contexts, Ownby, Goossaert and Ji (2017: 3–4) show that the terminologies used to describe such figures include 'god' (*shen*), a term used especially after the physical deaths of such charismatic figures, as well as 'living Buddha' (*huo fo*) and 'living immortal' (*huo shen xian*) that are used to indicate 'flesh-and-blood' saints. These indicate that the idea of the founder as a living deity (or, in Japanese terms, *ikigami*) is not limited to Japan; nor is the idea promulgated in Kōfuku no Kagaku, among others, of their leader as the Buddha reincarnate or as a living Buddha.

Founders may also be enshrined and venerated as main figures of worship and as continuing, living, presences in their movements after death in Chinese contexts just as they have in Japan. In his study of Patriarch Zhang Tianran (1889–1947) of Yiguandao (The Way of Pervading Unity), a millenarian movement in late Imperial China, Sébastien Billoud (2017: 230) has shown that, despite having died in 1947, the Patriarch 'is more alive than ever as a source of authority in the movement'. His death and deification have transformed and considerably strengthened his authority; at the same time his authority is disseminated through the intense emotional attachment of the adepts to elderly leaders of their branches. Indeed, Billoud argues that the veneration of the Master (i.e. Patriarch Zhang Tianran) serves as a model or a matrix for the veneration of elderly leaders, while emotional attachment to these elderly leaders also reinforces the authority of the Master. This has produced a successful preservation and extension of charisma at a time when the Yiguandao has become a much more routinized religious organization. As such, Billoud states that 'forms of charisma today at work within the Yiguandao are still largely linked to Zhang's authority' (240). In Yiguandao, Zhang's presence and omniscience continue to be felt by devotees, for example, in the belief that he still intervenes directly in the organization during spirit-writing sessions – something that appears not dissimilar to the ways in which Goi Masahisa in Byakkō Shinkōkai and Kiriyama in Agonshū both relay messages from the spiritual realms to their successors.

A new religion, a new mainstream?

As we have shown in this book, what 'new' religions such as Agonshū do is reflect practices, concepts and ideas that are very much in the mainstream of Japanese religiosity. Concerns about the spirits of the dead, the importance of karma and the need to deal with its negative effects are central to Agonshū as they are to many other new movements in Japan – and to established Buddhism. Intercessionary practices to ameliorate the situation of the living and bring about worldly benefits, too, as offered by Agonshū, are normative in Japan, found in Shinto and Buddhism as well as in new movements. Agonshū deals with divination – another element of the folk stratum and evident also in popular practices at shrines and temples. It uses ritual forms drawn from the Japanese environment; its fire rituals and *yamabushi* attire are derived from esoteric Japanese Buddhism and Japanese mountain religion. It incorporates both Buddhist figures of worship and, more recently, Shinto deities into its pantheon, and while utilizing the universalized imagery of Buddhism, places a significant focus on Japanese issues of identity and emphasizes the significance and spiritual value of Japan as an entity. The emphasis on incorporating Shinto and Buddhist themes and figures – and Kiriyama's claims (see Chapter 4) that in this way Agonshū is restoring a mode of religiosity that was central to Japan and underpinned its spiritual and moral standing until the Meiji period – further serves to reiterate the point that it is seeking to reiterate what it sees as the normative and traditional. Its founder has, in a common Japanese pattern, become a figure of worship after death. To such degrees, it could be argued, Agonshū looks like a very normative mainstream type of Japanese religion, more so, perhaps, than it could be seen as a departure from them, a radically different vision of the world, or, indeed, something specifically 'new'.

This brings us back to the issue we touched on in Chapter 1, and that scholars such as Nancy Stalker and Byron Earhart have raised when they have questioned the category of the 'new'. Stalker's questioning of the term in relation to Oomoto was based in her assessment that it used Shinto rituals and could well be included in the Shinto rubric rather than being categorized alongside groups that drew their focus from other traditions such as Buddhism. Earhart's comments about Gedatsukai argued that it reinforced the values of and manifested continuities with older traditional religions, and in particular Buddhism. Such views also question the standard portrayal of new religions in Japan, which sets them apart from the mainstream and in essence marginalizes them.

We concur to a great degree with such critiques and concerns about the terminology of the 'new' and its implications. What, after all, is specifically 'new' about Agonshū? Historically, of course, there is a clear case to be made for associating Agonshū with this term. It was founded only a few decades ago in 1978, albeit with roots going back to 1954 and the beginning of the Kannon Jikeikai, and it is 'new' by comparison with traditions that have been around for many centuries. It fits into the wider historical rubric used to refer to 'new religions' in Japan, as a product of the period from the nineteenth century onwards in which Japan has become a modern nation state. It stands apart from the so-called mainstream established (*kisei*) traditions of Shinto and Buddhism that have long been associated with customary belonging not so much through belief and individualized commitment as through social structures and associations via households and communities.

Until little more than a year ago (as we write in early 2018) it was first-generational in nature, with its founder still its living leader. That, in turn, would locate it within the framework of the 'new' not just in Japanese terms but also more broadly in the study of new religions. One of the definitional frameworks for analysing new religions that scholars such as Eileen Barker (2004) who work in the wider field of the study of new movements have used is based in the very concept of 'newness' in which first-generational membership is a defining feature of what should be incorporated under the rubric of 'new religions'.

However, the idea of the 'new' may not be that clear-cut. Thomas Robbins (2005: 104), writing about the concept of 'new religions' in Western contexts, has noted that a 'degree of incoherence has marked discourse about "new religions". This is partly because of a tendency to equate "new religions" with "alternative religions" '. The incoherence Robbins complains about in great part revolves around the question of whether the 'new' can be limited to first-generational movements – the perspective supported by Barker (2004) – and whether once their founder has died, they cease to be 'new'. Yet Western studies of new movements have tended still to include movements that are in their second (or more) generation of leadership. The point made by Robbins is perhaps even more evident in Japanese contexts, where the term has been applied to just about any movement founded there since the beginning of the nineteenth century. The discussion we outlined in Chapter 1 about how the notion of 'new religions' is expressed in Japan certainly serves to contradict the notion of the new as limited to first-generation movements.[3] Yet it also reflects the incoherence that Robbins complains about. Movements that are almost two centuries old, with fourth or beyond generational leaders and members, and with memberships that have been born rather than converted into them – much in the way that people may in Japan continue to see themselves for customary reasons as being Buddhist – are clearly not new in any real temporal or structural way. As newer groups appear – as they are likely to do and as they have for much of the period since the first 'new religion' emerged in the early nineteenth century – the problem of the 'new' becomes even more intense. It is a problem that has been evident ever since different eras have produced new movements that fit with the ethos of their time while looking out of date in succeeding decades as subsequent generations of movements arises. The terminological struggles we referred to in Chapter 1, of scholars who added an additional 'new' to the terminology in the 1980s to differentiate movements like Agonshū, that at the time looked so new and abreast of the age, from the 'older' new religions, and of scholars who even sought to use the term 'old' new religions, are indications of such incoherence.

An alternative view of 'new religions' argues that, rather than being simply newly founded movements with their first-generation leaders in place, they are primarily defined by being alternatives to the mainstream traditions. Newness is thus associated with being alternative, and with movements that may be relatively new compared to the established traditions of a society while standing apart from them.[4] This perspective certainly has influenced the framing of the 'new religions' in Japan, as we discussed in Chapter 1.

Yet here again the case of Agonshū raises questions. Agonshū certainly appeared as an alternative that criticized established Buddhism for restricting its practices to the elite priesthood. It offered a democratizing of religious powers to those who were prepared to make the sacrifices of time and money to join Agonshū. And yet it also drew extensively on the old, using concepts, beliefs and ritual practices that are normative within the traditional domain of the established Japanese religious world. One can hardly be more normative than emphasizing the spirits of the dead and *genze riyaku* or talking of a union between the kami and Buddhist figures of worship. It is 'old' in terms of its incorporation of the veneration of relics and its focus on ancient Buddhist texts, while in its more recent associations with Shinto and its nationalism it articulates themes close to the Shinto establishment.

New religions have often been portrayed (especially in the Japanese media) as discordant anomalies from the established norms. Agonshū is an example of the movements that have been included under this rubric, yet as our study has shown, in many ways it is far more evidently an extension of those norms than of radical departures from them. That, we suggest, is common for the movements generally included under the catchall rubric of the 'new' in Japan. To that extent, it is not just the concept of 'newness' that proves a problem in the broader definitional framework but also that of being alternative.

Agonshū appeared to pose a threat to the established order by opening up the practices that established Buddhism restricted to religious orders, to a wider public. Yet in doing this Agonshū replicated the frameworks and structures of the older orders; one had to acquire the appropriate status (whether by initiation or payment or both) to carry out *yamabushi* rituals. In other words, it offered alternatives, but alternatives that resembled the established frameworks, rather than radically diverging from them. It became increasingly conservative and nationalistic, emphasizing the importance of Japanese spirits and affirming ties to and cooperation with established Shinto shrines. From challenging the existing order it has become (or at least has striven to become) part of that order.

Agonshū, in its short existence and in the wake of its founder's death, challenges the notion of the 'new religions' insofar as the term 'new' relates in any way to a sense of being abreast of the times, of being in the first generation of development or even of being in any real sense truly alternative. This is of course a problem because the term 'new religions' and its Japanese concomitant *shinshūkyō* have become so entrenched in academic and media vocabularies. Yet even if we can recognize that there are (as we commented in Chapter 1) commonalities that can be identified among the movements so labelled and 'lumped' together (as Stalker [2008: 196] has phrased it), we should also be conscious not just of the differences between movements but of the highly problematic nature of the catch-all terms 'new' and *shin*.

Concluding comments: trajectories and the ageing of religions

There comes a time in the life trajectories of movements when they move from being young and dynamic to becoming established, normally around the figures that founded them. In earlier eras in Japan we have seen charismatic and inspired figures emerge, often from within the Buddhist tradition in Japan, to develop new strands of teaching and practice. They have often done so while criticizing the existing established mainstream as out of touch and positing new alternatives (alternatives that are at times portrayed as going back to an original ideal, or true way of Buddhism). One can see this in the various Kamakura Buddhist reformist movements that developed around figures such as Dōgen, Shinran and Nichiren, all of whom broke away from the Tendai sect to develop new forms of Buddhism. They were new and revolutionary in their era, critical of the old and keen to pave new paths to transcendence. The sects that their activities gave rise to have all, in subsequent eras, become parts of what we view as the mainstream, the established religious traditions of Japan. They are the religious establishment that new movements such as Agonshū then criticize as they claim to have found new (or to have revived old forgotten) truths that the old are no longer capable of expressing. The new, critical and revolutionary thus can in time become the established and the old.

Movements that are new do not stay that way for long. They age, as our example of Agonshū indicates, and especially when they lose their founder and turn him/her into a figure of worship, can become increasingly akin to the ways in which mainstream and established traditions operate. The new becomes the old – especially if and when newer more dynamic movements, with new, younger charismatic founders, appear – just as happened when the so-called new new religions of the 1980s appeared to make the existing 'new religions' look dated and 'old'. The once-new can quickly move from being exciting and challenging the old and established, to replicating it.

How Agonshū will develop in future is of course not something we can say. Its loss of momentum in recent years could indicate that it might follow the course of some charismatic movements that, within a relatively brief period, or within a few generations after their founder dies, fade away altogether. It could become established in the way other 'new' religions such as Tenrikyō have, or it might retain a following that continues across generations and retains support in the customary ways evident in much of Japanese Buddhism. What is clear is that its time of major growth has come to an end along with the ageing and demise of its founder. As this has happened it has become more and more apt to consider it as a founder-veneration movement that has aged within the lifetime and in the immediate aftermath of the demise of its founder. It is an example of how the charismatic and spectacular are driving forces in the formation of religious movements – forces that provide a dynamic of newness that attracts new followers and appears to offer alternatives to the staid and old. At the same time it is evidence of how the new can lose its lustre as founders age and die, as charisma becomes memorialized and as movements become increasingly focused on holding on to their founder and the images of their past. Agonshū, within the lifetime and immediate demise of its founder, provides an example of how the supposedly new and alternative can age and replicate the established, and shows how problematic the conceptualization of 'new' religions in Japan has come to be.

Notes

Introduction

1 These observations have been made by the authors of this book in their interactions with Agonshū particularly from around 2010. We discuss these issues further in Chapter 4.

2 Star Festival is direct translation of *Hoshi Matsuri*, although, as we note in Chapter 4, Agonshū developed a new official English title for the event in the mid-1990s. In this book, we normally will refer to the festival by using its Japanese title.

3 Here we would like to thank Birgit Staemmler, of Tübingen University, Germany, for her help and support in these projects. The website is run under the auspices of the World Religions and Spirituality Project, overseen by David Bromley, of Virginia Commonwealth University, and we thank him for his help and support. See http://wrldrels.org/SpecialProjects/JapaneseNewReligions/JapaneseNewReligions.htm.

4 Studies about the 'new religions of Japan' have been numerous in Western languages (notably English) and Japanese, both treating the idea of 'new religions' (*shinshūkyō*) as a collective phenomenon, and dealing with particular movements as examples of this collectivity. See, for example, in English, Thomsen (1963); McFarland (1967); Davis (1980); Hardacre (1984; 1986); Earhart (1989); Astley (2006); Staemmler and Dehn (2011); Reader (2015); in Japanese, Murakami (1975); Numata (1988); Inoue et al. (1991); Inoue (1992); and Shimazono (1994).

5 Although we, in Chapters 1 and 6 in particular, raise questions about the use of the term 'new religion' we use it here and elsewhere in this book as a matter of convenience, given that the term has become so widely used that it is essentially normative in Japan.

1 Situating Agonshū: The Concept of 'New Religions' in Modern Japan

1 See Reader (2015) for a downloadable and extensive overview of this topic, along with the various sources cited thus far in this chapter.

2 These include having a designated responsible person who is answerable legally for the movement's activities and affairs, possessing a belief system, nurturing followers, performing religious rites and having places of worship.

3 In the most recent *Shūkyō Nenkan* (Bunkachō 2017) it is listed in administrative terms under the category of a single self-standing Buddhist organization (p. 137) and under 'other' (*sono ta*) as a Buddhist group.

4 We stress 'Japanese roots' here because as a rule religious traditions (notably Christianity) that come from outside Japan and may be 'new' in Japanese terms tend not to be portrayed as 'new religions'.

5 Nishiyama (1990) himself later rejected the term, for example.
6 The *Shinshūkyō Jiten* (Dictionary of New Religions) compiled by Japanese scholars in 1991 (Inoue et al. 1991) had entries for over 300 movements and the data base of the Religious Information Research Center in Tokyo numbers between 300 and 400 groups in this category (Staemmler and Dehn 2011: 5).
7 See the series of articles in *Nova Religio* on this issue by Barker (2004), Melton (2004), Bromley (2004) and Reader (2005).
8 Buddhism's entry into Japan is generally dated as in around 538 CE. While scholars debate when it is viable to refer to an independent Shinto tradition, it is clear that *kami* worship (a basis of Shinto) and Shinto shrines predate Buddhism's entry.
9 For more discussions on such issues and the image of established traditions such as Buddhism being out of touch, see Murai (2010), Nelson (2012), Reader (2011) and Ukai (2015).
10 See Reader (1994: 58 fn. 32) for further discussion.
11 On the use of *jakyō*, see Dorman (2012: 25); Ketelaar (1993: 42). See also Sawada (2004).
12 For a discussion of such state suppressions, see Stalker (2008) and Staemmler (2011a: 27) (the latter of which lists several other suppressions in this period). For a discussion of another case, Renmonkyō, see Inoue (1992); Sawada (2004).
13 See Dorman 2012 (esp. pp. 135–6) for a discussion of the media's self-perceived role in guarding society against new movements both in prewar and postwar Japan.
14 Various officials of new religions have highlighted their social welfare activities to the authors, especially in the aftermath of disasters such as the 2011 Tōhoku tsunami and earthquake, and complained that these are never featured in the media – even as the media draws attention to volunteering and relief efforts in general.
15 For a general discussion of media and establishment responses to Aum, see Baffelli and Reader (2012); for discussions of media constructions about 'the next Aum', see Wilkinson (2009); and for Panawave and its treatment by the media, see Dorman (2005).
16 Among the studies that have helped develop this more balanced assessment are several we have already mentioned, such as the works of Hardacre (1984, 1986) and Earhart (1989) in English and Murakami (1975), Shimazono (1992a), Inoue (1992) and Numata (1988) in Japanese.
17 The work of Kitagawa (1966: 333) is typical here in his comment that new religions 'offer nothing new, as far as their religious contents are concerned'.
18 Hubbard (1998: esp. 87–8). Hubbard also suggests that Buddhist Studies scholars have not taken this approach because they did not want to have to acknowledge such things.
19 For example, the *Besseki* lectures (a set of ten lectures for members) outline core teachings and can be attended at Tenrikyō's headquarters at Tenri on a regular basis. The healing ritual called Sazuke (the Divine Grant) can only be administered by a *yoboku* (an initiated member), who has attended the *Besseki* nine times. For details, see Katō (2017).
20 Konkōkyō is a good example here, as it publishes a glossary that accompanies its canonical text, the *Konkōkyō Kyōten*, and explains the nuances and meanings of terms used in the writings of its founder (Konkōkyō Honbu Kyōchō 1983).
21 Both authors, when interviewing figures from Kōfuku no Kagaku, have had this phrase directed at them; Shimada (1995), too, notes its usage when he questioned Kōfuku no Kagaku's representatives about the group. In its early years the group also introduced a system of examinations based on knowledge of Ōkawa's books.

22 According to the group, Ōkawa entered the Guinness Book of Records in 2011, having published 52 books in 2010. His production increased to 161 books in 2014 and the total number currently is 2,600 volumes. See https://happy-science.jp/ryuho-okawa/book/ and http://happy-science.org/ryuho-okawa/ (both accessed 3 July 2017).

23 In the early 1950s, for example, officials in the Sōtō Zen sect referred to the need to adopt the methods of new religions in order to remain relevant, and the sect thereafter began producing a variety of publicity and teaching materials that were very similar to those of the new religions. As a result Sōtō began to produce a large amount of pamphlets, monthly magazines and so on – in a similar vein to the new religions – in order to try and counter the appeal of the new religions and maintain the loyalty of their existing followers (Reader 1983). Other Buddhist sects have done similarly – although the general pattern of declining affiliation in the older Buddhist sects suggests that this strategy has not always worked (Reader 2011).

24 See also Shimada (2005 and 2010) for two highly critical discussions of the costs of death rituals in the context of Buddhism in Japan.

25 This was a recurrent criticism of Aum Shinrikyō, for example (Reader 2000a: 131–2), while numerous magazines and popular books by academics and journalists have focused expressly on the topic of new religions and money (e.g. Shimada 2008; Sakurai 2011; Yamada 2012).

26 Debates about the nature of 'being Japanese' have of course been discussed widely through analyses of the '*nihonjinron*' (discourses about being Japanese) debates that were prevalent especially in the period – the 1980s – when Agonshū became popular.

27 GLA is the official name of the movement. It is an acronym for 'God Light Association' and is, as far as we are aware, the only movement in Japan to use solely an English-language title for itself. This usage in itself is striking and conveys an implication that, while being Japanese (and its focus on spirits, healing and the like locates it very much within the Japanese new religions spectrum), it also embraces Western and modern notions and themes.

28 We use these three to illustrate the diversity of types of movement alongside some unifying themes. Each was formed at a different era – Agonshū in 1978, Kurozumikyō in the early nineteenth century and Reiyūkai in 1924 – and has a different doctrinal orientation: Agonshū has an esoteric Buddhist framework supplemented by Shinto deities and folk concepts; Reiyūkai is a Nichiren Buddhist movement; and Kurozumikyō emerged from and has close ritual and other links with Shinto.

29 Although this theme emerged most potently in Aum (see Reader 2000a for some examples, notably p. 108), it was a theme that could be found among members of other groups such as Agonshū and Kōfuku no Kagaku that we have met. This does not mean they rejected the materialistic world (indeed, Agonshū and Kōfuku no Kagaku followers we have met often have emphasized an interest in such things but have also sought to augment this with what they see as spiritual development).

30 Oomoto under Deguchi Nao's leadership is a good example of a movement that was both xenophobic and hostile to Western medical practices such as vaccinations; Stalker (2008: 210, fn. 121), for example, notes that Deguchi Nao refused to allow her granddaughter to be vaccinated against smallpox because she thought the vaccination was a foreign pollutant.

31 Or, perhaps, although we have been unable to fully ascertain this, only at such institutions.

32 These positions are set out in pamphlets Agonshū produces as introductions to the faith, such as its dual language publication (Agonshū, ed., nd., pp. 11–13 of the English section and pp. 11–12 of the Japanese).

2 The Story of a Religious Founder: Kiriyama Seiyū, Turmoil, Charisma and Experience

1 We note also that Japanese scholars have commonly used 'charisma' (Japanese: *karisuma*) as a foreign loanword in their discussions. See, for example, Kawamura (1981); Numata (1987 and 1988); Shūkyō Shakaigaku Kenkyūkai (1987). More generally, on leaders of Japanese new religions, see Ooms (1993); Baffelli (2005); Stalker (2008); McLaughlin (2009); Dorman (2012); and Chilson (2014).

2 We are not suggesting that female founders such as Nakayama and Deguchi *only* became religious founders because other avenues were shut off to them but are noting that the new religions offered scope for female participation that was not available in some other public spheres.

3 For this reason Staemmler and Dehn (2011) use the phrase 'establishing the revolutionary' in the title of their overview of Japanese new religions.

4 We should note that there are exceptions, such as, for example, Sōka Gakkai, whose political activism led to the establishment of a political party, the Kōmeitō. On Kōmeitō, see Ehrhardt et al. (2014). On religion and politics in postwar Japan, see also Nakano (2003) and Tsukada (2015).

5 A striking example, of course, is Asahara Shōkō of Aum Shinrikyō, venerated as a guru and spiritual master by his disciples and pilloried in multiple ways as a charlatan and worse in the media and in general public view (Reader 2000a).

6 At the 2017 Hoshi Matsuri one of the authors was approached by a *Japan Times* journalist seeking comments about the event from non-Japanese visitors; he confirmed to us that the article he had been commissioned to write was, indeed, a paid-for advertisement and that Agonshū had been doing this annually for some time.

7 This phrase, initially reported in the *Mainichi Daily News* in October 1987, has been recycled by Agonshū and used as a self-description as well as becoming a phrase commonly cited in academic studies of the group (see, e.g. Reader 1988).

8 For an analysis of the text, see Baffelli (2005).

9 See Ooms (1993: 21–33) for an account of Nao's life that draws on Oomoto sources.

10 This account is drawn together from narratives in Yajima (1985), Murō (1987), Reader (1994) and Benod (2013), along with sermons and publications by Kiriyama and testimonies and interviews with Agonshū officials at various periods from 1987 to 2017. It also incorporates narratives of his life produced by Agonshū and broadcast at his funeral and at the 2017 Hoshi Matsuri. The first two cited authors were involved, we understand, with Agonshū at the time of writing their accounts.

11 It is unclear how long he spent in prison. While Benod (2013: 162) says he served ten months in prison, both Reader (1988: 246) and Yajima (1985: 48–9) say it was six months. The account of the leader's life presented in the text *Genze jōbutsu* (Kiriyama 1983) does not specify how long the sentence was.

12 This was how it was portrayed in 1987 and 1988 in sermons attended by one of the authors (see Reader 1988, 1991).

13 See Reader (1994: 59, fn. 33). Although Kakida (1984: 63–4) claims that Kiriyama's account of his practices and links with Shingon Buddhism was false, there appears sufficient evidence to show that he did undertake various practices in the Kongōin branch of Shingon Buddhism and received an ordination there; see also Benod (2013: 164, fn. 345).

14 It was in this area that one of the authors had a chance encounter in 2010 with an Agonshū priest, who confirmed that the movement was struggling to gain new followers (see Reader 2012: 20, fn. 10); interestingly, the movement's centre there still had the old name, Kannon Jikeikai, on its door.

15 It is unclear how many people were involved in it though it probably was only a few hundred at most. One of us (Reader) in 1987 met members of Agonshū who had been in the Jikeikai in the 1960s, so it is evident that Kiriyama did at least get some followers early on. According to the annual religious yearbook published by the Agency for Cultural Affairs in Japan, the recorded membership for Kannon Jikeikai rose from 500 to 18,500 between 1976 and 1977. In 1978 they claimed 20,200 members (Bunkachō 1977: 197; 1979).

16 The *goma* ritual is also used in a number of new religions as well that draw inspiration from the esoteric tradition, such as Bentenshū and Shinnyoen.

17 This is, of course, the Agonshū view. See Reader (1994: 49).

18 The term 'boom' (*būmu*) is widely used in Japanese media to indicate popular trends, which tend to disappear rather quickly, being replaced with a new fashion or popular topic. According to Skov (1995: 175), '[T]he Japanese word boom refers to more than consumer trends: environmental problems, economic fluctuations, political issues, cultural debates – along with television series, writers and models – have been popularized and then forgotten according to the same temporal logic.'

19 In this dual-language booklet the Japanese text translates the same as the English cited here except that in Japanese the term 'Shaka' (i.e. Shakyamuni) is used whereas in English it is 'Laud' (*sic*) Buddha.

20 Ōkawa Ryūhō's claim to the mantle of original Buddhism did not appear to be grounded in the type of study and reading that both Aum and Agonshū claimed went into their understandings. For example, Ōkawa and his followers disciples – after a fractious televised debate with Aum members that involved each group making claims that they represented true Buddhism – for not having a sound grasp of Buddhist texts (Watanabe 1997: 37–8).

21 Reader (2018). On Oomoto and millennialism, see Ooms (1993) and Berthon (1985).

22 The Western calendar is used in Japan alongside the traditional one based on Imperial reigns.

23 We will look more clearly at these issues of millennialism and hopes for world salvation (which were a cardinal element in Agonshū's teaching) in the next chapter.

24 This pattern of attribution (materialism and hence destruction as a product of Western civilization, while the solution is grounded in the 'spirituality of the East') is a recurrent theme in Japanese cultural discourses, notably in the highly nationalistic *Nihonjinron* ('debates about being Japanese') discourses: on this issue, see Befu (2001 and 2009).

25 Nostradamus Quatrain X.72; see http://www.predictions-nostradamus.com/x72.htm. This phrase is often rendered or thought to refer to a 'King of the Mongols' – hence the way it was translated into Japanese linked the rise of this king to a figure 'from the East'.

26 On 'spirituality' in Japan, see also Horie (2009 and 2011). On New Age in Japan see Haga and Kisala (1995)

27 http://www.agon.org/en/about/page_b3.html. Retrieved 7 August 2017.

28 See Reader (1988: 242, fn. 5) for further discussion about the difficulties of finding out what motivated the Sri Lankans in this context.

29 http://www.agon.org/en/about/page_b3.html. Retrieved 7 August 2017.

30 Some scholars have argued that this pattern of according divine (or similar) status to founders of new religions is grounded also in the notion, prevalent in prewar Japan and affirmed by State Shinto (and still found in some nationalist circles thereafter) that the Emperor was a living deity. For some scholars, this reverence for the founders of new religions and their portrayal as living deities was a replacement of the prewar veneration of the Emperor who, in post-1945 Japan, had renounced his divinity. For a critical account of this theory, see Rajana (1975).

31 Agonshū also has produced a booklet that it hands out to prospective followers, and that has the same Japanese title as the 1993 book. It contains the text of a sermon by Kiriyama in 1992, and outlines the themes developed in the 1993 book.

32 Subsequently, we should note, Agonshū has emphasized that its prime links with the Tibetan form of Buddhism has come via Bhutan and Bhutanese Buddhism (see Chapter 5).

33 For a photographic account, accompanied by a narrative text, of the Hoshi Matsuri, see http://nirc.nanzan-u.ac.jp/en/publications/photo-archive/nc-cat/1/. Especially for Kiriyama's activities at the festival, see http://nirc.nanzan-u.ac.jp/en/publications/photo-archive/nc-image/109/.

34 www.hirakawa-shuppan.co.jp.

35 For an example of advertisement text using these statements, see *Shūkan Sunday* July 1987: 232.

36 http://www.agon.org/en/books/. The book in question is Kiriyama (2000b), a translation of Kiriyama (2000c).

37 Fukami was a major donor to the International Shinto Foundation, which was involved in supporting the conference.

38 http://happy-science.org/ryuho-okawa/. Accessed 15 August 2017.

3 Teaching as Practice: Ritual, Benefits and the Costs of Devotion

1 Officials have noted that, at the peak of the movement's growth in the 1980s, every year a number of members of the general public who came to watch the Hoshi Matsuri signed up to join Agonshū on the day.

2 These are the translations as given in Reader (1988: 244).

3 It has been a common feature of new movements that they have a hierarchic dimension in which senior disciples who have been in the movement for some time and who have helped introduce new members, in effect become their teachers and guides. This pattern (often referred to as the *oyabun* framework), in which earlier members become the 'parent' (*oya*) for new recruits they have brought in, is found widely among new movements in Japan (Hambrick 1974: 237).

4 On ancestor rituals in Agonshū, see also Prohl (2004).

5 See Kiriyama's (*Agon Magazine* 2012: 18) response, in the Question and Answer session in *Agon Magazine*, to a question about whether those who fall into the hells at

death remain there eternally. Kiriyama affirms the notion of transmigration and says any spirit can in time attain higher realms, but he implies this is easier for Agonshū and that those who are non-believers are likely to initially go to the hells. As with the world of Japanese Buddhism, there seems to be a somewhat indistinct area here, in which Agonshū speaks of the spirits of the dead remaining present in and affecting this world, and going in a cycle of rebirths to other realms at death.

6 Also cited in Benod (2013: 323). See also the series of videos on Agonshū on YouTube that express this notion: https://www.youtube.com/watch?v=C0P08rtAGy8).

7 See Ambros (2015); Inose (2017); Kawahashi (2017); and Kawahashi and Kobayashi (2017) for discussions of gender-related issues, and notably, the prejudices in gender terms against women across the religious spectrum in Japan, and notably in Buddhism and Buddhist-related movements.

8 Not all of the movements of the 1980s were so 'modern' in this sense; Kōfuku no Kagaku, for example, appears more conservative in terms of gender issues than, for instance, Aum or Agonshū.

9 On Shugendō and gender issues, see Kobayashi (2017) and also Blacker (1999; (1975): 215–16), who outlines how female practitioners on the Yoshino-Kumano Shugendō pilgrimage had to follow a different route at some points because certain sacred mountains were (and some still are) prohibited for females.

10 In Japanese 'magic' can be rendered by terms such as *majutsu* (a term with underlying negative implications associated with 'black magic' and sorcery) and *jujutsu*, neither of which are used in Agonshū (for recent uses of these terms, see Horie [2015]). Agonshū does at times use the word *fushigi* (wonder, marvel) to refer to the ability of its rituals to help people realize their wishes (e.g. leaflets for the Hoshi Matsuri we collected in 2017 talk of how '*fushigini onegaigoto ga kanau!*' 'wonderfully, one's requests are realised' [Agonshū 2017] but the pamphlet emphasizes that such realization of wishes is based in identifying particular unhappy spirits, performing correct rituals for them and thus making them benevolent).

11 This term was used by Kiriyama in a sermon delivered on 16 January 1992 and printed in Agonshū's membership magazine (*Agon Magazine* 2017, 5/6: 5–22).

12 This was the case in 2012, and is the sum reported also in Yamada (2012: 161) and Benod (2013: 183); as far as we are aware, it remains so.

13 Around £260 as of December 2017 prices. Benod (2013: 233–6) also provides a full description of the items involved.

14 However, we should note that we are not and have never been members but we have attended various Agonshū rituals without being asked to provide a card. How closely the issue of membership is enforced is unclear to us but we have not come across any examples of people being excluded from a centre for such reasons.

15 The eightfold path (right view, right thought, right speech, right action, right livelihood, right effort, right mindfulness and right concentration) is set out along with other elements in what Agonshū designates as the true Buddhist path on its website http://www.agon.org/en/about/page_a4.html.

16 For a more detailed discussion of this issue and the ways in which the term '*shugyō*' may be used in Japanese contexts, see Reader (1991: 128).

17 See, for example, the movement's website account of a training event for members in which those who took part in a particular event in 2017 are referred to as *shugyōsha*: http://www.agon.org/blog/hokkaido/blog000715.php.

18 This outline of practices comes from a standard Agonshū publication, titled simply Agonshū, and published in 2014 as a basic guide to the religion.

19 For a further discussion of the role and symbolism of cleaning such spaces in Japanese religious contexts, see Reader (1995).

20 These points were made to one of the authors during interviews on 1 July 1987, with three young Agonshū devotees who worked for one of the movement's magazines.

21 Benod (2013: 229–31) even suggests, based on his experiences, that sometimes one can short-circuit the need for extensive training by just paying a fee; in his case he also seems to have negotiated a lower fee, doubtless because he was a foreign researcher and the movement was keen to get him involved in Agonshū.

22 For a discussion of cold water–related austerities and standing under waterfalls, see Blacker (1999 (1975): passim, esp. 142–5 and 171–2); and Reader (1991: 122–3). The statement about such water austerities disciplining the mind and body (*shinjin o tanren shimasu*) comes from Agonshū (nd. but probably 2014: 7).

23 This is unless they are at the very highest ranks within the movement, when they wear purple. At the 2017 Hoshi Matsuri, Wada Naoko wore purple robes.

24 These initially were carried out under the auspices of one of the smaller Shingon Buddhist sects (Reader 1994).

25 It also encourages *gomagi kanjin* for other of its rituals (such as the aforementioned monthly rituals) that involve *goma* fires and sticks, but it is the Hoshi Matsuri on which the main *kanjin* activities and expectations are centred.

26 Benod (2013), for example, does not discuss the term and nor do earlier studies such as Reader (1988, 1994) or Numata (1988). Agonshū's website does not mention the term in its English section and while mention is made in several places about the act of doing *gomagi kanjin* (i.e. soliciting sales and donations of *goma* sticks) for various rituals, there appears to be no explanation per se about the practice anywhere on the site.

27 The site is http://agama.zouri.jp and the text is available at http://agama.zouri.jp/gomabook_top.html. Accessed October 2017. The booklet that has been uploaded on this site was probably produced in 1995 or 1996.

28 http://www.agon.org/blog/osaka/blog000670.php.

29 http://www.agon.org/blog/hiroshima/blog000590.php.

30 One of the authors recalls being at the Hoshi Matsuri in the late 1980s with some visitors from outside Japan, who decided to purchase and write *gomagi* for world peace because it seemed, to them, to be a good thing to do and be part of. Neither of the current authors has ever felt the inclination to do this.

31 See, for example, Yamada (2012: 160–8). This is one of numerous populist publications in Japan – usually focused on new religions – that depict religions largely through the guise of money-making (or money-grubbing) organizations. Agonshū is normally one of the movements featured in such types of publication.

32 Discussion about and criticisms of *kanjin* and donations in Agonshū are frequent in online forums such as Yahoo Chiebukuro, Q&A sites and 2channel.

33 For accounts of this ritual, see Reader (1991: 225–8) and Baffelli (2016: 74–6).

34 Agonshū publishes a regular newsletter (*Meitoku Nyu-su*) about the *meitokusai* rituals; issue 245, in May 2012, for example, paid homage to the Japanese war dead and stated that Japan's later prosperity was built on their sacrifice.

35 This description comes from Agonshū's website: http://www.agon.org/schedule/schedule_000019.php.

36 http://nirc.nanzan-u.ac.jp/en/publications/photo-archive/nc-cat/1/. This is the Photo Archive of Japanese Religions, housed in the Nanzan University website: http://nirc.nanzan-u.ac.jp/en/activities/photo-archive-of-japanese-religions/.

37 http://www.agon.org/hoshimatsuri/e/about.html and http://www.agon.org/ hoshimatsuri/about.html. Both accessed 7 November 2017.

38 On the worship of stars in Japan, see also Dolce (2006).

39 While Hayek (2011: 368) has commented that divination in Japan has not received much substantive academic treatment compared to that given to the topic in Chinese contexts, there have been a number of useful accounts of the practice, including several on Taoist-related divinatory systems (e.g. Hayashi 2006) while Blacker (1999) makes a number of references to astrology and divination as elements in Japanese ascetic and folk culture. See also Hayashi and Hayek (2013) and Suzuki (1995) for a general overview of divination in contemporary Japanese religious contexts.

40 This is the term used on its website (http://www.agon.org/en/schedule/page_b.html) and in promotional literature for the event. Kiriyama (2005: 7 and 58–9) outlines how this change of name and increased focus on Shinto came about – a theme we discuss further in the following chapter.

41 It was as a result of finding a flier for the 1987 Hoshi Matsuri in his mailbox in Kobe (where he lived at the time) that Reader first became interested in Agonshū and studying it.

42 For example, one non-Japanese visitor to the festival, cited in Agonshū's members' magazine, commented that he had been made aware of the event by the Kyoto Tourist office (*Agon Magazine* 2012: 60).

43 In this context we draw attention to other means of making wishes and praying for the deceased in Japan, such as amulets, votive tablets (*ema*) and the like (see Reader and Tanabe 1998).

44 According to Agonshū, this development came after it had conducted a major fire ritual at Ise in October 1993, to commemorate the rebuilding of the Ise Shinto shrines. In interviews with officials of the movement in February 2017 they stated that the pyres still represented the *taizōkai* and *kongōkai* as well as the more recent designations, even if the former terms were less prominent now.

45 While this is something of a simplified generalization (Buddhism, e.g. has a strong this-worldly orientation in Japan alongside its concerns with the dead), it represents a standard perspective noted about Japan (see Reader 1991).

46 In 1988, for example, a delegation of Egyptian religious leaders was present and in 2017 Bhutanese monks played a role in the rituals. Agonshū's membership magazine often, after the annual festival, contains reports in which members of the public are cited as expressing their gratitude at being able to aid in the mission of world peace by attending the festival.

47 http://www.agon.org/history/history_000035.php. Interestingly Agonshū's website does not, in either its English-language or Japanese-language history pages of the movement, refer to any of its earlier (i.e. pre-2000) overseas fire rituals but only mentions those from 2000 onwards.

48 Agonshū's website states that the 2008 event was in Israel, whereas the 2013 one was in Jerusalem (without mentioning a country for the latter): http://www.agon.org/ history/.

49 See the full-page article that appeared (as a paid advertisement) in the *Japan Times*, 20 December 2010, for an account of this event, and, for a live stream of the ritual, see http://commonpassion.org/announcement/ one-peace-live-the-buddhist-maya-aura-festival-for-world-peace-november-7-2010/.

50 *Agon Magazine* (2012: 2). The term '*bunmei*' can have nationalist connotations and was used by activists in the period after the 1868 Meiji Restoration who were intent on building a new civilization in Japan (Gluck 1985).

51 See the report in *Agon Magazine* (2012: 8–12).

4 From the World to Japan: The Nationalism of an Ageing Movement

1 See Reader (2000a: 260 n. 71) for further discussion.

2 The term 'catastrophic millennialism' – indicating a form of millennialism in which disaster was an essential precursor of the advent of a new spiritual age – was initially suggested by Catherine Wessinger (1997) and developed further by her (Wessinger 2000: 8–9). It has come to be widely accepted in studies of millennialism and was used, for example, by Reader (2000a) in his analysis of Aum.

3 See http://fakty.interia.pl/malopolskie/news-guru-sekty-w-oswiecimiu,nId,1128408. Retrieved 14 August 2017. The authors would like to thank Paulina Kolata for translating this article for us. Other Polish magazine and online groups reported critical comments about the Agonshū event. See, for example: http://auschwitz.org/en/museum/news/who-donated-money-for-the-remembrance-mound-museum-rejected-support-from-a-questionable-donor,98.html. Retrieved 14 August 2017.

4 By 2000 Nostradamus was, in effect, out of date, no longer a voice in the popular cultural context – a point brought home to one of the authors who, in 2002, came across a shelf of remaindered books about Nostradamus and his prophecies, outside a second-hand bookshop in the Jimbochō bookshop area of Tokyo. On sale for derisory sums of 100 yen each, the books had clearly passed their sell-by date.

5 It is not just new religions that face such problems or that resort to stratagems to boost their numbers and maintain a facade of continued success. Established Buddhist sects can also interpret their figures in inventive ways. As such, reported figures do not convey any realistic depiction of a movement's strength at any time.

6 Data on Kōfuku no Kagaku's membership are not published in the *Shūkyō Nenkan*. Current figures reported in Kōfuku no Kagaku's publications claim around eleven million members.

7 Sometimes organizations do recognize the problem of numbers and accept there are gaps between official figures and active members; in the 1980s the Sōtō Buddhist sect reported membership figures well over 6 million in the annual Agency report but, at the same time, in a study carried out within the sect, it stated that it had only 287,000 active followers (Reader 1991: 9). Isaac Gagné (2013) reports that Kagamikyō amended its official membership numbers downwards from 140,000 to 6,000 in 2010 to reflect actual active engagement.

8 See also Reader (2012: 20 fn 10) for a conversation with an Agonshū priest who said the movement was experiencing similar problems of decline as other religious groups.

9 These observations of the 2017 festival were made by Reader, along with photographic evidence that contrasts with the crowds depicted in the 1987 and 1988 events and portrayed in the Nanzan photo archive: http://nirc.nanzan-u.ac.jp/en/publications/photo-archive/nc-cat/1/.

10 Katō's account of Tenrikyō's problems has been confirmed in interviews with officials in the movement (Reader 2012: 20), while the authors have also heard numerous

similar reports from officials in new religious movements about their problems in recent times. For further discussion of the issue of decline in religious organizations in Japan, see Reader (2012) and (on Buddhism in particular) Reader (2011) and Nelson (2012).

11 This was to an extent because many religious organizations, notably new movements in the wake of the Aum Affair, were concerned about the attacks that had been made on them in the media over many decades and were reluctant to expose themselves to the new online media (Baffelli, Reader and Staemmler 2011: 20–34); see also Fukamizu (2011: 39–61) for an example of an older established religious organization that faced similar problems that hampered its use of the internet.

12 Reader (1983) examines Sōtō Zen strategies to deal with such problems, showing that playing on a sense of loyalty and on retaining the bonds of existing members has been the way this has been handled, while his subsequent discussion of Buddhist problems in Japan (2011) indicates that this has not been a great success.

13 During a visit to Tenri headquarters on 26 January 2006, on the occasion of the anniversary of Nakayama Miki's death, one of the authors had discussions with various Tenrikyō priests and officials about their strategies and was shown a new anime film about the origins and teaching of the movement that had been commissioned recently by Tenrikyō. The aim was to present its teachings in a modern accessible form for a new generation. The recognition that it still is losing large numbers of members (see earlier in this chapter) suggests that thus far this new anime strategy has not been a success.

14 It was involved in the formation of the *Nihon o Mamorukai* (Society to Protect Japan), a right-wing grouping that was one of the two groups that merged in 1997 to form the Nippon Kaigi, the right-wing nationalist organization that has become prominent in recent times (McNeill 2015). Staemmler (2013) describes it as 'more overtly patriotic than many new religions', which is a polite way of putting it.

15 This was the view of the leader of another new religious movement that one of the authors talked to in February 2017. He was extremely impressed with Seichō no Ie's new direction and what its leader was trying to do – but he was also not sure how successful it would be, and he recognized that if he tried any similar innovations in his movement, it would upset older members upon whom the movement relied.

16 Gagné uses a pseudonym to refer to this group because of its small size and in order to maintain the privacy of those who provided him with information.

17 Other groups have sought to do this as well. In 2010 one of the authors was contacted by a PR company in the United Kingdom seeking advice (which the author felt unable to provide) because it was bidding for a contract to work for a Japanese new religion. The religion in question similarly was worried about declining membership in Japan and was looking to expand overseas to counterbalance this problem, and to do so wanted to engage a PR company to mastermind its activities. This strategy is used in World Mate, as Kawakami (2008) has indicated; in Chapter 2 we mentioned how its leader Fukami portrayed himself as a leading figure on the international stage, and this, as Kawakami indicates, helps attract followers in Japan.

18 Sōka Gakkai is the main outlier here, with a following in the United States and elsewhere, while some movements have built followings among Japanese diaspora communities notably in South America, and some (e.g. Sekai Kyūseikyō) have sought to establish followings in Africa; Sekai Kyūseikyō claims to have around 80,000 followers in that continent, although this is hardly a great number given Africa's population is, as of 2018, estimated to be 1.2 billion people:

http://worldpopulationreview.com/continents/africa-population/. Retrieved 20 March 2018. Sakashita (1998) provides another example of the apparent lack of major success by Japanese new religions abroad in showing that Shinnyoen – one of the most successful movements in Japan – had not, by the late twentieth century, managed to attract any following among the local population in places such as the United Kingdom.

19 On the wider issues of Yasukuni, see the collection of essays in Breen (2008).

20 See Mullins (2012a, b) for a discussion of the links between right-wing political groups and Shinto nationalists, and John Breen (2015: 5–6, 174) for the links between Abe Shinzō, the right-wing nationalist politician who has been elected as Japan's Prime Minister, and the Shinto shrines at Ise.

21 This theme, known as the *honji suijaku* theory, posits that the Shinto gods are localized manifestations awaiting the coming of Buddhism so as to become enlightened. On various issues related to the complex relationship of the Buddhist and Shinto figures of worship, see Matsunaga (1969); Rambelli and Teeuwen (2003); and Sueki (2007).

22 The ritual was not actually held within the precincts of the shrines but adjacent to them. In publications Agonshū tends to be somewhat vague on this point, so that casual readers might well assume that the ritual was actually held at and hosted by the Ise shrines. On the themes of the Ise shrine rebuilding processes that take place every twenty years, and the ways in which the rebuilding is portrayed in different ways and with different meanings, see Breen (2015).

23 Details on Koizumi, who died in 1989 aged 83, are unclear, and we have had to rely largely on internet sources that provide some basic materials. For example, http://blog.kawashima-seitai.com/?eid=1248343. Accessed 27 March 2018. It appears that he was born in northern Japan, had Shinto connections, was associated with divination practices (which may have influenced Kiriyama) and opened a number of kendō training centres in Japan, including one in Ise in 1961, where he normally resided. The account of his meeting with Kiriyama comes from Kiriyama (2005), in which Kiriyama says he had mentioned this event often when speaking to disciples, but we have found no corroborative accounts beyond that of Kiriyama himself.

24 This identification is because the ideograms for *daikoku* can also be read as *ōkuni* (Reader and Tanabe 1998: 154).

25 *Sore wa kuyashii. kuni no tame ni mo shinu koto mo dekinai no dakara.*

26 *Sankei Shinbun* 15 August 2012 Advertisement special.

27 The text in Japanese states: *Watashi wa, ima no nihonjin zenin ga taiheiyōsensō no izoku de aru to itte yoi to omoimasu* (Agonshū 2012: 1).

28 *Yasukuni sanpai wa nihonjin toshite atarimae da to omoimasu.*

29 See, for example, the following news articles about Ishihara: https://www.japantimes.co.jp/news/2014/12/16/national/politics-diplomacy/ishihara-bows-wants-war-china-compares-hashimoto-young-hitler/#.WfiESRh0dqc and http://www.nytimes.com/2012/12/09/world/asia/shintaro-ishihara-right-wing-japanese-politician-makes-gains.html.

30 Although the term 'sensei' is widely used in Japan to refer especially to those who are older than oneself, the recurrent use of the term by Ishihara has been taken by some Agonshū members to indicate the extent to which the politician respected and took inspiration from religious leader. It is unclear when the association began and thus far we have not been able to discover when the two first met. Ishihara had links with

a number of new movements with nationalist orientations and this may in part be because of his many years in politics and his period as governor of Tokyo; see on all these points the discussion among members at https://detail.chiebukuro.yahoo.co.jp/qa/question_detail/q12165689432. Accessed 31 October 2017.

31 This dialogue was published also in the *Sankei shinbun* of 7 June 2012, and summarized online at https://togetter.com/li/316770. Accessed 31 October 2017.

32 The *Sankei Shinbun* company, for example, published an English-language book titled 'History Wars' in 2015 that was sent to many foreign academics and that disputed records of Japanese wartime misdeeds and claimed such records were politically motivated propaganda used by foreign governments to keep Japan subservient (McNeill 2015).

33 The *Sankei* and its affiliates (such as Sankei Square, its online outlet) appear to be the main (if not sole) area in which Agonshū places its paid Japanese-language articles; on its website Agonshū provides links to (sponsored and supportive) items about the movement in the press and these appear, in Japanese-language terms, to be invariably in the Sankei media conglomerate. In English Agonshū uses the *Japan Times*, the widest selling English daily in Japan.

34 http://www.sankeisquare.com/event/agon/index.html. The Japanese here is: *Yasukuni de auo" to itteyutta karera e no kansha o wasurete wa nihon ni mirai wa nai.*

35 http://www.agon.org/en/history/.

36 *Japan Times.* https://www.japantimes.co.jp/news/2006/07/07/national/rites-set-for-fallen-siberia-prisoners/#.WfmwgxhOdqc.

37 http://www.agon.org/history/history_000051.php. The text reads *Shiberia ni yokuryū sare gisei ni narareta kyū nihongun heishi yaku rokumannin (issetsu ni sujūmannin) no gorei o go kuyō suru tame ni)* (In order to perform a memorial ritual for the 60,000 soldiers [according to some, many tens of thousands] of the former Japanese army who were interned and sacrificed in Siberia).

38 There is thus a discrepancy with the English-language website, to the extent that this just mentions 'victims' and thus implies that the ritual did not single out and focus specifically on the Japanese dead; this may be an example of how sometimes Japanese movements use different vocabularies and modes of editing to convey a different nuance in materials focused more at a non-Japanese audience.

39 http://www.agon.org/history/history_000071.php. The Japanese text reads: *go-eirei o rokujūnannen buri ni kokoku e otsureshita.*

40 http://www.agon.org/history/history_000071.php. It remains unclear to us whether the repatriated spirits of Agonshū's voyages are also enshrined at Yasukuni, which is where the spirits of the war dead are normally enshrined, or whether Agonshū is trying to act like Yasukuni by doing such rituals of repatriation. We have sought to clarify the relationship between Yasukuni and Agonshū and have received a lengthy email communication from a shrine priest at Yasukuni on this matter. The email managed to carefully skirt around our questions in a polite Japanese manner, affirming that Kiriyama, as a well-known religious leader, was received (as would any such figure) at Yasukuni Shrine and that the institution knew him and naturally sent condolences at his funeral and so on. The communication was a masterpiece that graciously and politely managed to avoid providing any actual information on issues related to the enshrinement of spirits by Agonshū, or related to the links existing between Yasukuni and Agonshū.

41 http://www.agon.org/history/. Accessed 5 January 2018.

42 The literature on these issues is immense; see Breen and Teeuwen (2010); Hardacre (1989, 2016); Isomae (2014); Maxey (2014); Murakami (1970); Okuyama (2011); Scheid (2013); Shimazono (2010).

43 Again there is an extensive and growing literature on these issues; see Victoria (1997, 2012); Sharf (1993); Hur (1999; for Buddhism and colonialism); Heisig and Maraldo (1994); Ives (2009).

44 http://archives.dailynews.lk/2012/11/13/fea22.asp. Retrieved 5 January 2018.

45 http://www.agon.org/img_group/news/20150730_tjt.pdf. In both the Sri Lankan and Bhutanese cases it is difficult to establish exactly how these awards and titles were bestowed, although it is evident that Agonshū has donated money to Sri Lanka over the years (via the Sri Lanka Agonshū Friendship Foundation, a foundation established and financially supported by Agonshū; see http://archives.dailynews.lk/2012/11/13/fea22.asp). The background details to these transactions are obscure and hard to ascertain, as Reader (1988) noted when trying to find out what, if any, transactional arrangements occurred prior to the Sri Lankan presentation of the Buddha relic to Kiriyama in 1986. Regarding the Bhutanese connection, we have been unable to find any details of the nature of this arrangement, although the remarks made by the Bhutanese monks – that they were invited by Agonshū – make us think that Agonshū funded their visits.

46 http://www.agon.org/img_group/news/20150730_tjt.pdf.

47 On issues of globalization and Japanese issues, see, for example, Dessi (2013) and Inoue (2007, 2014).

5 Transcending Death: The Birth and Spiritual Messages of the Second Buddha

1 A detailed chart of the lineages of new movements that have emerged from Tenrikyō, Oomoto, Sekai Kyūseikyō and Reiyūkai is given in Inoue et al. (1996).

2 On some discussion boards, as we mention later, some people claiming to be long-term members have expressed discontent with the leadership of Wada in particular, and claim she is using Kiriyama's spirit to enhance her own position.

3 One online poster (who may be a member) in a discussion forum related to Agonshū also claimed on 2 January 2017 that for the five years prior to his death Kiriyama had been unable to deliver sermons (http://rio2016.2ch.net/test/read.cgi/psy/1482223360/l10 post 189 in thread).

4 This point was reiterated to us by members, especially during larger events such as the *Hatsugoma* in January, when the Tokyo centre tended to be crowded.

5 Benod (2013: 156) has made a similar point: 'Il y a bien un culte de la personne de Kiriyama, mais il reste mesuré comparé à d'autre chefs spirituels comme Ōkawa. Aucun texte, ni parole n'exposent un transcendantalisme ontologique de Kiriyama.'

6 We would like to thank Lucia Dolce for this information. In addition some online discussion forums related to Agonshū have also mentioned this, albeit with very little substantive information or reference to Kiriyama's own writings.

7 Since his death *Agon Magazine* has on occasions repeated the story of Koizumi proclaiming Kiriyama to be the reincarnation of Susanoo (*Agon Magazine* 2017, 1/2: 35, and 3/4: 37) but without going any further by directly stating that Kiriyama was Susanoo.

8 As we have noted elsewhere (Baffelli and Reader 2011) there appears to be a degree of competition in terms of these claims of past lives by Asahara and

Ōkawa – competition that served to increase the emphasis each gave to their visions of the past and that also led each to disparage the others' claims.

9   See, for example, Kyoto shinbun: http://www.kyoto-np.co.jp/politics/article/20160912000069; and Asahi shinbun: http://www.asahi.com/articles/ASJ9D5DBZJ9DPLZB012.html. Both retrieved 10 August 2017.

10   It has been difficult to find any clear and accurate information about who knew the news and when, and thus far Agonshū sources we have had contact with have not made matters any clearer. We have heard, albeit from secondary sources, that staff at some Agonshū centres, including those overseas, were only informed several days after the event.

11   www.agon.org. The website was later amended to indicate that Fukuda Seia would be the chief ritual officer at the event. As it happens, Kiriyama did preside over the 2017 Hoshi Matsuri, albeit in spirit.

12   It is possible that the magazine had been printed and distributed before the death was known, especially since it is common for Japanese monthly magazines to be published sometime before their stated monthly date.

13   This section is based on interviews with Agonshū officials in Tokyo and Yamashina on 8 and 11 February 2017.

14   http://www.sankeisquare.com/event/agon/index.html. Accessed 25 November 2017.

15   This is purely speculative but we are struck by how the narrative of Kiriyama's death resembles that surrounding Kūkai's death, in which the Shingon Buddhist founder foresaw his imminent death, and died with his disciples around him (Hakeda 1972: 59; Tanabe 2002: 676–7).

16   We stress that we simply do not know about this. However, we have both heard comments and questions about his state of being from a variety of people involved in the religious studies field in Japan – including leaders and senior officials of other movements. We have heard also from others that the initial withdrawal might have been Ikeda's own decision and that he gave instructions to those around him at the time about how the movement was to handle future succession. We would like to thank an anonymous reviewer for this comment.

17   See, for example, the thread at https://detail.chiebukuro.yahoo.co.jp/qa/question_detail/q12165689432 in which the original poster notes that despite being a long-term member who had been having reservations about Agonshū in recent times, he wept on seeing Kiriyama's body. Other posters also affirm similar emotions.

18   According to *Agon Magazine* 2017, 5/6: 1, Kiyokawa Hakuhō oversaw the anniversary ritual celebration of the movement's Great Buddha statue on 5 May 2017.

19   http://www.agon.org/hatsugoma/pdf/hatsugoma_2017.pdf. Retrieved 11 August 2017.

20   See https://detail.chiebukuro.yahoo.co.jp/qa/question_detail/q12165689432 notably the posts from *hanhannichi* and *teltagiannto*, the former reporting the sighting of the golden dragon (*kinryū*), and the latter various miracle stories claimed by people at the funeral and that were attributed to Kiriyama.

21   Agonshū officials have also confirmed to us that *kaiso* is the normative term used now in the movement for Kiriyama.

22   According to one source (interviewed in Tokyo, 8 February 2017) both Wada and Fukada are able to receive messages from Kiriyama's spirit, although the official concerned was unclear as to which of them received the message outlined in the leaflet about the pendant that we refer to in this chapter, and which gave rise to our asking the official concerned who received such messages. There is no information provided in the *Agon Magazine* (where the *kaiso reiyu* are reported) or elsewhere in

Agonshū publications, whether in print or online at the time of writing, to indicate how they are transmitted, or whether any special ritual process is undertaken in order to receive them.

23 We should also note that channelling spirits became popular in Japanese religious culture in the era when Agonshū came to the fore and other movements (notably Kōfuku no Kagaku) have made great play about their leaders' ability to communicate with and transmit the thoughts of figures (including past religious leaders) from the spiritual realms. Ōkawa Ryūhō has been especially prominent in this context, claiming to channel messages from and hold conversations with the spirits of numerous famous figures both from past and present times (Astley 1995; Baffelli 2005).

24 This is the first such message we have been able to discover and we have seen no references in Agonshū to any earlier message. Online discussions (which, as we stress, cannot be verified for accuracy) have also implied that the December *kaiso reiyu* was the first one in the movement; see comments in the thread http://rio2016.2ch.net/test/read.cgi/psy/1482223360/l10. Accessed 8 January 2018. Unlike later messages reported in *Agon Magazine*, this had no specific date apart from the month (December 2016) on it. It has not been printed in totality, as far as we are aware, in any other official Agon publication, although sections have appeared elsewhere in Agonshū magazines and pamphlets. It was printed and circulated only among members, so we have been informed, and was not supposed to be seen by non-members. However, it is clear that some copies have been circulated beyond the movement and found their way into the public domain, where we were able to access it.

25 For reasons of style when reporting these messages we use terms such as 'Kiriyama' and 'he' to indicate that (in the view of Agonshū) this is Kiriyama's voice we are hearing.

26 These citations come from the unpublished *kaiso reiyu* text circulated in December 2016, using the page numbers of that text. The Japanese text here states: *Watashi wa nikutai o hanare, kanzeni reikon to natte nirubāna ni iri, saikō saijō no reikai sunawachi bukkai ni itta.*

27 *Shinu made ni kanzen ni budda ni naru. Kanzen ni budda ni natte shinu koto ga dekiru.*

28 While this is speculative on our part, we cannot but help note a similarity to Pure Land Buddhism in Japan, in which people are instructed to invoke Amida Buddha, and to popular cults centred on the bodhisattva Kannon and on Kōbō Daishi, both of whom may be called out to for aid at times of crisis.

29 Tōzan is the *onyomi* (Chinese-style reading) of the ideograms Kiriyama, and giving them this reading clearly confers a formality to this term.

30 As far as we can ascertain, this is the first use of the term *Tōzanryū gomahō* to refer to Agonshū's fire rituals and as such appears to be a post-death development in the movement.

31 *Ikite iru kaiso sonomono de aru watashi no shinjinshari.*

32 *Daga Nihon wa, Agonshū no gohō ga sonzai suru kuni de aru.*

33 *Kotoshi mo, watashi to tomoni ganbarō!*

34 Agonshū follows a pattern found in Japanese Buddhism of giving the deceased (through a ritual process) a *kaimyō* or preceptual/posthumous name for the next realm that supposedly indicates the deceased's nature and qualities.

35 Again this allusion to the diamond further suggests an implicit association with or mirroring of the image of Kūkai (see above, note 15).

36 These details are taken from the undated leaflet *Gomagi kanjin 2000 hon tokubetsu gohōse* available at the Agon centre in Tokyo in February 2017.

37 http://www.agon.org/hoshimatsuri/. Accessed 4 October 2017: *Daireiriki no hotoke ni inori!*

38 http://www.agon.org/hoshimatsuri/. Accessed 4 October 2017.

39 This account is based on observations made at the event itself, coupled with reports published in the *Agon Magazine* 2017, 3/4: 2–45.

40 Sadly, despite one of us being in attendance at the event, we cannot recall this sudden transformation in the weather at this point.

41 *Hoka ni hirui no nai kanzen bukkyō no seichi de aru.*

42 This term 'true law' (*shōbō*) has been used historically in Japanese Buddhism by those who claim that they have brought to Japan the true, correct transmission of Buddhism; it was a term used, for example, by Dōgen (1200–53), the founder of the Sōtō Zen tradition in Japan, on his return from China and reiterated in his magnum opus the Shōbōgenzō.

43 http://www.agon.org/about/about_000010.php.

44 The point of interest here is that according to the *kaiso reiyu* we reported earlier, Kiriyama's attainment of complete Buddhahood occurred on 29 August 2016 at the point of death – which was not, as far as we are aware, during an Agonshū ritual.

45 Kiyokawa's actual words are: *Dai ichi no budda yorimo sarani ookikuna kyūsairiki ga hakki saremasu.*

46 These reports, in the *Japan Times* and the *Sankei Shinbun*, are, like the newspaper reports we cited in Chapter 2, paid advertisements.

47 http://www.agon.org/news/news000724.php, also on http://www.sankeisquare.com/event/agon2017/index.html.

48 This account of the voyage is based on reports in *Sankei Square* (in Japanese) http://www.sankeisquare.com/event/agon2017/index.html and the *Japan Times* http://info.japantimes.co.jp/ads/pdf/20170831-Agonshū.pdf, both of which are linked to Agonshū's web pages. Interestingly the *Sankei Square* article account is written by Kamijima Yoshirō; it mentions the visit to Yasukuni whereas the *Japan Times* one does not.

49 See http://www.buddhism-dict.net/cgi-bin/xpr-ddb.pl?q=%E6%87%89%E4%BE%9B. We would like to thank Ian Astley for helping us understand the meaning of this term.

50 We are unclear exactly when during 2017 this new addition occurred. We first heard it chanted at the first *goma* ritual of 2018, although it appears that this was not the first time it had been used. It had not been in use in our previous attendance at Agonshū rituals in February 2017.

51 This account of the *hatsugoma* is based on attendance at the event in Tokyo on 1 January 2018.

52 We were unable to attend this event; the outline here is from a flyer of the event produced by Agonshū.

53 We also draw attention to the study by Sharf (1992) who discusses the mummification and preservation of the bodies of Ch'an Buddhist masters in China

54 For example, such concerns have been raised in threads such as https://detail.chiebukuro.yahoo.co.jp/qa/question_detail/q14168762729 and http://rio2016.2ch.net/test/read.cgi/psy/1482223360/l10. In one of these, the original participant specifically requested criticisms of the movement and in the other, comments alleging that Wada was taking over the movement appeared to have a gender-discriminatory orientation

to them, complaining that since Kiriyama's death the movement had become 'strange' (*okashikunaru*) because a female figure was relaying the messages from Kiriyama. We have also had informal conversations with followers who feel uneasy about her role, about the apparent emphasis being made on soliciting *gomagi* and about what they fear might be increased financial demands in terms of membership fees in future.

55 The case of Deguchi Ōnisaburō is in many ways an anomaly, in which Oomoto, founded by Deguchi Nao, produced a second highly charismatic and dynamic leader with new insights – but it is widely known that Ōnisaburō and Nao in effect engaged in a power struggle in Oomoto, with Ōnisaburō changing many of its orientations, to the extent that one could argue it became a rather different movement under his leadership. Another example is Ikeda Daisaku, Sōka Gakkai's third leader, but the one who has most encapsulated themes of charisma into his leadership.

6 Concluding Comments: Founder Worship and the Problem of the 'New'

1 For fuller discussion of Kōbō Daishi and the role of this figure in the growth of Shingon and of Kōyasan, see Miyata (1988) and Kitamura (1988); for ascetics associated with Kōyasan, see Gorai (1975); and in connection with pilgrimage see Reader (2004b and 2005: 41–5).

2 The sect's constitution portrays them both as sect founders and places them alongside the main object of worship of Sōtō, namely, Shakyamuni (Reader 1983: 172).

3 See Reader (2005) for a contribution to this discussion.

4 For an example of this perspective, see the essay by Melton (2004) in the same series of essays in Nova Religio debating the terminology of the 'new'.

References

Agon Magazine. 2012. 3/4 bimonthly Agonshū members' magazine.

Agon Magazine. 2017. 1/2 bimonthly Agonshū members' magazine.

Agon Magazine. 2017. 3/4 bimonthly Agonshū members' magazine.

Agon Magazine. 2017. 5/6 bimonthly Agonshū members' magazine.

Agon Shu. 2017. *Agon Shu's Hoshi Matsuri: The Combined Shinto-Buddhist Fire Rites Festival.* Tokyo: Agonshū. Also available at www.agon.org/hoshimatsuri/e/.

Agonshū. nd. (probably 1995–96). *Gomagi kanjin shugyō tokuhon.* Tokyo: Agonshū. Available at http://agama.zouri.jp/gomabook_top.html.

Agonshū. nd. (possibly 2014). *Gomagi kanjin 2000 hon tokubetsu gohōse.* Available at the Agon centre in Tokyo in February 2017.

Agonshū (ed.). nd. *Agonshū to wa/The Agon-shū* (undated Agonshū Japanese- and English-language booklet given to prospective members and inquirers).

Agonshū (ed.). 1986. *Senzo kuyō.* Tokyo: Agonshū Kyōkabu.

Agonshū. 1992. *Kimi wa dare no umarekawari ka* (pamphlet/booklet report of a lecture delivered by Kiriyama Seiyū 1 November 1992, during the Tsuitachii goma ritual service).

Agonshū. May 2012. *Meitokusai Nyūsu* 245.

Agonshū. 2014. *Agonshū* Kyoto: Agonshū (booklet outlining Agonshū practices, teachings and activities).

Akiya Kōhei. 2015. *Kōfuku no Kagaku.* Tokyo: Taibundō.

Ambros, Barbara. 2015. *Women in Japanese Religions.* New York: New York University Press.

Asahara Shōkō. 1986. *Chōnōryoku: himitsu no kaihatsuhō.* Tokyo: Oumu Shuppan.

Asahara Shōkō. 1988. *Mahayāna sūtora.* Tokyo: Oumu Shuppan.

Asahara Shōkō. 1991. *Nosutoradamasu himitsu no yogen.* Tokyo: Oumu Shuppan.

Asahara Shōkō. 1992. *Tathāgatha Abhidhamma: The Ever-Winning Law of the True Victors Book 1.* Trans. by the Aum Translation Committee. Tokyo: Aum Publishing.

Asahara Shōkō. 1994. *Vajrāyana kōsu. Kyōgaku shisutemu kyōhon.* Internal Aum Shinrikyō unpublished 368-page training manual.

Asahara Shōkō and Yamaori Tetsuo. 1992. Interview. *Bessatsu Taiyō.* pp. 94–101.

Astley, Ian. 2016. 'Space, Time and Heritage on a Japanese Sacred Site: The Religious Geography of Kōyasan'. In *The Changing World Religion Map*, ed. Stanley D. Brunn, pp. 523–44. Dordrecht: Springer.

Astley, Trevor. 1995. 'The Transformation of a Recent Japanese New Religion: Ōkawa Ryūhō and Kōfuku no Kagaku'. *Japanese Journal of Religious Studies* 22, 3–4: 343–80.

Astley, Trevor. 2006. 'New Religions'. In *Nanzan Guide to Japanese Religions*, ed. Paul L. Swanson and Clark Chilson, pp. 91–114. Honolulu: University of Hawai'i Press.

Baffelli, Erica. 2005. *Vendere la felicità. Media, marketing e nuove religioni giapponesi. Il caso del Kōfuku no Kagaku.* PhD diss., Università Ca' Foscari di Venezia.

Baffelli, Erica. 2011. 'Charismatic Blogger? Authority and New Religions on the Web 2.0'. In *Japanese Religions on the Internet: Innovation, Representation, and Authority*, ed. Erica Baffelli, Ian Reader and Birgit Staemmler, pp. 118–35. New York: Routledge.

Baffelli, Erica. 2012. 'Hikari no Wa: A New Religion Recovering from Disaster'. *Japanese Journal of Religious Studies* 39, 1: 29–49.

Baffelli, Erica. 2016. *Media and New Religions in Japan*. New York and London: Routledge.

Baffelli, Erica. 2017. 'Contested Positioning: "New Religions" and Secular Spheres'. *Japan Review* 30: 129–52.

Baffelli, Erica and Ian Reader. 2011. 'Competing for the Apocalypse: Religious Rivalry and Millennial Transformations in a Japanese New Religion'. *International Journal for the Study of New Religions* 2, 1: 5–28.

Baffelli, Erica and Ian Reader. 2012. 'Impact and Ramifications: The Aftermath of the Aum Affair in the Japanese Religious Context'. *Japanese Journal of Religious Studies* 39, 1: 1–28.

Baffelli, Erica, Ian Reader and Birgit Staemmler (eds). 2011. *Japanese Religions on the Internet: Innovation, Representation and Authority*. New York and London: Routledge.

Barker, Eileen. 2004. 'What Are We Studying? A Sociological Case for Keeping the "Nova"'. *Nova Religio: The Journal of Alternative and Emergent Religions* 8, 1: 88–102.

Befu, Harumi. 2001. *Hegemony of Homogeneity: An Anthropological Analysis of Nihonjinron*. Melbourne: Trans-Pacific Press.

Befu, Harumi. 2009. 'Concepts of Japan, Japanese Culture and the Japanese'. In *The Cambridge Companion to Modern Japanese Culture*, ed. Yoshio Sugimoto, pp. 21–37. Cambridge: Cambridge University Press.

Benod, Alexandre. 2013. *Les Feux du Goma: du Traitement de la Souffrance Sociale par la Nouvelle Religion Japonaise Agonshū*. PhD diss., Université de Lyon.

Berthon, Jean-Pierre. 1985. *Omoto: Espérance millénariste d'une nouvelle religion japonaise*. Paris: Atelier Alpha Bleue.

Berthon, Jean-Pierre and Kashio Naoki. 2000. 'Les nouvelles voies spirituelles au Japon: état des lieux et mutations de la religiosité'. *Archives de Sciences Sociales des Religions* 109: 67–85.

Billoud, Sébastien. 2017. 'Yiguandao's Patriarch Zhang Tianran: Hagiography, Deification and Production of Charisma in a Modern Religious Organization'. In *Making Saints in Modern China*, ed. David Ownby, Vincent Goosaert and Ji Zhe, pp. 209–40. New York: Oxford University Press.

Blacker, Carmen. 1999 (1975). *The Catalpa Bow: A Study of Shamanstic Practices in Japan*. London: George Allen and Unwin.

Breen, John (ed.). 2008. *Yasukuni, the War Dead and the Struggle for Japan's Past*. New York: Columbia University Press.

Breen, John. 2015. *Shinto monogatari: Ise Jingū no kindaishi*. Tokyo: Yoshikawa Kōbunkan.

Breen, John and Mark Teeuwen. 2010. *A New History of Shinto*. Malden, MA; Oxford and Chichester, UK: Wiley-Blackwell.

Bromley, David. 2004. 'Whither New Religious Studies: Defining and Shaping a New Area of Study'. *Nova Religio: The Journal of Alternative and Emergent Religions* 8, 2: 83–97.

Bunkachō. 1977; 1978; 1979; 2017. *Shūkyō Nenkan*. Tokyo: Gyōsei.

Castiglioni Andrea. Forthcoming. 'Devotion in Flesh and Bone: The Mummified Corpses of Mount Yudono Ascetics in the Edo Period'. *Asian Ethnology*.

Chilson, Clark. 2014. 'Cultivating Charisma: Ikeda Daisaku's Self Presentations and Transformational Leadership'. *Journal of Global Buddhism* 15: 65–78.

Comaroff, Jean. 1994. 'Defying Disenchantement: Reflections on Ritual, Power and History'. In *Asian Visions of Authority*, ed. Helen Hardacre, Laurel Kendall and Charles F. Keyes, pp. 305–7. Honolulu: University of Hawai'i Press.

Cornille, Catherine. 1999. 'Nationalism in New Japanese Religions'. *Nova Religio: The Journal of Alternative and Emergent Religions* 2, 2: 228–44.

Covell, Stephen G. 2005. *Japanese Temple Buddhism: Worldiness in a Religion of Renunciation.* Honolulu: University of Hawai'i Press.

Covell, Stephen G. and Mark Rowe. 2004. 'Editors' Introduction: Traditional Buddhism in Contemporary Japan'. *Japanese Journal of Religious Studies* 31, 2: 245–54.

Davis, Winston. 1980. *Dojo: Magic and Exorcism in Modern Japan.* Stanford, CA: Stanford University Press.

Dawson, Lorne. 2006. 'Psychopathologies and the Attribution of Charisma: A Critical Introduction to the Psychology of Charisma and the Explanation of Violence in New Religious Movements'. *Nova Religio: The Journal of Alternative and Emergent Religions* 10, 2: 3–28.

Dehn, Ulrich. 2011. 'Risshō Kōsei-kai'. In *Establishing the Revolutionary: An Introduction to New Religions in Japan,* ed. Birgit Staemmler and Ulrich Dehn, pp. 221–38. Zurich: LIT.

Dessi, Ugo. 2013. *Japanese Religions and Globalization.* London: Routledge.

Dolce, Lucia (ed.). 2006. 'The Worship of Stars in Japanese Religious Practice'. Special Issue of *Culture and Cosmos* 10, 1–2.

Dorman, Benjamin. 2005. 'Pana Wave The New Aum Shinrikyō or Another Moral Panic?' *Nova Religio: The Journal of Alternative and Emergent Religions* 8, 3: 83–103.

Dorman, Benjamin. 2012. *Celebrity Gods: New Religions, Media, and Authority in Occupied Japan.* Honolulu: University of Hawai'i Press.

Earhart, H. Byron. 1989. *Gedatsukai and Religion in Contemporary Japan.* Bloomington: University of Indiana Press.

Ehrhardt, George, Axel Klein, Levi McLaughlin and Steven S. Reed (eds). 2014. *Kōmeitō: Politics and Religion in Japan.* Berkeley: Institute of East Asian Studies.

Faure, Bernard. 1987. 'The Daruma-shū, Dōgen and Sōtō Zen'. *Monumenta Nipponica* 42, 1: 25–55.

Feuchtwang, Stephan. 2008. 'Suggestions for a Redefinition of Charisma'. *Nova Religio: The Journal of Alternative and Emergent Religions* 12, 2: 90–105.

Feuchtwang, Stephan and Mingming Wang. 2001. *Grassroots Charisma: Four Local Leaders in China.* New York: Routledge.

Fukamizu Kenshin. 2011. 'The Situation of Traditional Buddhism in the Web 2.0 Era: Who Attacks and Who Guards the Religion?' In *Japanese Religions on the Internet: Innovation, Representation and Authority,* ed. Baffelli et al., pp. 39–61. New York and London: Routledge.

Gagné, Isaac. 2013. *Private Religion and Public Morality: Understanding Cultural Secularism in Late Capitalist Japan.* PhD diss., Yale University.

Gagné, Isaac. 2017. 'Religious Globalization and Reflexive Secularization in a Japanese New Religion'. *Japan Review* 30: 153–77.

Gaitanidis, Ioannis. 2012. 'Gender and Spiritual Therapy in Japan'. *International Journal for the Study of New Religions* 3, 2: 269–88.

Gluck, Carol. 1985. *Japan's Modern Myths: Ideology in the Late Meiji Period.* Princeton: Princeton University Press.

Goodwin, Janet R. 1994. *Alms and Vagabonds: Buddhist Temples and Popular Patronage in Medieval Japan.* Honolulu: University of Hawai'i Press.

Goosaert, Vincent. 2008. 'Mapping Charisma among Chinese Religious Specialists'. *Nova Religio: The Journal of Alternative and Emergent Religions* 12, 2: 12–28.

Goosaert, Vincent and David Ownby (eds). 2008. 'Special Issue: Mapping Charisma in Chinese Religion'. *Nova Religio: The Journal of Alternative and Emergent Religions* 12, 2.

Gorai Shigeru. 1975. *Kōya hijiri*. Tokyo: Kadokawa Sensho.

Haga, Manabu and Robert J. Kisala. 1995. 'Editors' Introduction. The New Age in Japan'. *Japanese Journal of Religious Studies* 22, 3–4: 235–47.

Hakeda, Yoshito S. 1972. *Kukai: Major Works*. New York: Columbia University Press.

Hambrick, Charles. 1974. 'Tradition and Modernity in the New Religious Movements of Japan'. *Japanese Journal of Religious Studies* 1, 2–3: 217–52.

Hardacre, Helen. 1984. *Lay Buddhism in Contemporary Japan: Reiyūkai Kyōdan*. Princeton: Princeton University Press.

Hardacre, Helen. 1986. *Kurozumikyō and the New Religions of Japan*. Princeton: Princeton University Press.

Hardacre, Helen. 1989. *Shinto and the State 1868–1988*. Princeton: Princeton University Press.

Hardacre, Helen. 1994. 'Conflict between Shugendō and the New Religions of Bakumatsu Japan'. *Japanese Journal of Religious Studies* 21, 2–3: 137–66.

Hardacre, Helen. 2016. *Shinto: A History*. New York: Oxford University Press.

Hayashi Makoto. 2006. *Kinsei onmyōdō no kenkyū*. Tokyo: Yoshikawa Kōbunkan.

Hayashi Makoto and Matthias Hayek. 2013. 'Editors' Introduction: Onmyōdō in Japanese History'. *Japanese Journal of Religious Studies* 40, 1: 1–18.

Hayek, Matthias. 2011. 'The Eight Trigrams and Their Changes: An Inquiry into Japanese Early Modern Divination'. *Japanese Journal of Religious Studies* 38, 2: 329–68.

Heisig, James W. and John Maraldo (eds). 1994. *Rude Awakenings: Zen, The Kyoto School, and the Question of Nationalism*. Honolulu: University of Hawai'i Press.

Hori, Ichiro. 1968. *Folk Religion in Japan*. Chicago: University of Chicago Press.

Horie, Norichika. 2009. 'Spirituality and the Spiritual in Japan: Translation and Transformation'. *Journal of Alternative Spiritualities and New Age Studies*. Available at http://www.asanas.org.uk/journal.htm. Accessed 13 December 2017.

Horie Norichika. 2011. *Supirichuariti no yukue: wakamono no kibun*. Tokyo: Iwanami Shoten.

Horie Norichika. 2015. 'Sabukaruchā no majutsushi tachi – shūkyōgakuteki chishiki no shōhi to kyōyū'. In '*Jujutsu*' *no jubaku* vol.1, ed. Egawa Jun'ichi and Kubota Hiroshi. Tokyo: Lithon.

Horie, Norichika. 2017. 'The Making of Power Spots: From New Age Spirituality to Shinto Spirituality'. In *Eastspirit: Transnational Spirituality and Religious Circulation in East and West*, ed. Jørn Borup and Marianne Qvortrup Fibiger. Leiden: Brill.

Huang, Julia C. 2009. *Charisma and Compassion*. Cambridge, MA: Harvard University Press.

Hubbard, Jamie. 1998. 'Embarrassing Superstition, Doctrine, and the Study of New Religious Movements'. *Journal of the American Academy of Religion* 66, 1: 59–92.

Hur, Nam-Lin. 1999. 'The Sōtō Sect and Japanese Military Imperialism in Korea'. *Japanese Journal of Religious Studies* 26, 1–2: 107–34.

Inose, Yuri. 2017. 'Gender and New Religions in Modern Japan'. *Japanese Journal of Religious Studies* 44, 1: 15–35.

Inoue Nobutaka. 1992. *Shinshūkyō no kaidoku*. Tokyo: Chikuma Shobō.

Inoue Nobutaka. 1997. '"Shinshinshūkyō" gainen no gakujutsuteki yūkōsei ni tsuite'. *Shūkyō to shakai* 3: 3–24.

Inoue, Nobutaka. 2007. 'Globalization and Religion: The Cases of Japan and Korea'. In *Religion, Globalization, and Culture*, ed. Peter Beyer and Lori Beaman, pp. 453–71. Leiden: Brill.

Inoue Nobutaka (ed.). 2011. *Jōhō jidai no Oumu shinrikyō*. Tokyo: Shunjūsha.

Inoue, Nobutaka. 2014. 'New Religious Movement in Global Context'. In *Controversies in Contemporary Religion: Education, Law, Politics, Society, and Spirituality Volume 3: Specific Issues and Case Studies*, ed. Paul Hedge, pp. 223–48. Santa Barbara, Denver, Oxford: Praeger.

Inoue Nobutaka et al. (eds). 1991. *Shinshūkyō jiten*. Tokyo: Kōbundō.

Inoue Nobutaka et al. (eds). 1996. *Shinshūkyō kyōdan, jinbutsu jiten*. Tokyo: Kōbundō.

Ishii Kenji. 2007. *Dētabukku: Gendai nihon no shūkyō*. Tokyo: Shinyōsha.

Isomae, Jun'ichi. 2014. *Religious Discourse in Modern Japan: Religion, State, and Shintō*. Translated by Galen Amstutz and Lynne E. Riggs. Leiden: Brill.

Ives, Christopher. 2009. *Imperial-Way Zen: Ichikawa Hakugen's Critique and Lingering Questions for Buddhist Ethics*. Honolulu: University of Hawai'i Press.

Ji, Zhe. 2008. 'Expectation, Affection and Responsibility: The Charismatic Journey of a New Buddhist Group in Taiwan'. *Nova Religio: The Journal of Alternative and Emergent Religions* 12, 2: 48–68.

Kakida Mutsuo. 1984. 'Hoshi matsuri no himitsu'. *Bunka hyōron* 280: 56–66.

Kamijima Yoshirō. 2017. 'Hoppō no eirei e no omoi'. *Agon Magazine* 5, 6: 33–49.

Katō, Masato. 2017. 'Tenrikyō' World Religion and Spirituality Project. Available at https://wrldrels.org/2015/03/22/tenrikyo/. Accessed 14 December 2017.

Kawahashi, Noriko. 2017. 'Women Challenging the "Celibate" Buddhist Order: Recent Cases of Progress and Regress in the Sōtō School'. *Japanese Journal of Religious Studies* 44, 1: 55–74.

Kawahashi, Noriko and Kobayashi Naoko. 2017. 'Editors' Introduction: Gendering Religious Practices in Japan: Multiple Voices, Multiple Strategies'. *Japanese Journal of Religious Studies* 44, 1: 1–13.

Kawakami, Tsuneo. 2008. *Stories of Conversion and Commitment in Japanese New Religious Movements: The Cases of Tōhō no Hikari, World Mate, and Kōfuku no Kagaku*. PhD diss., Lancaster University.

Kawamura Kunimitsu. 1981. 'Karisumateki shūkyō shidōsha no keisei o megutte: Sutiguma kara karisuma e'. *Shūkyō kenkyū* 246: 5–6.

Ketelaar, James E. 1993. *Of Heretics and Martyrs in Meiji Japan*. Princeton: Princeton University Press.

Kiriyama Seiyū. 1957. *Kōfuku e no genri: shinkannongyō*. Tokyo: Kannon Jikeikai.

Kiriyama Seiyū. 1971. *Henshin no genri*. Tokyo: Kadokawa Bunsho.

Kiriyama Seiyū. 1981. *1999 nen: karuma to reishō kara no dasshutsu*. Tokyo: Hirakawa Shuppan.

Kiriyama Seiyū. 1983. *Gense jōbutsu: waga jinsei, waga shūkyō*. Tokyo: rikitomi shobō.

Kiriyama Seiyū. 1993. *Kimi wa dare no umarekawari ka*. Tokyo: Hirakawa Shuppan.

Kiriyama Seiyū. 1995a. *1999 nen shichi no gatsu ga kuru: Unmei no hi no yogen to yochi*. Tokyo: Hirakawa Shuppan.

Kiriyama Seiyū. 1995b. *Oumu Shinrikyō to Agonshū*. Tokyo: Hirakawa Shuppan.

Kiriyama Seiyū. 1997. *Shakai kagaku toshite no Agon Bukkyō*. Tokyo: Hirakawa Shuppan.

Kiriyama Seiyū. 2000a. *You Have Been Here Before: Reincarnation*. Tokyo: Hirakawa Shuppan.

Kiriyama Seiyū. 2000b. *21st Century: The Age of Sophia, the Wisdom of Greek Philosophy and the Wisdom of the Buddha*. Tokyo: Hirakawa Shuppan.

Kiriyama Seiyū. 2000c. *21seiki wa chie (sofia) no jidai: girisha tetsugaku no chie to budda no chie*. Tokyo: Hirakawa Shuppan.

Kiriyama Seiyū. 2001. *Nyūyōku yori sekai ni mukete hasshinsu*. Tokyo: Hirakawa Shuppan.

Kiriyama Seiyū. 2005. *Shugorei o motte: minna no shiawase no tame ni*. Tokyo: Hirakawa Shuppan.

Kiriyama Seiyū. 2013 (1965). *Hito wa donna innen o motsu ka*. Tokyo: Agonshū.

Kiriyama Seiyū. 2017 (1992). 'Shōja mo, shisha mo jōbutsu sase, niruvāna e michibikiireru makanizumu to wa?' Kaiso Hōwa shiri-zu No. 1, *Agon Magazine* 5, 6: 5–22 (text of sermon delivered on 16 January 1992).

Kisala, Robert J. 1997. 'Nostradamus and the Apocalypse in Japan'. *Inter-Religio* 32: 47–62.

Kisala, Robert J. and Mark R. Mullins (eds). 2001. *Religion and Social Crisis in Japan: Understanding Japanese Society through the Aum Affair*. New York: Palgrave.

Kitagawa, Joseph. 1966. *Religion in Japanese History*. New York: Columbia University Press.

Kitamura Satoshi. 1988. 'Daishi nyūjō shinko'. In *Nihon bukkyō no sekai*, ed. Kanaoka Shūyū et al. vol. 4, pp. 128–45. Tokyo: Shūeisha.

Kiyokawa Hakuhō. 2017. '"Dai ni no budda" oofukkatsusai kara sekai no karuma o tatsu reiseikangen no katsudō ga honkaku shidō suru'. *Agon Magazine* 3, 4: 47–57.

Kobayashi, Naoko. 2017. 'Sacred Mountains and Women in Japan: Fighting a Romaticised Image of Female Ascetic Practitioners'. *Japanese Journal of Religious Studies* 44, 1: 103–22.

Konkōkyō Honbu Kyōchō. 1983. *Konkōkyō Kyōten*. Okayama-ken Konkō-chō: Konkōkyō Honbu Kyōchō.

Lo Breglio, John. 1997. 'The Revisions to the Religious Corporations Law: An Introduction and Annotated Translation'. *Japanese Religions* 22, 1: 38–59.

Matsunaga, Alicia. 1969. *The Buddhist Philosophy of Assimilation*. Tokyo: Sophia University.

Maxey, Trent. 2014. *The 'Greatest Problem': Religion and State Formation in Meiji Japan*. Cambridge, MA: Harvard University Asia Center.

McFarland, H. Neill. 1967. *The Rush Hour of the Gods: A Study of New Religious Movements in Japan*. New York: Macmillan.

McLaughlin, Levi. 2009. *Sōka Gakkai in Japan*. PhD diss., Princeton University.

McLaughlin, Levi. 2012. 'Did Aum Change Everything? What Sōka Gakkai Before, During, and After the Aum Shinrikyō Affair Tells Us About the Persistent "Otherness" of New Religions in Japan'. *Japanese Journal of Religious Studies* 39, 1: 51–75.

McLaughlin, Levi. 2018. *Soka Gakkai's Human Revolution: The Rise of a Mimetic Nation in Modern Japan*. Honolulu: University of Hawai'i Press.

McNeill, David. 2015. 'Nippon Kaigi and the Radical Conservative Project to Take Back Japan'. *The Asia-Pacific Journal* 13/ 50: 4. Available at http://apjjf.org/-David-McNeill/4409. Accessed 3 November 2017.

Melton, J. Gordon. 2004. 'Towards a Definition of "New Religion"'. *Nova Religio: The Journal of Alternative and Emergent Religions* 8, 1: 73–87.

Miyamoto, Yuji. 2011. *Beyond the Mushroom Cloud: Commemoration, Religion, and Responsibility after Hiroshima*. New York: Fordham University Press.

Miyata Noboru. 1988. 'Daishi shinkō to nihonjin'. In *Kōbō Daishi shinkō*, ed. Hinonishi Shinjō, pp. 19–48. Tokyo: Yūzankaku.

Morioka, Kiyomi. 1994. 'Attacks on the New Religions: Risshō Kōseikai and the "Yomiuri Affair"'. *Japanese Journal of Religious Studies* 21, 2–3: 281–310.

Morris-Suzuki, Tessa. 1998. *Re-inventing Japan: Time, Space, Nation*. New York: M. E. Sharpe.

Mullins, Mark R. 2012a. 'Secularization, Deprivatization, and the Reappearance of "Public Religion"'. In Japanese Society'. *Journal of Religion in Japan* 1, 1: 61–82.

Mullins, Mark R. 2012b. 'The Neo-nationalist Response to the Aum Crisis: A Return of Civil Religion and Coercion in the Public Sphere?' *Japanese Journal of Religious Studies* 39, 1: 99–125.

Munakata Masako. 2010. *Nijūsai kara no 20 nenkan: Oumu no seishun no makyō o koete*. Tokyo: Sangokan.

Murai Kōzō. 2010. *Obōsan ga kakusu otera no hanashi*. Tokyo: Shinchōsha.

Murakami Shigeyoshi. 1970. *Kokka shintō*. Tokyo: Iwanamishinsho.

Murakami Shigeyoshi. 1975. *Shinshūkyō*. Tokyo: Hyōronsha.

Murō Tadashi. 1987. *Agonshū: sekai heiwa he no michi*. Tokyo: Seiunsha.

Nagaoka Takashi. 2015. *Shinshūkyō to sōryokusen: Kyōso igo o ikiru*. Nagoya: Nagoya Daigaku Shuppankai.

Nakano Tsuyoshi. 2003. *Sengo nihon no shūkyō to seiji*. Tokyo: Taimeidō.

Nelson, John. 2012. 'Japanese Secularities and the Decline of Temple Buddhism'. *Journal of Religion in Japan* 1, 1: 37–60.

Nicoloff, Philip L. 2008. *Sacred Kōyasan: A Pilgrimage to the Mountain Temple of Saint Kōbō Daishi and the Great Sun Buddha*. Albany, NY: SUNY Press.

Nishijima Takeo. 1988. *Shinshūkyō no kamigami*. Tokyo: Kōdansha.

Nishimura, Akira. 2013. 'The Engagment of Religious Groups in Postwar Battlefield Pilgrimages'. *Bulletin of the Nanzan Institute for Religion and Culture* 37: 42–51.

Nishiyama Shigeru. 1979. 'Shinshūkyō no genkyō'. *Rekishi kōron* 5, 7: 33–7.

Nishiyama Shigeru. 1986. 'Shin shinshūkyō no shutsugen'. In *Shūkyō: Riidingsu Nihon no shakaigaku*, ed. Miyake Hitoshi et al., vol. 19, pp. 198–204. Tokyo: Tōkyō Daigaku Shuppankai.

Nishiyama Shigeru. 1988. 'Gendai no shūkyō undō: "reijitsu" kei shin shūkyō no ryūkōyuku to "futatsu no kindaika"'. In *Gendaijin no shūkyō*, ed. Ōmura Eishō and Nishiyama Shigeru, pp. 169–210. Tokyo: Yuikaku.

Nishiyama Shigeru. 1990. 'Reijutsuteki shinshūkyō no taitō to futatsu no kindaika'. In *Kindaika to shūkyō būmu*, ed. Kokugakuin Daigaku Nihonbunka Kenkyūjo, pp. 93–8. Kyoto: Dōhosha.

Numata Ken'ya. 1987. 'Gendai shinshūkyō ni okeru karisuma: Takahashi Shinji to Jīeruei ni kansuru ichikōsatsu'. In *Kyōso to sono shūhen*, ed. Shūkyō Shakaigaku Kenkyūkai, pp. 70–90. Tokyo: Yūzankaku.

Numata Ken'ya. 1988. *Gendai Nihon no shinshūkyō*. Osaka: Sōgensha.

Numata Ken'ya. 1995. *Shūkyō to kagaku no neoparadaimu*. Osaka: Sōgensha.

Offner, Clark B. and Henry van Straelen. 1963. *Modern Japanese Religions, with Special Reference upon Their Doctrines of Healing*. Tokyo: Enderle.

Ōkawa Ryūhō. 1988. *Nosutoradamasu no shinyogen*. Tokyo: Kōfuku no Kagaku Shuppan.

Ōkawa Ryūhō. 1995a. *Buddha Speaks: Discourses with the Buddha Incarnate* Tokyo: Kōfuku no Kagaku Shuppan.

Ōkawa Ryūhō. 1995b. *Sōka Gakkai make inuron: Gendai nihon no jubaku o toku*. Tokyo: Kōfuku no Kagaku Shuppan.

Ōkawa Ryūhō. 2001a. *Shin taiyō no hō*. Tokyo: Kōfuku no Kagaku Shuppan.

Ōkawa Ryūhō. 2001b. *The Laws of the Sun: The Spiritual Laws & History Governing Past, Present & Future*. New York: Lantern Books.

Okuyama, Michiaki. 2011. '"State Shinto" in Recent Japanese Scholarship'. *Monumenta Nipponica* 66: 123–45.

Ooms, Emily Groszos. 1993. *Women and Millenarian Protest in Meiji Japan: Deguchi Nao and Ōmotokyō*. Ithaca: Cornell University East Asia Series.

Ownby, David, Vincent Goosaert and Ji Zhe (eds). 2017. *Making Saints in Modern China*. New York: Oxford University Press.

Prohl, Inken. 1995. *Die Agonshū: Eine Neue Religion in Japan*. Berlin: Freie Universität Berlin, Ostasiatisches Seminar/Japanologie.

Prohl, Inken. 2004. 'Solving Everyday Problems with the Help of the Ancestors: Representations of Ghosts in the New Religions Agonshū and World Mate'. In *Practising the Afterlife: Perspectives from Japan*, ed. Susanne Formanek and William LaFleur, pp. 461–83. Wien: Verlag der Österreichischen Akademie der Wissenschaften.

Pye, Michael. 1986. 'National and International Identity in a Japanese Religion (Byakko Shinkokai)'. In *Identity Issues and World Religions: Selected Proceedings of the XVth Congress of the International Association for the History of Religions*, ed. V. Hayes, pp. 234–41. South Australia: Australian Association for the Study of Religion.

Rajana, Eimi Watanabe. 1975. 'New Religions in Japan: An Appraisal of Two Theories'. In *Modern Japan: Aspects of History, Literature and Society*, ed. W. G. Beasley, pp. 187–97. Berkeley: University of California Press.

Rambelli, Fabio and Mark Teeuwen. 2003. *Buddhas and Kami in Japan: Honji Suijaku as a Combinatory Paradigm*. London: Routledge.

Reader, Ian. 1983. *Contemporary Thought in Soto Zen Buddhism: An Investigation of the Publications and Teachings of the Sect in the Light of Their Cultural and Historical Context*. PhD diss., University of Leeds.

Reader, Ian. 1988. 'The "New" New Religions of Japan: An Analysis of the Rise of Agonshū'. *Japanese Journal of Religious Studies* 15, 4: 235–61.

Reader, Ian. 1991. *Religion in Contemporary Japan*. Basingstoke, UK: Macmillans, and Honolulu: University of Hawai'i Press.

Reader, Ian. 1994. 'Appropriated Images: Esoteric Themes in a Japanese New Religion'. *Esoteric Buddhism in Japan*, ed. Ian Astley, pp. 36–63. Copenhagen and Aarhus: Seminar for Buddhist Studies.

Reader, Ian. 1995. 'Cleaning Floors and Sweeping the Mind: Cleaning as a Ritual Process'. In *Ceremony and Ritual in Japan: Religious Practices in an Industrialized Society*, ed. Jan van Bremen and D. P. Martinez, pp. 227–45. London: Routledge.

Reader, Ian. 1996. 'Pilgrimage as Cult: The Shikoku Pilgrimage as a Window on Japanese Religion'. In *Religion in Japan: Arrows to Heaven and Earth*, ed. P. F. Kornicki and I. J. McMullen, pp. 267–86. Cambridge: Cambridge University Press.

Reader, Ian. 2000a. *Religious Violence in Contemporary Japan: The Case of Aum Shinrikyō*. Richmond and Honolulu: Curzon Press and University of Hawai'i Press.

Reader, Ian. 2000b. 'Scholarship, Aum Shinrikyō, and Academic Integrity'. *Nova Religio: The Journal of Alternative and Emergent Religions* 3, 2: 368–82.

Reader, Ian. 2002. 'Identity and Nationalism in the "New" New Religions: Buddhism as a Motif for the New Age in Japan'. In *Religion and National Identity in the Japanese Context*, ed. Klaus Antoni, Hiroshi Kubota, Johann Nawrocki and Michael Wachutka, pp. 13–36. Zurich: LIT.

Reader, Ian. 2004a. 'Consensus Shattered: Japanese Paradigm Shifts and Moral Panic in the Post-Aum Era'. In *New Religious Movements in the 21st Century: Legal, Political and Social Challenges in Global Perspective*, ed. Philip Charles Lucas and Thomas Robbins, pp. 191–201. New York and London: Routledge.

Reader, Ian. 2004b. 'Weaving the Landscape: The Shikoku Pilgrimage, Kōbō Daishi and Shingon Buddhism'. *Bulletin of the Research Institute of Esoteric Buddhist Culture* 139–64.

Reader, Ian. 2005. 'Chronologies, Commonalities and Alternative Status in Japanese New Religious Movements: Defining NRMS outside the Western Cul-de-Sac'. *Nova Religio: The Journal of Alternative and Emergent Religions* 9, 2: 84–96.

Reader, Ian. 2011, 'Buddhism in Crisis? Institutional Decline in Modern Japan'. *Buddhist Studies Review* 28, 2: 233–63.

Reader, Ian. 2012. 'Secularisation R.I.P? Nonsense! The "Rush Hour Away from the Gods" and the Decline of Religion in Contemporary Japan'. *The Journal of Religion in Japan* 1, 1: 7–36.

Reader, Ian. 2015. 'Japanese New Religions: An Overview'. Available at http://wrldrels. org/SPECIAL%20PROJECTS/JAPANESE%20NEW%20RELIGIONS/Japanese%20 New%20Religions.WRSP.pdf.

Reader, Ian. 2018. 'Millennialism with and without the Violence: An Examination of Late Twentieth-Century Japanese New Religions (or Why Aum Is Rather Unique in Japan)'. In Michael Wachutka, Monika Schrimpf and Birgit Staemmler eds. *Religion, Politik, Ideologie: Beitraäge zu enier kritischen Kulturwissenschaft* pp. 103–17. Munich: Iudicum.

Reader, Ian and George J. Tanabe Jr. 1998. *Practically Religious: Worldly Benefits and the Common Religion of Japan* Honolulu: University of Hawai i Press.

Reid, David. 1991. *New Wine: The Cultural Shaping of Japanese Christianity* Berkeley, CA: Asian Humanities Press.

Robbins, Thomas. 2005. 'New Religions and Alternative Religions'. *Nova Religio: The Journal of Alternative and Emergent Religions* 8, 3: 104–11.

Rowe, Mark M. 2011. *Bonds of the Dead: Temples, Burials, and the Transformation of Contemporary Japanese Buddhism* Chicago: University of Chicago Press.

Saitō Akitoshi. 1984. 'Kōbō Daishi shinkō ni kansuru jittai chōsa'. *Bukkyō bunka ronshū* 4: 400–79.

Sakashita, Jay. 1998. *Shinnyoen and the Transmission of Japanese New Religions Abroad.* PhD, University of Stirling, Scotland.

Sakurai, Yoshihide. 2011. 'New Religions: Economic Aspects'. In Birgit Staemmler and Ulrich Dehn eds. *Establishing the Revolutionary: An Introduction to New Religions in Japan* pp. 89–118. Wien, Zurich: LIT.

Sankei Shinbun .15 August 2012 Advertisement special: 'Nihonjin toshite, inochi wo kangaeru hi'.

Sasagase, Yuji and Sato Kei. 2015. 'Japan's Largest Right-Wing Organization: An Introduction to Nippon Kaigi'. *The Asia-Pacific Journal* 13/ 50:5. Available at http:// apjjf.org/-Mine-Masahiro/4410. Accessed 14 December 2017.

Satō, Hiroo. 2016. *How Like a God: Deification in Japanese Religion* Tokyo: International House of Japan.

Sawada, Janine Tasca. 2004. *Practical Pursuits: Religion, Politics, and Personal Cultivation in Nineteenth-Century Japan* Honolulu: University of Hawai'i Press.

Scheid, Bernard with Kate Wildman Nakai (eds). 2013. *Kami Ways in Nationalist Territory: Shinto Studies in Prewar Japan and the West* Wien: Austrian Academy of Sciences Press.

Schopen, Gregory. 1987. 'Burial "ad sanctos" and the Physical Presence of the Buddha in Early Indian Buddhism'. *Religion* 17, 3: 193–225.

Schrimpf, Monika. 2011. 'Shinnyo-en'. In Birgit Staemmler and Ulrich Dehn eds. *Establishing the Revolutionary: An Introduction to New Religions in Japan* pp. 239–58. Wien, Zurich: LIT.

Sekimori, Gaynor. 2006. 'Star Rituals and Nikko Shugendo'. In Lucia Dolce ec. Special Issue of *Culture and Cosmos* 10, 1–2: 217–50.

Sharf, Robert. 1992. 'The Idolization of Enlightenment: On the Mummification of Ch'an Masters in Medieval China'. *History of Religion* 32, 1: 1–31.

Sharf, Robert. 1993. 'The Zen of Japanese Nationalism'. *History of Religions* 33, 1: 1–43.

Shimada Hiromi. 1995. *Shinji yasui kokoro. Wakamono ga shinshin shūkyō ni hashiru riyū.* Tokyo: PHP Kenkyūjo.

Shimada Hiromi. 2005. *Kaimyō: Naze shigo ni namae o kaeru no ka.* Tokyo: Hōzōkan.

Shimada Hiromi. 2008. *Nihon no 10 dai shin shūkyō.* Tokyo: Gentosha.

Shimada Hiromi. 2010. *Sōshiki wa iranai.* Tokyo: Gentosha.

Shimazono Susumu. 1987. 'Kyōso to shūkyōteki shidōsha sūhai no kenkyū kadai'. In *Kyōso to sono shūhen*, ed. Shūkyō Shakaigaku Kenkyūkai, pp. 11–35. Tokyo: Yūzankaku.

Shimazono Susumu. 1992a. *Gendai kyūsai shūkyō ron.* Tokyo: Seikyūsha.

Shimazono Susumu. 1992b. *Shinshinshūkyō to shūkyō boom.* Tokyo: Iwanami shoten.

Shimazono Susumu. 1993. 'Shūkyōteki Monogatari toshite no Taikendan'. In *Shūkyō no Kotoba*, ed. Tsuruoka Yoshio and Shimazono Susumu, pp. 118–45. Tokyo: Taimeidō.

Shimazono Susumu. 1994. 'Shinshūkyō no gainen to hassei'. In *Shinshūkyō jiten*, ed. Inoue et al., pp. 2–13. Tokyo: Kōbundō.

Shimazono Susumu. 1995. 'In the Wake of Aum: the Formation and Transformation of a Universe of Belief'. *Japanese Journal of Religious Studies* 22, 3–4: 381–415.

Shimazono Susumu. 1996. *Seishin sekai no yukue: Gendai sekai to shinreisei undō* Tokyo: Tokyodō Shuppan.

Shimazono Susumu. 1997. 'Gendai Nihon no han-sezokushugi to nashonarizumu'. In *Shūkyō to nashonarizumu*, ed. Nakano Tsuyoshi, Iida Takafumi and Yamanaka Hiroshi, pp. 217–35. Kyoto: Sekai Shisōsha.

Shimazono Susumu. 2001. *Posutomodan no shinshūkyō: Gendai nihon no seishin jōkyō no teiryū.* Tokyo: Tōkyōdō shuppan.

Shimazono Susumu. 2004. *From Salvation to Spirituality: Popular Religious Movements in Japan* Melbourne: TransPacific Publishers.

Shimazono Susumu. 2007. *Supirichuariti no kōryū: shin reisei bunka no shūhen.* Tokyo: Iwanami Shoten.

Shimazono Susumu. 2010. *Kokka shintō to Nihonjin* Tokyo: Iwanami shoten.

Shinnyoen (ed.), 1977. *Shinnyoen: The Way to Nirvana* Tachikawa: Shinnyoen.

Shūkyō Shakaigaku Kenkyūkai (ed.). 1987. *Kyōso to sono shūhen.* Tokyo: Yūzankaku.

Skov, Lise. 1995. 'Environmentalism Seen through Women's Magazines'. In *Women, Media and Consumption in Japan*, ed. Lise Skov and Brian Moeran, pp. 170–96. Honolulu: University of Hawai'i Press.

Staemmler, Birgit. 2011a. 'New Religions: The History'. In *Establishing the Revolutionary: An Introduction to New Religions in Japan*, ed. Birgit Staemmler and Ulrich Dehn, pp. 13–40. Zurich: LIT.

Staemmler, Birgit. 2011b. 'Ōmoto'. In *Establishing the Revolutionary: An Introduction to New Religions in Japan*, ed. Birgit Staemmler and Ulrich Dehn, pp. 121–40. Zurich: LIT.

Staemmler, Birgit. 2013. 'Seichō no Ie' World Religions and Spirituality Project. Available at https://wrldrels.org/2016/10/08/seicho-no-ie/. Accessed 14 December 2017.

Staemmler, Birgit and Ulrich Dehn (eds). 2011a. *Establishing the Revolutionary: An Introduction to New Religions in Japan.* Zurich: LIT.

Staemmler, Birgit and Ulrich Dehn. 2011b. 'Introduction'. In *Establishing the Revolutionary: An Introduction to New Religions in Japan*, ed. Birgit Staemmler and Ulrich Dehn, pp. 1–9. Zurich: LIT.

Stalker, Nancy. 2008. *Prophet Motive: Deguchi Onisaburō, Oomoto and the Rise of New Religions in Imperial Japan*. Honolulu: University of Hawai'i Press.

Strong, John. 2004. *Relics of the Buddha*. Princeton: Princeton University Press.

Sueki Fumihiko. 2007. *Chūsei no kami to hotoke*. Tokyo: Yamakawa.

Suzuki, Kentarō. 1995. 'Divination in Contemporary Japan: A General Overview and an Analysis of Survey Results'. *Japanese Journal of Religious Studies* 22, 3–4: 249–66.

Tabor, James D. and Eugene V. Gallagher. 1995. *Why Waco? Cults and the Battle for Religious Freedom in America*. Berkeley: University of California Press.

Tanabe, George J. 2002. 'The Foundiong of Mount Kōya and Kūkai's Eternal Meditation'. In *Religions of Asia in Practice: An Anthology*, ed. Donald S. Lopez, Jr., pp. 672–7. Princeton: Princeton University Press.

Tenrikyō. 1984. *Tenrikyō kyōten*. Tenri: Tenrikyō.

Tenrikyō. 2002. *The Doctrine of Tenrikyo*. Tenri: Tenrikyo Church headquarters (English version of Tenrikyō 1984).

Tenrikyō. 2006 (1967). *The Life of Oyasama, Foundress of Tenrikyo* Tenri: Tenrikyo. Church Headquarters.

Tenshō Kōtai Jingū Kyō. 1954. *The Prophet of Tabuse*. Tabuse, Yamaguchi, Japan: Tenshō Kōtai Jingū Kyō.

Thomsen, Harry. 1963. *The New Religions of Japan*. New York: Charles Tuttle.

Trainor, Kevin. 2007. *Relics, Ritual, and Representation in Buddhism: Rematerializing the Sri Lankan Theravada Tradition*. Cambridge: Cambridge University Press.

Tsukada, Hotaka. 2012. 'Cultural Nationalism in Japanese Neo-New Religions: A Comparative Study of Mahikari and Kōfuku no Kagaku'. *Monumenta Nipponica* 67, 1: 133–57.

Tsukada Hotaka. 2015. *Shūkyō to seiji no tentetsuten: Hoshu gōdō to seikyō ittchi no shukyō shakaigaku*. Tokyo: Kadensha.

Tsukada, Hotaka and Ōmi Toshihiro. 2011. 'Religious Issues in Japan 2010 A Deluge of "Religious" Information on New Religions, Power Spots, Funeral Services, and Buddhist Statues'. *Bulletin Nanzan Institute for Religion and Culture* 35: 24–47.

Ukai Hidenori. 2015. *Jiin shōmetsu*. Tokyo: Nikkei BP sha.

Umehara Takeshi and Yamaori Tesuo. 1995. *Shūkyō no jisatsu: Nihonjin no atarashii shinkō o motomete*. Tokyo: PHP Kenkyūjo.

Victoria, Brian. 1997. *Zen at War*. New York: Weatherhill.

Victoria, Brian. 2012 (2003). *Zen War Stories*. London: Routledge.

Vogel, Ezra. 1979. *Japan as Number One: Lessons for America*. Cambridge MA: Harvard University Press.

Watanabe, Manabu. 1997. 'Reactions to the Aum Affair: The Rise of the Anti-Cult Movement in Japan'. *Bulletin of the Nanzan Institute for Religion and Culture* 21: 32–48.

Watanabe, Masako. 2011. 'New Religions: A Sociological Approach'. In *Establishing the Revolutionary: An Introduction to New Religions in Japan*, ed. Birgit Staemmler and Ulrich Dehn, pp. 69–88. Zurich: LIT.

Weber, Max 1968 (1947). 'The Nature of Charismatic Authority and Its Routinization'. In *On Charisma and Institution Building*, ed. S. N. Eisenstadt, pp. 48–65. Chicago, IL: University of Chicago Press.

Wessinger, Catherine. 1997. 'Millennialism With and Without the Mayhem'. In *Millennium, Messiahs, and Mayhem*, ed. Thomas Robbins and Susan J. Palmer, pp. 47–59. New York: Routledge.

Wessinger, Catherine. 2000. 'Introduction: The Interacting Dynamics of Millennial Beliefs, Persecution, and Violence'. In *Millennialism, Persecution, and Violence: Historical Cases*, ed. Catherine Wessiner, pp. 3–39. Syracuse, NY: Syracuse University Press.

Whelan, Christal. 2007. *Religious Responses to Globalization in Japan: The Case of the God Light Association*. PhD diss., Boston University.

Whelan, Christal. 2015. 'God Light Association'. World Religion and Spirituality Project. Available at https://wrldrels.org/2016/10/08/god-light-association/. Accessed 10 August 2017.

Wilkinson, Gregory. 2009. *The Next Aum: Religious Violence and New Religious Movements in Twenty-First Century Japan*. PhD thesis, University of Iowa.

Winter, Franz. 2013. 'A "Greek God" in a Japanese New Religion: On Hermes in Kōfuku no Kagaku'. *Numen* 60: 420–46.

Yajima Teruo. 1985. *Agonshū to Kiriyama Seiyū Tokyo*. Akimoto Shobō.

Yamada Naoki. 2012. *Shūkyō to kane*. Tokyo: Tetsujinsha.

Yamaori, Tetsuo. 1995. 'Aum Shinrikyō Sounds the Death Knell of Japanese Religion'. *Japan Echo* 22, 3: 48–53.

Yoshii Toshiyuki. 1996. 'Saikoku junrei no seiritsu to junrei jiin no soshikika'. In *Honzon Junrei*, ed. Shinno Toshikazu, pp. 46–67. Tokyo: Yūzankaku.

Young, Richard Fox. 1988. '*Gokyō-dōgen* to *bankyō-dōkon*: A Study in the Self-Universalization of Ōmoto'. *Japanese Journal of Religious Studies* 15, 4: 263–86.

Index